TRANSLATION OF
CONTEMPORARY JAPANESE
SCHOLARSHIP
ON
SOUTHEAST ASIA

READING SOUTHEAST ASIA

VOLUME I

Southeast Asia Program
120 Uris Hall
Cornell University
Ithaca, New York 14853-7601

Project Leader
  George Kahin

Participating Researcher
  Takashi Shiraishi

Assistant Researchers
  Jose Cruz
  Saya Shiraishi
  Sadako Taylor

Translation
  EDS (Tokyo)

Editing and Production
  Audrey Kahin
  Roberta Ludgate
  Dolina Millar

Published under the auspices of the Toyota Foundation

CONTENTS

INTRODUCTION

Born as "Southern Studies" (*Nampo Kenkyu*) in the late 1930s and early 1940s, Southeast Asian studies in Japan is now passing from the second to the third generation, while the fourth generation of scholars in their twenties and early thirties is now emerging on the horizon. The preceding generations have produced excellent works, only some of which are available in English. Tatsuro Yamamoto's classic, *Recherches sur l'histoire de l'Annam*, and the "Overseas Chinese" studies by scholars affiliated with the East Asia Economic Research Bureau of the Manchurian Railway are among the best works of the first generation, while the writings of such scholars of the second generation as Akira Nagazumi, Yoneo Ishii, and Toru Yano represent Japanese scholarship on Southeast Asia at its best.[1] These and other studies, cross-bred with non-Japanese language works on Southeast Asia, have formed a beautifully mestizo scholarly tradition of Japanese research on Southeast Asia, now rebaptized as *Tonan Ajia Kenkyu* (Southeast Asian Studies), in which the succeeding generation of Japanese Southeast Asianists, among whom I belong, have worked over the last twenty years.

Yet each generation of Japanese scholars working on Southeast Asia carries its own historical birth marks. Many members of the first generation entered "Southern Studies" in the 1930s when Japan was starting its fatal southward expansion. No wonder, then, that one of the major contributions of these scholars lay in their work on the "Overseas Chinese" and on the anti-Japanese Chinese national salvation movement in Southeast Asia.[2] Members of the second generation started to study Southeast Asia in the 1950s and early 1960s when Japan was notable by its absence from the region and when American scholarship was fast replacing the old colonial studies of Southeast Asia. Akira Nagazumi, the first Japanese to obtain a PhD in

---

[1]Tatsuro Yamamoto, *Recherches sur l'histoire de l'Annam* (Tokyo: Yamakawa, 1950); Mantetsu Toa Keizai Chosakyoku, *Tai-koku ni okeru Kakyo* [Chinese in Thailand] (Tokyo, 1939); *Firipin ni okeru Kakyo* [Chinese in the Philippines] (Tokyo, 1939); *Ranryo Indo ni okeru Kakyo* [Chinese in the Dutch Indies] (Tokyo, 1940); *Eiryo Marai, Biruma oyobi Goshu ni okeru Kakyo* [Chinese in British Malaya, Burma and Australia] (Tokyo, 1941); *Futsuryo Indo-shina ni okeru Kakyo* [Chinese in French Indochina] (Tokyo, 1943); Akira Nagazumi, *The Dawn of Indonesian Nationalism: The early years of the Budi Utomo, 1908-1918* (Tokyo: Institute of Developing Economies, 1972); Yoneo Ishii *Jozaha Bukkyo no Seiji-Syakai-gaku: Kokkyo no Kozo* (Tokyo: Sobunsha, 1975) Translated by Peter Hawkes, under the title *Sangha, State, and Society: Thai Buddhism in History* (Honolulu: University of Hawaii Press, 1986); Toru Yano, *Tai Biruma Gendai Seijishi Kenkyu* [A study of Thai and Burmese political history] (Tokyo: Sobunsha, 1968) and *"Nanshin" no Keifu* [The lineage of "southward expansion"] (Tokyo: Chuo Koronsha, 1975).

[2]Aside from the works on "Overseas Chinese" cited in fn. 1, see also Toa Kenkyujo, Dai 3 Chosa Iinkai, *Nan'yo Kakyo Konichi Kyukoku Undo no Kenkyu* [A Study on the Nanyang Chinese Anti-Japanese National Salvation Movement] (Tokyo: Toakenkyujo, 1944).

Southeast Asian history at an American university, thus clearly marked the coming-of-age of the second generation.

The third generation of Japanese Southeast Asianists, some of whose works appear in this and future volumes of this series, also display special characteristics. In terms of age they are now in their forties, and they entered Southeast Asian studies in the mid-1960s to early 1970s, when Japan was fast returning to Southeast Asia, and there were expanding opportunities for conducting research in the region and/or graduate studies abroad. Many of this generation spent one or more of their formative years outside Japan—in Southeast Asia, in the United States, in Australia, and in Europe. They viewed a knowledge of all the languages needed for their studies as a self-evident requirement, "translation works" (those based on non-Japanese works) were no longer acceptable, and many were well aware of most recent research by non-Japanese Southeast Asianists. Yet when they first entered Southeast Asian studies Southeast Asia was still remote and it remained so for some time. Scholars of this generation felt themselves fortunate to visit the region once in five years; library collections on Southeast Asia were poor, a book or a journal article had to be pursued from one library to another. Besides, there were few places where one could learn Southeast Asian languages. At the same time, events were moving swiftly in Southeast Asia: the killings and the establishment of the New Order in Indonesia in 1965-1966, the American war in Vietnam, the 1969 riot in Malaysia, the anti-Japanese movement and the revolution in Thailand in the early 1970s, the anti-Japanese riot in Jakarta in 1974. Since then things have changed very much. But scholars of the third generation have not forgotten this past and the contrast it presents with the way things now are. And this memory still leaves its marks on many of their studies—on the questions they ask, on the approaches they take, and on the sources they use.

The essays included in the four volumes of the present series, *Contemporary Japanese Scholarship on Southeast Asia*, are chosen to illuminate the scholarship of this third generation, especially in fields where few Japanese works are available in English. The studies included in the first volume, *Reading Southeast Asia*, are attempts to read Southeast Asian "texts" in the broader sense: Noriaki Oshikawa has written on Indonesia's "Scarlet Pimpernel" popular novels of the 1930s; Saya Shiraishi on Acehnese historical texts; Teruo Sekimoto on the huge signs which appear on the roofs of village houses commemorating August 17, Indonesia's independence day; Kenji Tsuchiya on Dutch Javanology; and Setsuho Ikehata on a nineteenth century Tagalog religious text. All the essays are undoubtedly inspired in one way or another by the kind of textual reading exemplified by scholars such as Ben Anderson, Reynaldo Ileto, and James Siegel, but they also represent an attempt to go beyond the scholarly tradition created by the preceding generations.

The essays to be included in the second volume of the series will explore Japanese language sources on Vietnam in the 1940s, and the articles based on these sources represent an effort by the Japanese authors to make their own contributions to Vietnamese history. Most of the works in the third volume were originally written by the research group led by Hajime Shimizu at the Institute of Developing Economies. Building on Toru Yano's pioneering work on Japan's southward expansion they investigate the origins of the Japanese presence in Southeast Asia. And, finally, the fourth volume will include works on Suharto's New Order in Indonesia, the country where since the late 1960s the Japanese presence in the form of aid, investment, and trade has been the most pronounced in Southeast Asia.

This project to make Japanese works on Southeast Asia available to English readers has been carried out by a team at Cornell, headed by Professor George McT. Kahin and funded by the Toyota Foundation. All the draft translations were done by EDS (Editorial and Design Services) in Tokyo with great care. For all this, I would like to thank Ms. Kazue Iwamoto of the Toyota Foundation who first brought up the idea; Ms. Yoshiko Wakayama who patiently saw the project through to completion; Ms. Suzanne Trumbull and her colleagues at EDS who put so much work into the translation effort; Dr. Audrey Kahin, without whose effort this project would have never got off the ground; and Jose Cruz, Roberta Ludgate, Dolina Millar, Saya Shiraishi, and Sadako Taylor who contributed to the project in many and valuable ways.

Finally, many Japanese scholars of the third generation owe an enormous intellectual debt to the late Prof. Akira Nagazumi in whose seminar some of us, including myself, were initiated into Southeast Asian studies and whose works set a standard to which all of us have had to aspire. His untimely death in 1988 was an enormous loss for us all. But his works are still with us, and his soft voice, his gentle and quiet manner, and his rigorous scholarship are still in our memory. To his memory we would like to dedicate this book.

Takashi Shiraishi
Ithaca
February 1990.

1

PATJAR MERAH INDONESIA AND TAN MALAKA: A POPULAR NOVEL AND A REVOLUTIONARY LEGEND

Noriaki Oshikawa

INTRODUCTION

Patjar Merah Indonesia [The Scarlet Pimpernel of Indonesia] is a five-volume popular novel published in Medan, East Sumatra, between 1938 and 1940. As the title suggests, the work is inspired by *The Scarlet Pimpernel*, Baroness Orczy's famous 1905 novel about the French Revolution and a secret society led by Sir Percy Blakeney (the Scarlet Pimpernel) that rescues French monarchists from the guillotine and smuggles them to England.[1] *Patjar Merah Indonesia* is a similar tale of adventure with political overtones on an international scale about Indonesian nationalists of the 1930s who pursued an underground struggle against the oppressive power of the Dutch colonial government, namely imperialism, and against Stalinism. The Patjar Merah, or Scarlet Pimpernel, is the nationalists' exiled leader, an elusive and protean hero.[2]

Swinging back and forth between historical fact and incredible fantasy, the story is peopled with characters who are for the most part readily identifiable historical figures whose names are only thinly disguised. Some of the leading figures in the PKI (Partai Komunis Indonesia; Indonesian Communist Party) of the 1920s—Semaun (1899–1971), Alimin (1889–1964), Musso (1897–1948), and Darsono (1897–?)—appear in supportive roles under the Russian-style names Semounov, Alminsky, Mussotte, and Darsonov, respectively. The Scarlet Pimpernel himself uses a variety of aliases, depending on where he happens to be: Vichitra in Thailand, Tan Min Kha in China, Ibrahim el Molqa in Palestine. These names are on file in intelligence agencies around the world, but his true identity is never revealed. Nevertheless, through his actions,

---

[1] There is a Japanese version, *Benihakobe* [The Scarlet Pimpernel], translated by Nishimura Kōji (Tokyo: Sōgen Suiri Bunko, 1970), that is a translation of the 1950 popular edition published by Hodder & Stoughton, London. There is also an Indonesian version, *Patjar Merah*, translated by R. Poeradiredja and published as Balai Pustaka Serie 746 (Weltevreden: Balai Pustaka, 1930). However, this is the second edition; the publication date of the first edition is unknown.

[2] I first learned of the existence of this novel from Anas Ma'ruf (1922–1980) when he was a visiting professor at the Tokyo University of Foreign Studies in the 1960s. A native of West Sumatra like Tan Malaka, he belonged to the generation that fought for Indonesia's independence and was an admirer of *Patjar Merah Indonesia* in his youth. The novel is also discussed in Harry A. Poeze, *Tan Malaka: Strijder voor Indonesië's Vrijheid, Levensloop van 1897 tot 1945* (The Hague: Nijhoff, 1976), pp. 482–90.

his personality, and the settings in which he is placed, readers can easily discern that the Scarlet Pimpernel is supposed to be Tan Malaka, the second chairman of the PKI. Exiled from Indonesia by the Dutch colonial government in 1922, he was involved in revolutionary activities in China and Southeast Asia in the 1920s and 1930s. At the time that *Patjar Merah Indonesia* was written he was living secretly in Singapore, almost totally cut off from both the Indonesian nationalist movement and the international revolutionary movement.[3]

This novel's appeal lies in its clever meshing of fact and fiction and its thrilling story development, interweaving politics, adventure, and romance. The author's imaginative use of the Indonesian nationalists' *modus operandi* depicts the characters moving about freely within the boundaries of time and space dictated by historical reality, facing their enemies with valor, ingenuity, and camaraderie.

I believe an analysis of the character of the Scarlet Pimpernel reveals a great deal about the way in which this fictional character contributed to the legend that had grown up around Tan Malaka by the time he reappeared on the Indonesian political scene in 1945 at the time of Indonesia's independence revolution. Though he had been out of the country for two decades (his political career within Indonesia, excluding time spent in prison, actually lasted less than two years), Tan Malaka was welcomed by the people as the legendary revolutionary of the 1920s and was so adored as a glorious leader that imposters of Tan Malaka appeared. In tracing this process of mystification that merged fact and fiction within the *Patjar Merah Indonesia*, I hope also to define the place of the popular novel in Indonesia's colonial history and to show how the world of Indonesian nationalism and nationalists in the late 1930s was translated and interpreted.

Popular fiction has long been considered too vulgar a genre to include in the study of Indonesian literature. But if one accepts the premise that popular fiction reflects the aspirations and hopes of the readers of its day and reveals an approximation of the people's feelings toward politics and society, then *Patjar Merah Indonesia* serves as an important source for elucidating the character and evolution of Indonesian nationalism. It is within the broad context including the readers' active role in shaping literature and giving significance to the despised genre of popular fiction that I will discuss this well-known work and its portrayal of a major Indonesian hero.

I. TAN MALAKA THE REVOLUTIONARY

Sutan Ibrahim gelar Datuk Tan Malaka was born in 1897 in Minangkabau, West Sumatra.[4] A bright youth belonging to the local nobility, Tan Malaka attended a

---

[3]That the Scarlet Pimpernel is Tan Malaka can be surmised from the fictional character's aliases. In China he uses the name Tan Min Kha, which closely resembles the name Tan Malaka. Ibrahim, an alias used in Palestine, was Tan Malaka's childhood name.

[4]For more information on Tan Malaka's life, thought, and activities, see Ruth T. McVey, *The Rise of Indonesian Communism* (Ithaca, NY: Cornell University Press, 1965); Benedict Anderson, *Java in a Time of Revolution: Occupation and Resistance, 1944–1946* (Ithaca, NY: Cornell University Press, 1972); Rudolf Mrazek, "Tan Malaka: A Political Personality's Structure of Experience," *Indonesia* 14 (October 1972); Poeze, *Tan Malaka*; Alfian, "Ama kakeru kakumei no shisō—densetsu no kyōsanshugisha Tan Maraka" [A soaring philosophy of revolution: The legendary communist Tan Malaka], in Taufik Abdullah, ed., *Shinjitsu no Indoneshia* [The true Indonesia; original title *Manusia dalam Kemelut Sejarah*], trans. Masahide Shibusawa and Kenji Tsuchiya (Tokyo: Simul Shuppankai, 1978); Tan Malaka, *Rōgoku kara rōgoku e—Tan Maraka jiden* [From jail to jail: The autobiography of Tan Malaka; original title *Dari Pendjara ke Pendjara*], trans.

teachers' training school in Bukittinggi. There he came to the attention of one of the school's Dutch instructors, who arranged for him to go to the Netherlands in 1913 to study at the Haarlemse Rijks Kweekschool voor Onderwijzer, a state teachers' training school. Tan Malaka hoped to acquire a teaching certificate so that he could return to Indonesia as an instructor at a school for Dutch children. But life in a strange country was more trying than he had anticipated, and he contracted pulmonary tuberculosis. He was to be plagued by the disease off and on for the rest of his life.

He boarded with a poor steelworker's family. Influenced by their poverty and stoicism, the socialist thinking of a Belgian fellow boarder, the racial discrimination to which he was subject as a student from a Dutch colony, and the upheaval in European society brought about by World War I, Tan Malaka awoke to an awareness of being a son of a colonized people and to his country's oppressed status, and he lost interest in his original purpose in being in the Netherlands. The success of the Russian Revolution was another decisive influence. The young man who had once been enamored of Nietzsche's Superman now pored over Karl Marx's *Das Kapital*. His propensity for arguing over the validity of the colonial system quickly earned him the nickname "Mister Bolshevik" among his friends.

Upon his return to Indonesia in late 1919, after the end of the war, he was hired with the status of a European by the owner of a tobacco plantation in Deli, East Sumatra, to teach the children of the plantation's Indonesian contract coolies. The contradictions of colonialism were blatantly obvious in Deli, known as a capitalist's paradise and a worker's hell. The abstract concepts of class and racial conflict that Tan Malaka had acquired in the Netherlands became a painful reality in Deli, where he came into contact with both the labor leaders and the Dutch socialists of Medan. Before long, Tan Malaka was arguing with his Dutch colleagues over educational principles, and when he had finished paying the debts he had incurred in staying in the Netherlands to study, in March 1921, he quit his job to move to Java, the heart of the Indonesian nationalist movement.

Tan Malaka made his appearance on the scene at a time when the growing PKI (then known as the Perserikatan Komunis di India; Indies Communist Party), formed in May 1920 as the first communist party in Asia, was challenging the leadership of the Sarekat Islam (Islamic Union), which had led the Indonesian nationalist movement since the middle of the second decade of the century. The growing number of Sarekat Islam members who were also card-carrying communists contributed to PKI membership. It was not uncommon at the time for a person to belong to more than one political party. The leadership tug-of-war was at its peak when Tan Malaka met the PKI's first chairman, Semaun, at the Sarekat Islam national congress held in Yogyakarta in March 1921.

Responding to Semaun's invitation, Tan Malaka accompanied him to Semarang in Central Java—known at the time as the "Red City" because it was the center of the PKI movement. There Tan Malaka was asked to establish and manage a school for the children of the Semarang members of Sarekat Islam, then under the supervision of the Communist party. The school's focus was on the basic principles of reading, writing, and arithmetic, but Tan Malaka also endeavored to instill in his pupils a strong sense of responsibility toward the oppressed. The school opened with eighty

Noriaki Oshikawa, 3 vols. (Tokyo: Rokusaisha, vol. 1, 1979; vol. 2, 1981; vol. 3, forthcoming). My account is based mainly on these works.

pupils, but in a short time branches, popularly referred to as "Tan Malaka schools," had been built in Salatiga and Bandung.

His successful schools and the publication of his first political essay, "Sovjet atau Parlement?" [Soviet or Parliament?],[5] won Tan Malaka a reputation as both activist and theoretician and boosted his status within the party. In its earlier incarnation as the ISDV (Indische Social-Democratische Vereniging; Indies Social Democratic Association), the party had lost senior leaders to overseas exile. As its confrontation with the Sarekat Islam intensified, the PKI sought a new kind of leader, one well versed in European political style and theory. Though he had only recently joined the party, Tan Malaka was elected the second party chairman at the PKI congress held in Semarang in late December 1921.

Thus, at the age of only 25, Tan Malaka found himself in a leadership position, and he immediately set about repairing the rift between the Sarekat Islam and the PKI, urging them to join forces in the fight against colonialism.[6] Yet he had hardly had time to begin testing his new authority when he was arrested by the colonial government, ostensibly for having abetted a strike by the PPPB (Perserikatan Pegawai Pandhuis Bumiputera), the pawnshop workers' union, in Yogyakarta in January 1922. Sentenced to imprisonment, he was assigned to a penal colony in Kupang, on the island of Timor. But he appealed for and was granted exile and left Indonesia in March 1922. Tan Malaka was to undergo arrest, imprisonment, and exile three more times before he died. He remained overseas for twenty years, secretly returning only in 1942, when Indonesia was under Japanese occupation. This first exile was also to become the beginning of the "Tan Malaka myth."

Traveling through the Netherlands and Germany, Tan Malaka made his way to Moscow, where he attended the fourth congress of the Communist International, or Comintern, in November 1922 as a representative of the PKI. During the congress's discussion of national liberation in the East, Tan Malaka criticized the Comintern's hostility toward Pan-Islamism, stressing Islam's revolutionary role as a major driving force in the fight for national liberation and freedom from colonialism. Communists and Muslims, he believed, should seek to form a united front. Most of the European representatives were cool toward his argument, but Grigory Zinovyev and Karl Radek were taken with his strong personality and lucid analysis.

Tan Malaka stayed in Moscow about a year, during which time he published several essays on Indonesia. Toward the end of 1923 he was sent to China as a Comintern agent to form a network with the leftist Profintern to further the revolutionary cause in Southeast Asia. Arriving in December, Tan Malaka made his base in Guangzhou. His meeting around this time with Sun Yat-sen, to whom he was introduced by Tan Ping-shan of the Chinese Communist Party, made a deep impression on him. He had done little to achieve his assigned task, however, when he was struck down again by illness, and in June 1925 he went to the Philippines to convalesce.

---

[5]"Sovjet atau Parlement?" was written in Deli and serialized in the PKI organ *Soeara Ra'jat* [Voice of the People] between May and August 1921.

[6]For Tan Malaka, a devout Muslim, the coexistence of socialism (Marxism) and Islam was a major concern throughout his life, as can be seen by his later attempt to convince the Comintern that this was possible. Some Indonesian Muslims even consider Tan Malaka one of their major religious leaders. See, for example, Hamka's preface to Tan Malaka's posthumously published *Islam dalam Tindjauan MADILOG* [Islam in the MADILOG view] (Jakarta: Widjaya, 1951). The fictional Scarlet Pimpernel is also portrayed as a pious Muslim.

While recovering in Manila, Tan Malaka spent much of his time trying to turn the PKI away from the radical course it had adopted in his absence. An ultraleftist faction led by such radicals as Alimin and Musso, both former Sarekat Islam members, had pushed the PKI to change its policy from one directed at expanding a mass movement through a united front to one that focused on revolutionizing the labor movement. In accordance with directives decided upon at their party congress in June 1924, which included the establishment of a soviet, they disbanded the Sarekat Rakjat (People's Union), the PKI's mass organization, in an effort to make the party more proletarian, and in the process took the party underground.

The Comintern frowned upon this trend and urged the PKI to abandon its radical line. Despite this, at a secret December 1925 meeting of the PKI leadership held at the Prambanan temple complex in Central Java, it was decided to instigate an armed rebellion within six months, beginning in Padang, West Sumatra, and moving from there into Java, to bring down the colonial government and establish a soviet in its stead. Alimin was sent to Manila to secure Tan Malaka's approval of the plan. Condemning the scheme as a *Putsch*, Tan Malaka handed Alimin an opinion paper based on his analysis of the situation to be presented at the meeting of party leaders that was to be held in Singapore. But Alimin suppressed the paper, reporting to his fellow leaders that Tan Malaka had been too ill to discuss the plan for an uprising. Unopposed, the party leaders reasserted their resolve and sent Alimin and Musso to Moscow to get the Comintern's endorsement. When Tan Malaka learned of this, he rushed to Singapore. He tried frantically to get the party members to change their minds, but was only able to secure their agreement to delay the revolt.

Between November 1926 and January 1927 the PKI launched attacks on government officials and the police, and on railroad and communications facilities in West Sumatra and Java. As Tan Malaka had feared, the rebellion was suppressed in just a few days. Some thirteen thousand people were arrested, and the party organization was left a shambles.

In June 1927 Tan Malaka and two of his most loyal comrades, Djamaluddin Tamin and Subakat, organized Pari (Partai Republik Indonesia; Republic of Indonesia Party) in Bangkok. The new party dissociated itself from the reckless radicalism that had brought about the PKI's downfall and declared itself independent of the Comintern, which was subordinate to the Soviet Union's interests. Tan Malaka sought to strengthen the new organization by publishing propaganda pamphlets and smuggling cadres trained overseas into Indonesia to rally the remnants of the PKI and establish a new organization of intellectuals. Unfortunately, the bulk of the propaganda materials sent into Indonesia were confiscated by the colonial government, and the arrests of the major activists, including Tamin and Subakat, greatly hampered the new party's attempts to stir up popular support.

Tan Malaka was arrested by the American authorities in August 1927 when he entered Manila to attend the Pan-Malay Congress. Manuel Quezon and other Philippine nationalists rallied to his defense, but despite their efforts to gain his release, he was deported. Unable to return to Indonesia, he traveled on to Xiamen in China's Fujian Province, where he was welcomed by Chinese friends. He spent most of the next decade in southern China, weakened by recurrent bouts of tuberculosis and hounded by the intelligence agents of several countries. Some of this time was spent convalescing in a Fujian farming village, and in the early years of Japan's invasion of China he lived in Shanghai. In October 1932 he was discovered in Hong Kong and arrested and deported by the British. He returned to Xiamen, where he opened an English-language school.

While in Shanghai, Tan Malaka was sought out by Alimin, who persuaded him to work once again with the Comintern,[7] but after 1933 Tan Malaka had very little to do with either the international or the Indonesian communist movement. In August 1937 he fled the advancing Japanese forces and made his way to Singapore, where he obtained a teaching job in a Chinese school. He was to remain there for roughly the next five years. When Singapore fell to the Japanese, he fled to Penang and then Medan, finally arriving in Jakarta in July 1942, two decades after he had been exiled.

For nearly a year Tan Malaka remained in hiding in the *kampung* of Rajawati in southern Jakarta, observing Indonesia's transformation under the Japanese military occupation. It was during this interlude that he completed his masterpiece, *MADILOG*.[8] For the rest of the war he worked under the alias Hussein at the Bayah coal mine in southern Banten, which was then under the management of Sumitomo Mining. He was not to reemerge upon the Indonesian political scene until just before Sukarno's declaration of independence on August 17, 1945. While keeping his true identity hidden, he managed to make contact with the radical young nationalists, known collectively as *pemuda* (youth), who goaded Sukarno, Mohammad Hatta, and other older leaders who had collaborated with the Japanese to declare the independence of the Republic of Indonesia. When armed confrontation between the nationalists and the Dutch, who had the support of the British forces, broke out in September, Tan Malaka was working behind the scenes, gradually increasing his influence over the radicals and making overtures toward the leaders of the Republican government with regard to leadership of the revolution.

Though he lacked his own organizational base within Indonesia, Tan Malaka was able to rely on his reputation as the shining leader of the nationalist movement since the 1920s and the legendary revolutionary hero returned from exile. His presence was made known through the local newspapers and other media sometime between late November and early December.[9] A revolutionary radio station also reported that Tan Malaka (actually an impostor) led the armed resistance in the November battle of Surabaya between the people and British India Army forces.[10] This battle was a milestone in the Indonesian fight for independence and provided Tan Malaka with the opportunity to gain his position as the liberation movement's primary spokesman and theoretician.

Deeply affected by the people's revolutionary spirit, Tan Malaka wrote a series of three pamphlets, including one on battle strategy entitled *Moeslihat* [On strategy],

---

[7] See Poeze, *Tan Malaka*, p. 416.

[8] *MADILOG* is a word coined by Tan Malaka by combining the first few letters of the words *materialisme, dialektika,* and *logika* (materialism, dialectics, and logic).

[9] The *Kedaulatan Rakjat*, published in Yogyakarta, was among the leading Indonesian newspapers during the period of the independence movement. In an article probably written in late November or early December 1945 the paper reported that Tan Malaka had returned from his two-decade exile to join in the fight for independence, but many readers questioned the story's credibility. To dispel their doubts, the *Kedaulatan Rakjat* had Tan Malaka himself write a front-page article, titled "Tan Malaka," which was published on December 13 (see note 60). On December 28 and 29 the *Kedaulatan Rakjat* also reprinted Muhammad Yamin's "Tan Malaka, Father of the Indonesian Republic" (*Tan Malaka, bapak Repoeblik Indonesia*) from the *Ra'jat*, a Jakarta newspaper.

[10] See Anderson, *Java in a Time of Revolution*, p. 283.

urging a long-term strategy of armed resistance to the Dutch. His advice ran counter to that of Sutan Sjahrir, who sought to negotiate independence through diplomatic channels. Sjahrir became prime minister of the newly declared Republic in December 1945. Tan Malaka's call for armed resistance had a profound effect upon the more radical revolutionaries, however, and in January 1946 when the Persatuan Perdjuangan (Struggle Union), whose slogan was "One hundred percent independence!" was established, he became the symbol of the struggle.

The Persatuan Perdjuangan, a united front made up of 141 political and military groups seeking complete independence for all of Indonesia, was vehemently opposed to the more moderate Sjahrir faction (the diplomatists), which aimed only to free the islands of Java and Madura. So powerful was this militant group that at first, from January through March, it completely eclipsed Sjahrir's cabinet as a force. Fearing Tan Malaka's influence, Sjahrir had him and the other leaders of the Persatuan Perdjuangan arrested in March 1946. Tan Malaka was forced to remain in prison until September 1948. It was during this time that he wrote his three-volume autobiography, *Dari Pendjara ke Pendjara* [From jail to jail]. Upon his release he and a number of *pemuda* radicals formed the Partai Murba (Proletarian Party) in an attempt to continue the policy of armed resistance, but the party did not have the power to change the course of diplomatic negotiations that Sjahrir had laid out. In February 1949 Tan Malaka, then 52 years old, was shot to death by Indonesian Army forces, as he was leading a guerrilla battle near Kediri, East Java.

Today, Tan Malaka is primarily a figure of legend. Very few Indonesians have any knowledge or understanding of his ideology and activities. In the postwar PKI's official history, he is condemned as a traitor and Trotskyite who opposed the 1926–1927 uprising.

II. The Development of the Indonesian Popular Novel

The term "popular literature" came into use in Indonesia with the appearance, in the late 1930s, of *roman picisan*—cheap, mass-published books providing light reading. These were contrasted with "serious" or "pure" literature, by which was meant the modern Indonesian novel, which had begun to undergo major development in the 1920s.[11] However, if popular literature is defined broadly as reading material designed to appeal to the tastes of an unspecified mass readership,[12] the Indonesian prototype of this genre can be said to have emerged in the late nineteenth century.[13]

---

[11]The popular novel is referred to in Indonesian as *novel pop*, short for *novel populer*. See Ajip Rosidi, *Pembinaan Minat Baca, Bahasa Dan Sastera* (Surabaya: Bina Ilmu, 1983), pp. 238–39, for a discussion of the evolution of this term. The "serious," or literary, novel is called *novel serius*.

[12]In Japan, Shunsuke Tsurumi has defined the popular novel as "a literary genre to be distinguished from literature read only by the people of a certain occupational or age group." The popular novel, he writes, "is a form of fiction widely, and continuously, read by members of the general public. . . . In other words, *it is a type of novel that ordinary people read because they wish to, regardless of their educational level and regardless of whether they are interested in the arts*" (emphasis added). See Shunsuke Tsurumi, *Taishū bungaku ron* [On popular literature] (Tokyo: Rokkō Shuppan, 1985), pp. 191–92. In Indonesia, on the other hand, the popular novel is defined more by its quality than by its readership. See A. Teeuw, *Pokok dan Tokoh dalam Kesusasteraan Indonesia Baru*, 2 vols. (Jakarta: Pembangunan, 1955), vol. 1; Bakri Siregar, *Sedjarah Sastera Indonesia Modern* (Jakarta: Akademi Sastera dan Bahasa "Multatuli," 1964).

[13]Pramoedya Ananta Toer refers to this kind of turn-of-the-century literature as *sastra pra-Indonesia* (pre-Indonesian literature). See Pramoedya Ananta Toer, ed., *Tempo Doeloe: Antologi Sastra Pra-Indonesia* (Jakarta: Hasta Mitra, 1982). He uses the prefix *pra* (pre) to designate the

Below I will trace the development of the Indonesian popular novel from its origins to the publication of *Patjar Merah Indonesia*.

1. THE TRANSLATED NOVEL AND *PERANAKAN* CHINESE LITERATURE

The earliest novels published in the East Indies were colloquial-Malay (pre-Indonesian) translations of foreign novels. This genre made its appearance at the end of the nineteenth century, and the favored works were European (primarily French) popular novels and Chinese historical novels and action-packed adventure tales, the last known as *wuxia xiaoshuo* or *jianxia xiaoshuo*. Some of the major works translated into Malay were *Around the World in Eighty Days* (translated in 1880) and *Twenty Thousand Leagues Under the Sea* (1895) by Jules Verne, *Robinson Crusoe* (1891, fourth edition) by Daniel Defoe, *The Count of Monte Cristo* (1894–1899) and *The Three Musketeers* (1914) by Alexandre Dumas *père*, *La Dame aux camélias* (1907) by Alexandre Dumas *fils*, and such Chinese works as *Sanguozhiyanyi* [The romance of the three kingdoms] (1883–1885), *Shuihuchuan* [All men are brothers] (1885), and *Xiyouji* [Pilgrims to the west] (1886). The Chinese historical works were especially popular among *peranakan* Chinese (Indies-born Chinese), who could no longer read their ancestral language.[14]

The translators and publishers during this period were for the most part *peranakan* Chinese, Dutch nationals, and Eurasians.[15] Over the years the translations were reprinted and retranslated, and after 1910 the repertoire was expanded to include the Sherlock Holmes stories and such fantastic adventure tales as the Rocambole stories of Ponson du Terrail.[16] An expanding readership among the Indonesians helped establish a commercial foundation for the publication of such novels, and there emerged a growing appetite for native adaptations of popular foreign works and eventually for original novels set in Indonesia (principally Java).

The proliferation of popular-literature magazines published by *peranakan* Chinese from the latter half of the 1920s until the end of the colonial era testifies to the popu-

---

time prior to the use of the word *Indonesia* to indicate a single political and cultural entity. Other studies of the literature of that period include Nio Joe Lan, *Sastera Indonesia-Tionghoa* (Jakarta: Gunung Agung, 1962); C. W. Watson, "Some Preliminary Remarks on the Antecedents of Modern Indonesia Literature" (*Bijdragen tot de Taal-, Land- en Volkenkunde* 127, no. 4 [1971]); W. V. Sykorsky, "Some Additional Remarks on the Antecedents of Modern Indonesian Literature" (*Bijdragen tot de Taal-, Land- en Volkenkunde* 136, no. 4 [1980]); Claudine Salmon, *Literature in Malay by the Chinese of Indonesia: A Provisional Annotated Bibliography* (Paris: Editions de la Maison des Sciences de l'Homme, 1981); Jakob Sumarjo, *Novel Populer Indonesia* (Yogyakarta: Nur Cahaya, 1982). While these scholars focus on different authors and works, they all tend to emphasize the continuity of Indonesian literature rather than accept conventional Indonesian literary historians' treatment of the literature of the 1920s and later as completely divorced from the Indonesian literary tradition that preceded it.

[14]See Watson, "Preliminary Remarks," p. 417.

[15]One of the most prolific *peranakan* Chinese, active in a diversity of fields, was Lie Kim Hok. He was the translator of numerous Chinese and Western works and the author of several original works, in addition to being a journalist and publisher. Tio Ie Soei provides a detailed account of his life and work in *Lie Kimhok: 1853–1912* (Bandung: Good Luck, 1959).

[16]Later the Balai Pustaka, the publishing agency of the colonial government, also began publishing translated works, which were made available to the public through the government-run Volksbibliotheken, or "people's library" (called the Taman Pustaka in Indonesian). The most popular translated works were *The Three Musketeers*, *Around the World in Eighty Days*, and Rudyard Kipling's animal stories. See Nidhi Aeusrivongse, "Fiction as History: A Study of Pre-war Indonesian Novels and Novelists (1920–1940)" (PhD dissertation, University of Michigan, 1976), p. 92.

larity of the genre. Issued once or twice a month, they had such titles as *Tjerita Roman* [Romance novels], *Goedang Tjerita* [A godown (warehouse) of novels], *Hiboeranku* [My pleasure], *Boe Hiap* [Warriors], and *Kiam Hiap* [Swordsmen], averaged eighty to a hundred pages, and were circulated widely in the major cities of Java: Jakarta, Surabaya, Bandung, Tasikmalaya, and Yogyakarta. Their content included adventure, mystery, romance, and picaresque novels, collectively referred to as *cerita silat*. These popular novels, made available to the public through the privately run lending libraries known as the *taman bacaan*, presented a formidable rival to the works issued by the colonial government's publishing agency, the Balai Pustaka.[17] They also helped stimulate the birth of *roman picisan* written by Indonesian authors.

So far, the *peranakan* Chinese literature of translations, adaptations, and original works[18] has been studiously ignored by orthodox scholars of Indonesian literary history. As Claudine Salmon points out, among the major reasons for this neglect are that the authors and translators were not ethnic Indonesians and that by Western scholarly standards on Indonesian literary history, which tend to place the emphasis on belles-lettres, popular novels are not worthy of study or analysis.[19] But exclusion of authors and their works on ethnic grounds is hardly valid. What would Japanese literature be without its writers of Korean ancestry? Even aside from this, the role of *peranakan* Chinese in the development of Indonesian literature goes far beyond their influence on plot and style. It is not an exaggeration to say that fiction written in Malay, starting from the end of the nineteenth century, might never have come to be, had it not been for the pioneering efforts of the *peranakan* Chinese in creating a commercial market for popular novels, establishing distribution channels, introducing new genres, and building the habit of reading itself.

2. The Nonfiction Novel

The nonfiction novel, particularly the genre known as the *nyai* novel, was as popular as *cerita silat*. *Nyai* were the native wives and mistresses of Europeans in the East Indies. Usually prefaced by a claim of being a record of actual events, *nyai* novels were generally based on newspaper crime reports and court transcripts relating to contemporary scandals involving *tuan*, "masters," and their *nyai*. The *nyai* tales catered to a taste for the lurid and macabre, entangling their characters in the passions of terror, suspicion, jealousy, and revenge, and reveling in situations of menace and intimidation, appeasement and enticement, and obsessive attachment.[20] Favored props were poisons, drugs, sorcery, nightmares, and pestilence that enhanced their obsession with darkness.

One of the best known *nyai* novels is the 1896 work *Tjerita Njai Dasima* by G. Francis, based on an incident that occurred in Batavia (Jakarta) about 1813. Dasima, the beautiful native wife of the British landowner Edward Williams, is taken in by

---

[17]According to a 1936 study made by the Balai Pustaka, the most popular books in the *taman bacaan*, which developed as a privately run alternative to the Taman Pustaka (see note 16) were popular novels written by *peranakan* Chinese. See Salmon, *Literature in Malay*, p. 112. For more information on the *taman bacaan* and the Taman Pustaka, see also Zubaidah Isa, "Printing and Publishing in Indonesia: 1602–1970" (PhD dissertation, Indiana University, 1972); Aeusrivongse, "Fiction as History."

[18]Salmon counts 806 *peranakan* Chinese authors and translators producing 3,005 works between the 1870s and the 1960s. See Salmon, *Literature in Malay*, p. 10.

[19]Ibid., pp. 93–94.

[20]See Kenji Tsuchiya, "Nyai Dashima" [*Njai Dasima*] (*Hon'yaku no sekai*, June 1986), p. 59.

the lies and flattery of the native youth Samioen, who covets her wealth. In the end she is murdered and her body thrown in a river. It is the curiosity and jealousy directed at Dasima by other natives and the details of the bizarre and horrifying circumstances of her death that are depicted in this novel.[21]

The *nyai* novel was by no means a static genre; it changed as its authorship switched from European to *peranakan* Chinese and Indonesian writers.[22] For example, Francis's voiceless and hence, in Indonesian eyes, ill-fated Dasima became a stronger, more self-aware heroine, like Nora in Henrik Ibsen's play *A Doll's House,* when the novel was rewritten in a time of intensifying nationalism.[23] The self-awareness of the *nyai* in Indonesian fiction from the 1920s onward reflects the transformation of hapless young women, sold without voicing a protest by poverty-stricken and debt-ridden parents, into strong-willed vocal women rebelling against the feudalistic custom of forced marriage. The epitome of the new breed of fictional *nyai* is seen in Takdir Alisjahbana's portrayal of a woman completely freed of traditional trammels in his 1936 novel *Lajar Terkembang* [With sails unfurled]. Nationalism's emancipation of the *nyai* also had the side effect of diluting the lasciviousness and bizarreness that had been the major attraction of the early *nyai* novels.

The *nyai* genre has established for itself a unique position in popular Indonesian literature and drama. Even today, a bridge in Jakarta is said to be haunted by the ghost of a *nyai*, probably the tragic Dasima.[24] After the initial 1896 fictionalization of Dasima's story, it became the favorite subject of traditional four-line *syair* poems, was adapted to the stage by the Komedi Stambul troupe, and was made into a movie four times (in 1929 and in a 1930 sequel, and again in 1940 and 1970). The image of the *nyai* Dasima has spread among the people and she has become a folk heroine in various media. Much more than a heroine in the printed world, she has become a symbol independent of both fiction and reality, a figure of popular imagination suspended in a world with no boundaries separating fact from fiction.

3. The *Roman Picisan*

A *picisan* is a ten-cent coin; the *roman picisan* is thus the dime novel, a genre of popular fiction published mainly in Medan, Padang, and Bukittinggi in Sumatra between 1938 and 1942 during the colonial period. Sometimes these works are referred to as "*roman* Medan" because so many were published in that city. *Roman picisan* represented pure commercial mass publication of cheap books. They were characteristically open to readers because the stories were serialized and sold by subscription, a system called *langganan*, and publishers encouraged letters and contributions from readers. Story themes also centered on contemporary issues that attract readers, and

---

[21]Pramoedya recapitulates *Tjerita Njai Dasima* and other *nyai* novels in *Tempo Doeloe*. For a detailed analysis of these novels and the social context in which they were written and read, see Tsuchiya, "Nyai Dashima"; Kenji Tsuchiya, "Nyai Dashima monogatari ron" [On *Tjerita Njai Dasima*] (*Tōyō bunka* 67 [1987]).

[22]*Peniti-dasi barlian* by Tan Tjin Kang, a *peranakan* Chinese novel published in 1922, is an extremely optimistic story about the happy triangular relationship of a *nyai*, her master, and the Chinese woman whom the *nyai* urges her master to marry. See Salmon, *Literature in Malay*, p. 38.

[23]A comparison of the G. Francis and S. M. Ardan versions of *Tjerita Njai Dasima* makes this transformation clear. See Tsuchiya, "Nyai Dashima monogatari," on the changing content of the *nyai* novel.

[24]See Tsuchiya, "Nyai Dashima," p. 59.

the action was often set in a new urban milieu. These handy paperback pocket books of eighty to a hundred pages had lavishly illustrated covers (usually suggesting an exotic locale), in contrast with the plain covers of Balai Pustaka books.

Some four hundred *roman picisan* titles were published in the five-year period from 1938 to 1942[25] in series with such names as *Doenia Pengalaman* [The world of experience] (Medan: 1938–1941), *Loekisan Poedjangga* [A poet's sketches] (Medan: 1939–1942), *Roman Indonesia* [Indonesian novels] (Padang: 1939–1940), *Roman Pergaoelan* [Social novels] (Bukittinggi: 1939–1941), *Tjendrawasih* [Bird of paradise] (Medan: 1940–1942), and *Doenia Pergerakan* [The world of movement] (Medan: 1940–?). These series closely resembled in style the popular-literature magazines published by *peranakan* Chinese.

The production system of *Loekisan Poedjangga* was typical of the genre.[26] *Loekisan Poedjangga* was the name of a series (like Harlequin Romances in the United States or Tachikawa Bunko in Japan) of detective stories, a type of publication known as *madjallah roman detektip popoeler* (popular detective novel magazine). Two novels were published every month. Some were self-contained stories; others were serials. If the first part of a serial proved to be especially popular, it was not uncommon to change the publication schedule and publish the sequel the next month instead of the novel that had been originally announced. Series novels could be purchased individually or through the *langganan* subscription system, under which readers paid for three months' worth of books in advance. The price of a three-month subscription (six books) was 1 guilder in Indonesia and 1.20 guilders for overseas subscriptions. Individual books cost 0.18 guilder domestically and 0.20 guilder overseas.[27] The publisher retained a dozen or so writers, including the editor in chief, who took turns writing the stories. Some of the more popular writers were so adept that they could turn out a novel overnight.[28]

---

[25]This number is based on Jakob Sumarjo's calculations (see Sumarjo, *Novel Populer*, p. 14). The actual number of copies of each volume printed is not known. The books were published in Solo and Gorontalo as well as Medan, Padang, and Bukittinggi. That two series published in Solo, *Doenia Pengalaman* and *Doenia Pergerakan*, had the same titles and publication dates as two series published in Medan indicates that the Medan publisher probably had a branch in Solo.

[26]The following information is based on the front and back cover copy, prepublication announcements, and lists of publications of *Loekisan Poedjangga* 5 and 12 (both published in 1940). I also referred to R. Roolvink, "Roman Pitjisan Bahasa Indonesia," in Teeuw, *Pokok dan Tokoh dalam Kesusasteraan Indonesia Baru*, vol. 2; Faizah Soenoto, "Tinjauan Bahasa Roman Indonesia Sebelum Perang" (*Archipel* 20 [1980]); Sumarjo, *Novel Populer*.

[27]*Doenia Pengalaman* published three volumes a month. The prices were 1.50 guilders domestically for a three-month subscription (nine books) and 1.75 guilders for an overseas subscription. Single publications were sold at 0.18 and 0.20 guilder, respectively. The novel *Salah Asuhan* [A wrong upbringing] by Abdul Muis, a representative work of modern Indonesian literature, was published in three volumes averaging 90 pages by the Balai Pustaka in 1928. Each volume cost 0.45 guilder. Clearly, the *roman picisan* were considerably cheaper. *Salah Asuhan* has been translated into Japanese by Kenji Matsuura as *Seiyō kabure—kyōiku o ayamatte* [Mania for the West: A wrong upbringing] (Tokyo: Imura Bunka Jigyōsha, 1982).

[28]So stated one of *Loekisan Poedjangga*'s authors, Tamar Djaja (see Sumarjo, *Novel Populer*, p. 40). His fellow writers included Joesoef Sou'yb (the editor in chief), Hamka, Rifai Ali, Soeman Hs., Selasih, Matu Mona, Dali, I Made Otar, Yusdja, Merayu Sukma, Manu Turie, A. Damhoeri, and Shaffar Yasin (many of these are clearly pen names). Interestingly, some of these writers, such as Joesoef Sou'yb and Rifai Ali, were regular contributors to the "pure" literary magazine *Pudjangga Baru*, first published in 1933. Others, such as Hamka, Soeman Hs., Selasih, and A. Damhoeri, also had works published by the Balai Pustaka. For example, *Tuan Direktur*,

As noted above, most *roman picisan* consist of detective and other genre novels, collectively known as *cerita silat*. Interestingly, politics is often as important an element in this kind of fiction as romance, mystery, crime, and tragedy. Political events and ideologies do not appear as the main themes, but are used as stage settings to highlight the themes essential to every kind of *roman picisan*: friendship and camaraderie, heroism, betrayal, intrigue, and mystery. In politics such themes can be found in their most symbolic form.

The *Patjar Merah Indonesia* stories by Yusdja, which were published as numbers 5 and 12 of *Loekisan Poedjangga*, were advertised as political novels, *roman politik*, but their principal themes are love, friendship, and betrayal among the men and women engaged in the revolutionary movement; there is very little real political content. The colonial government that the novels' heroes are supposedly fighting is presented as little more than a backdrop, a vague image at best, and no attempt is made to explain why colonialism and imperialism are evils to be battled.[29] Unlike Semaun's 1920 novel *Hikajat Kadiroen* [The story of Kadiroen], written when the Indonesian nationalist movement was at its peak, Yusdja's *Patjar Merah Indonesia* is "a novel without a message."[30]

Nevertheless, while such *roman picisan* may not deal directly with the issues of colonialism and imperialism as ideologies, they do manifest the concrete realities of politics through their fictional portrayals, with satirical twists, of spies and secret police, and of the nationalists' loves, friendships, and betrayals. "Politics" in *roman picisan* means trickery and disguise, evasion of enemy tails, the transportation of secret documents, defamation and slander, separation and escape, and finally rescue. The political *roman picisan* are extremely colorful and often fantastic, full of just the kind of exaggerated detail that was certain to appeal to a mass readership.[31] *Patjar Merah Indonesia*, on which I have chosen to focus, belongs to this world of *roman picisan*.

Whether translated or *peranakan* Chinese fiction, *nyai* novel, or *roman picisan*, the popular Indonesian literature of the 1920s and 1930s was a spontaneous product of

---

Keadilan Ilahi, and *Didalam Lembah Kehidupan* by Hamka, a noted Muslim writer, were first published as *roman picisan*—or at least by *roman picisan* publishing houses. When the works proved popular, they were republished by the Balai Pustaka. See the list of publications in *Loekisan Poedjangga* 12; Soenoto, "Tinjauan Bahasa Roman Indonesia."

[29]The same can be said of the novel *Tan Malaka di Medan* [Tan Malaka in Medan] by Emnast (real name, Muchtar Nasution), published in Medan as *Doenia Pengalaman* 9 in 1940. Tan Malaka appears under his real name in this novel about the efforts of a young member of Tan Malaka's secret organization to clear his name after having been wrongly accused of betraying the group and sentenced to death. The group's secret conclaves, the love that binds its male and female members, and the accusations, slander, and betrayal that tear them apart are the principal themes.

[30]Jakob Sumarjo, "Tradisi Novel Pop Indonesia" (*Pikiran Rakyat*, May 25 and 26, 1977).

[31]Political novels based on the activities of real nationalists and mystery stories involving political intrigue enjoyed special popularity around this time. For example, Muhammad H. Thamrin, a Jakarta-born leader of the nationalist movement, was arrested by the colonial government in 1941 and died in prison under mysterious circumstances. Shortly after his death a mystery story was published in which a giant bubble of poison gas is blown into Thamrin's cell and bursts over his head, killing him. See Seidō Miyatake, *Nan'yō no gengo to bungaku* [The languages and literatures of the South Seas] (Osaka: Yukawa Kōbunsha, 1943), pp. 210–11. To this day, a rumor persists that Thamrin died of poisoning, and the rumor may well have originated in this story.

the popular urban culture and the publishing customs of the day,[32] and it maintained its hold on the Indonesian imagination in spite of, or perhaps because of, the colonial government's dislike of the genre.[33]

Because these forms of popular fiction do not address the universal theme of self-awakening, they are not considered part of the national literature of Indonesia's colonial era and are virtually ignored in orthodox (*resmi*) Indonesian literary history. A. Teeuw, one of the foremost authorities on Indonesian literary history, has aptly called the *roman picisan* a "wild literature" (*kesusasteraan liar*).[34] His characterization of the genre as *liar*, or wild, can be interpreted in two ways. One is that *roman picisan* cannot be judged by the modern Western literary standards on which Teeuw relies and therefore are not worthy of study. The other is that they run counter to everything represented by the Balai Pustaka and *Pudjangga Baru*, a "pure" literary magazine first published in 1933, having absolutely no relationship to the exalted theme of self-awakening addressed by both the colonial government and scholars of modern Indonesian literature. Teeuw is Dutch, but his definition of literature as the portrayal of self-awakening has also been embraced by Indonesian scholars as almost the only valid definition.[35]

Given these circumstances, it is not surprising that the study of Indonesian literature has tended to consist primarily of analyses of writers and their works, with some attention focused on the historical and social context. But it is my belief that literature comes to life only when it is read and that therefore one cannot discuss it without taking into consideration its readers,[36] the "sea of humans."[37] I am not referring simply to the fact that popular fiction has a much larger audience than "pure" literature. Literature is a mirror that reflects the world of human psychology resting on the delicate balance between truth and fiction. The question is whether popular fiction fulfills this function. Does it share a common world with the reader? Does it "give

---

[32] For more information on the colonial-period urban culture that gave rise to the popular novel, see Kenji Tsuchiya, "'Jawa' kara 'Indoneshia' e—Indoneshia nashonarizumu sairon" [From Java to Indonesia: Indonesian nationalism reconsidered], in Yoneo Ishii, ed., *Tōnan Ajia sekai no kōzō to hen'yō* [The structure and transformation of the Southeast Asian world] (Tokyo: Sōbunsha, 1986); Kenji Tsuchiya, "Karutini sairon—19 seiki Jawa bunka ron e no ichi shikaku" [Kartini reconsidered: Toward a view of nineteenth-century Javanese culture], in Nichi-Ran Gakkai (Japan-Netherlands Society), ed., *Oranda to Indoneshia—rekishi to shakai* [The Netherlands and Indonesia: History and society] (Tokyo: Yamakawa Shuppansha, 1986).

[33] How the *roman picisan*, with their political themes and sometimes pornographic content, were able to get by the colonial censors is a very interesting question. I do not at present have access to materials that explain this phenomenon. But a notice in *Doenia Pengalaman* 9 (1940), in which *Tan Malaka di Medan* appeared, informed readers that *Doenia Pengalaman*'s sister publication *Poernama* had been forced to suspend publication because the editor, M. Saleh Oemar, had been imprisoned three months earlier. It is not clear whether he was arrested for political reasons or because of the pornographic content of his publications.

[34] See Teeuw, *Pokok dan Tokoh dalam Kesusasteraan Indonesia Baru*, 1: 67–70.

[35] See, for example, H. B. Jassin, *Kesusastraan Indonesia Modern dalam Kritik dan Esei*, 4 vols. (Jakarta: Gunung Agung, 1967); Ajip Rosidi, *Ikhtisar Sejarah Sastra Indonesia* (Bandung: Binacipta, 1976).

[36] As far as I know, only Aeusrivongse has made a study of the kinds of readers for whom the Indonesian literature that emerged in the 1920s was written and how that in turn helped determine the content of literature. See Aeusrivongse, "Fiction as History."

[37] Tsuchiya, "Karutini sairon," p. 236.

wings to the reader's dreams"?[38] Surely it does, for the fantastic world of popular fiction, which is often discarded as worthless, brings to life, like a treasure island, our wildest dreams. What could be more worthwhile than exploring this treasure island? *Patjar Merah Indonesia* is part of this treasure, even though Teeuw may judge it to lack all literary value.[39]

III. Patjar Merah Indonesia

The five *Patjar Merah Indonesia* books, all published in Medan, are listed below in order of publication.[40]

1. *Spionnage-Dienst (Patjar Merah Indonesia)* [Espionage service (The Scarlet Pimpernel of Indonesia)], 1938; 179 pages
2. *Rol Patjar Merah Indonesia c.s.* [The role of the Scarlet Pimpernel of Indonesia and his company], 1938; 168 pages
3. *Panggilan Tanah Air* [Call of the fatherland], 1940; 98 pages
4. *Moetiara Berloempoer, Tiga kali Patjar Merah datang membela* [The soiled pearl: Three times the Scarlet Pimpernel comes to the rescue], 1940; 76 pages
5. *Patjar Merah Kembali ke Tanah Air* [The Scarlet Pimpernel returns to the fatherland], 1940; 78 pages

The first three books were written by Matu Mona, the fourth and fifth by Yusdja.[41] I have managed to acquire all but one, *Panggilan Tanah Air*. The first and second books form a pair, as do the fourth and fifth, which were published as numbers 5 and 12 of *Loekisan Poedjangga*. Each pair is set in a different period and has a different cast of characters except for the Scarlet Pimpernel himself. The first two books are by far the best in terms of the grandeur of plot, originality, and the intricate balance of truth and fiction, and it is probably these two that helped shape the legend of Tan Malaka. I should therefore like to discuss their plots in some detail, while I will only briefly summarize those of the fourth and fifth books.

The cast of characters in the first two books includes the Scarlet Pimpernel (alias Vichitra, Tan Min Kha, Puting Ulap, and Ibrahim el Molqa); Paul Mussotte; Ivan Alminsky; Semounov; Darsonov; Djalumin; Khun Phra Pha, head of the Thai PID (Politieke Inlichtingendienst [political intelligence agency]); Ninon Phao, daughter of Khun Phra Phao and secret worshipper of the Scarlet Pimpernel; Phya Sakhon, a Thai army officer, and Ninon Phao's fiancé; Francois d'Isere, a leader of the socialist labor movement in Paris and a friend of Mussotte's; Marcelle, daughter of d'Isere, and Alminsky's lover; and Agnes Paloma, the Scarlet Pimpernel's Filipina secretary.

---

[38]Hiroshi Ikeda, *Taishū shōsetsu no sekai to hansekai* [The world and antiworld of the popular novel] (Tokyo: Gendai Shokan, 1983), p. 137.

[39]See Teeuw, *Pokok dan Tokoh dalam Kesusasteraan Indonesia Baru*, 1: 68.

[40]The first two were published by Centrale Courant en Boekhandel; the last three, by Tjerdas, publisher of *Loekisan Poedjangga*.

[41]Matu Mona's real name was Hasbullah Parinduri; Yusdja's was Yusuf Djajad. Both were well-known *roman picisan* authors. Matu Mona took up writing after serving as editor of the Medan newspaper *Pewarta Deli*. In addition to *Patjar Merah Indonesia*, he is known for his biographies of Muhammad H. Thamrin, a leader of the nationalist movement, and Wage Rudolph Supratman, composer of the Indonesian national anthem, "Indonesia Raya."

1. SPIONNAGE-DIENST (PATJAR MERAH INDONESIA)

The story opens in Bangkok, in January 1930. A suspicious-looking man dressed like a tourist arrives on a train from Penang in the Straits Settlements. Ninon Phao has been instructed by her father, head of the Thai PID, to learn the identity of the mystery man. She takes advantage of her beauty and sex appeal to approach the stranger, but her face turns pale when he shows her a photograph. The stranger, who calls himself Tengkoe Rahidin, is actually a secret agent of the Dutch PID. He has come in search of the Scarlet Pimpernel and the underground organization he formed in Bangkok after the dissolution of the PKI. The photograph Rahidin shows Ninon is of the Scarlet Pimpernel.

Through the efforts of Rahidin and the Thai PID one of the leaders of the underground group, Soe Beng Kiat (Subakat) is arrested the very next day. Meanwhile, the Scarlet Pimpernel has been struck down by a recurrence of tuberculosis (*sakit dada*) and is convalescing in the attic of a fisherman's house in the port town of Songkhla, near the Thai-Malay border. The fisherman's wife, Kanya, is Ninon's former wet nurse. She has agreed to Ninon's request to hide the Scarlet Pimpernel, who is using the alias Vichitra.

Ninon first met the Scarlet Pimpernel three years earlier, when she was returning to Thailand by ship after studying in France. In Hawaii the Scarlet Pimpernel rescued her from the clutches of a "marriage swindler," a con man who promises to marry women and then swindles them out of their money, and accompanied her as far as Bangkok. She has been secretly in love with him ever since. As soon as she learns that intelligence agents are after him, she flies to Songkhla in her own plane to warn him of the danger. Kanya and her husband know that Ninon is betrothed to another and are worried by her infatuation with Vichitra. They also want the large reward of 50,000 *tical* that has been offered for the Scarlet Pimpernel's capture, and they inform the agents where he is hiding.

In Songkhla, Ninon chances upon an Indonesian crewman from the freighter *Seremban*, which happens to be in port at the time. He is a leader of the Perhimpunan Kaum Buruh Laut, a seamen's union, and is also one of the Scarlet Pimpernel's most trusted lieutenants. His real name is Djalumin (Djamaluddin Tamin). With the help of his fellow seamen, Djalumin deftly rescues the Scarlet Pimpernel in the nick of time. Disguised as an old woman, the Scarlet Pimpernel slips through the authorities' hands and is safely transported on the *Seremban* to neighboring Malaya.

While these events are taking place, Paul Mussotte (Musso) is in Paris plotting to disrupt a colonial exhibition. He is at the home of Francois d'Isere, a leader of the Paris socialist labor movement, when his old comrade Ivan Alminsky (Alimin) arrives with d'Isere's daughter, Marcelle. Sent to Paris on a mission for Moscow (the Comintern), Alminsky has taken lodgings in a cheap boardinghouse. He has just rescued the young woman, who turns out to be d'Isere's daughter, from a wealthy Don Juan who lured her into the boardinghouse and tried to rape her.

Mussotte and Alminsky are overjoyed to see each other again. Alminsky's mission is to seek out the Scarlet Pimpernel and persuade him to return to Moscow's fold. Knowing the Scarlet Pimpernel's determined character, they fear that he is unlikely to comply. Still, the command of the Moscow *diktator* is absolute. Though he has fallen in love with Marcelle and she with him, Alminsky feels compelled to continue his search for the Scarlet Pimpernel. Torn by the conflicting emotions of his love for Marcelle and his sense of duty to Moscow, Alminsky departs, promising to return and marry Marcelle as soon as he has accomplished his mission.

After this opening, the tale moves on to the first Pan-Malay Congress, held in Manila in July 1931, and flashes back to events surrounding the Scarlet Pimpernel's arrest in Manila three years earlier. Eventually the scene shifts again, this time to New York. Alminsky has arrived there on board a steamship crossing the Atlantic and headed for the Far East. By chance he runs into Djalumin in a Brooklyn hotel. He explains his mission and enlists Djalumin's help in finding the Scarlet Pimpernel. Djalumin, who maintains regular communication with the Scarlet Pimpernel, is certain the latter will never agree to Moscow's terms. Still, he promises to help Alminsky, who then continues his journey to the Far East.

Meanwhile, the Scarlet Pimpernel is busy dissuading the nationalists in French Indochina from the reckless path on which they are about to embark. Having achieved his aim, he returns to Songkhla, where Ninon Phao confesses her love for him. She says she will part from Phya Sakhon, to whom she has been betrothed by her parents, and go with the Scarlet Pimpernel wherever his travels may take him. He, however, says he does not want her to suffer the hardships of his life as a fugitive, always running from imperialist agents. Leaving Ninon in tears, he departs for China.

Six months have passed since Alminsky began his search for the Scarlet Pimpernel. He has run out of money and still has no inkling of the Scarlet Pimpernel's whereabouts. Berated by Moscow for his failure, Alminsky is filled with despair. He is in Shanghai, which is under attack by the Japanese, when he notices a small advertisement in the *North China Daily News:* "WANTED: Friend, who is for ever seeking me. Apply No.987 Foochowstreet, west station. TAN MIN KHA" (*sic*). This is the signal sent to Alminsky by the Scarlet Pimpernel after being contacted by Djalumin.

Disguised as a Chinese, Alminsky is captured by British intelligence agents as he makes his way to the designated address. Some passing Japanese soldiers help him escape, however, and he slips into the International Settlement. The Scarlet Pimpernel is hidden in Chapei in northwestern Shanghai, near the International Settlement, and the two men finally meet in the basement of a ruined building that has been bombed by the Japanese. Alminsky urges the Scarlet Pimpernel to do Moscow's bidding, but after heated debate he is forced to acknowledge that the Scarlet Pimpernel is right. A lull in the battle raging around them provides an opportunity for the two to escape from Chapei, the Scarlet Pimpernel making his way to Hong Kong and Alminsky to the United States and eventually Europe.

The Scarlet Pimpernel's health fails him once again in Hong Kong. Learning of this from Djalumin, Ninon Phao rushes from Bangkok to nurse the man she loves. When he has recovered, thanks to Ninon's loving care, she speaks once again of her love for him and begs him to live with her in Thailand. Telling her that he cannot return her love lest he lose sight of his duty as a patriot and his determination to devote his life to his fatherland and his people, he urges her to marry her fiancé, Phya Sakhon.

Sakhon has followed Ninon to Hong Kong. When he learns of the depth of her love for the Scarlet Pimpernel, he is overcome by jealousy and tips off the British to the Scarlet Pimpernel's hiding place. The Scarlet Pimpernel is arrested, but Ninon promises to marry Sakhon if he will get the Scarlet Pimpernel released. Repenting his own rashness, Sakhon does everything in his power to save the Scarlet Pimpernel and finally persuades the British to deport him.

Ninon and Sakhon are married in Bangkok, and the Scarlet Pimpernel attends their wedding. But the peaceful interlude is brief. Notice arrives from the Singapore underground that Djalumin has been arrested. Despite the couple's entreaties to stay out of danger, the Scarlet Pimpernel leaves for new adventures.

2. Rol Patjar Merah Indonesia c.s.

According to the November 1938 preface by the publisher, M. Sjarqawi, *Rol Patjar Merah Indonesia c.s.* was published in response to favorable reviews of *Spionnage-Dienst* in newspapers and magazines and readers' requests for a sequel. In both scale and fantasy, this second story is probably the best of the *Patjar Merah Indonesia* books. The plot unfolds as follows.

It is October 1936. Paris, under Léon Blum's Popular Front coalition government, is in political turmoil as the left- and right-wing factions confront each other. Mussotte and d'Isere are there to speak at a leftist rally when they are sought out by Darsonov (Darsono), who has come from Brussels under orders from Moscow to go to Spain, which is in the throes of civil war. By chance, Darsonov comes across *Semangat Moeda* [Youthful spirit],[42] a book by the Scarlet Pimpernel, in Mussotte's study. Darsonov and Mussotte recall with chagrin the Scarlet Pimpernel's accusation that they have taken refuge in Europe and forgotten their duty to their fatherland, Nusasia (Indonesia). Mussotte decides to return to Nusasia, but Darsonov wavers between his yearning for his own country and his duty to Moscow. He finally decides to go on to Madrid, as instructed.

Meanwhile, Marcelle has joined a volunteer corps to fight alongside the women of Catalonia for a republican Spain, but her beloved Alminsky remains in the Far East, unable to return to her as he has promised. After parting from the Scarlet Pimpernel in Shanghai, Alminsky attempts to return to Moscow by way of Vladivostok (in the first book he makes his way to Europe via the United States). He is arrested in Harbin by the GPU, the Soviet secret police, and charged with plotting against the Kremlin's Iron Man (*orang besi;* Joseph Stalin). Sentenced to lifetime exile in Siberia, Alminsky is in the Soviet consulate in Harbin when he is rescued by Japanese soldiers who force their way into the building. They are led by the Scarlet Pimpernel, who has risked his life by disguising himself as a Japanese soldier to save Alminsky.

Alminsky spends 1934 and 1935 in Tianjin. From there he goes to Colombo, Sri Lanka, eventually making his way to Calcutta disguised as a mendicant priest. Under the protection of the Bengal Terrorists League, he plans to attend the Pan-Malay Congress to be held in Jodhpur, India, in December 1936.

At this time tension is heightening between the British and the Arabs over the issue of Jewish settlers in Palestine, whom Britain supports. A mysterious man is supplying the Bedouins with arms to help them defend their claim to Palestine and is leading a hundred of Britain's best intelligence agents a merry chase. He uses ten doubles, is a master of disguise and "mysterious knowledge" (*ilmu gaib*), and has a thousand and one tricks (*akal*) up his sleeve. His picture appears on wanted posters throughout the region, and the British are offering a reward of fifteen thousand pounds for his capture. His life a legend, his name on file in all the world's secret services, this man is none other than Ibrahim el Molqa, the Scarlet Pimpernel of Indonesia. At times he is a theoretician writing fiery pamphlets on the defense of Pales-

---

[42]*Semangat Moeda* is a pamphlet on strategy for the Indonesian independence movement written by Tan Malaka in 1926.

tine; at other times he is a strategist designing schemes to blow up the British oil pipelines; and at still other times he is an arms merchant supplying weapons for the Arab cause.

One day the Scarlet Pimpernel receives a telegram from Alminsky in Calcutta. Preparations for the Pan-Malay Congress are complete, and all the delegates are awaiting the Scarlet Pimpernel's arrival. Under the alias Professor Martinez, famed ethnologist and linguist, the Scarlet Pimpernel flies to Jodhpur from Rhodes accompanied by his Filipina secretary, Agnes Paloma. After delivering a lecture on Java man at the request of a local cultural group, he is joyfully reunited with Alminsky, whom he has not seen for several years.

Having reconfirmed the ideal of pan-Malayism that has brought them together and agreed to make still greater efforts to publicize their goals, the forty delegates attending the congress of December 1936 scatter to return to their own countries—except for Alminsky, who vows to stay with the Scarlet Pimpernel wherever he may go.

Mussotte, meanwhile, has boarded a ship in Amsterdam disguised as a Jewish tourist, Aaron. Arriving in Java via Singapore, he finds that his home country has changed greatly in the decade of his absence. The independence movement has been forced underground by the colonial government, and the people are struggling merely to survive. Mussotte makes his way to the Parambanan temple complex, where the leaders of the PKI once plotted an armed uprising, and vows before the goddess Loro Jonggrang that he will give his life to free his country. Thus begins a life in which he works by night to revive the revolutionary underground network while by day he distributes rice, salt, sugar, and other supplies to the people in the name of the savior Ratu Adil. Rumors of Ratu Adil's coming spread like wildfire.

In January 1937 Darsonov has completed his mission in Spain and returned to Brussels, from where he writes to Alminsky in Calcutta. Marcelle, he reports, has been sent to Russia for surgery with her four-year-old son after having been gravely wounded by a hand grenade while fighting valiantly for the Spanish republican cause. "Tell Alminsky," she begged Darsonov when he visited her in a Valencia field hospital, "if he loves his son, to come get us in Russia." But Russia is embroiled in the Purge, and Darsonov has heard from a trusted source that Semounov has been arrested by the GPU as a traitor.

Alminsky weeps as he reads the letter. If he goes to Russia, he runs the risk of being captured and executed. At a loss, he turns to the Scarlet Pimpernel for help. The Scarlet Pimpernel decides that it is up to him to rescue Marcelle, her son, and his old comrade Semounov. He knows this may well be his last mission in life, but he shakes off Agnes's entreaties to abandon such a dangerous venture.

Accompanied by Alminsky and Agnes, the Scarlet Pimpernel flies from Calcutta to Karachi and then makes his way overland through Baluchistan and Kabul to Samarkand in the Soviet Union. Disguised as gypsies to evade the secret police, the three split up in Samarkand, Alminsky and Agnes going by train to Moscow via Tashkent and the Scarlet Pimpernel making his way alone on horseback to Siberia to rescue Semounov. Fighting sleeplessness and hunger, the Scarlet Pimpernel, now disguised as a Russian named Amru, makes his way past GPU checkpoints to the town of Krasnoyarsk in southwestern Siberia. From there he travels by train and horseback to his destination, where he is reunited with Semounov.

It turns out, however, that Semounov has not been exiled but has been sent to Siberia under direct orders from the Kremlin to oversee the political prisoners there. Darsonov's information that Semounov was arrested by the GPU and exiled to

Siberia was purposely leaked by the Kremlin's Iron Man to lure the Scarlet Pimpernel to Russia.

Warned by Semounov of the danger to his life, the Scarlet Pimpernel rushes to Moscow, where he searches for Alminsky, who should have already arrived. Meeting in a Moscow park, the two plot to escape but are arrested by the GPU. As they are being driven to GPU headquarters, the Scarlet Pimpernel recites a spell that paralyzes the GPU agents and the driver, and guides the car to Marcelle's hospital. There he reunites Alminsky with his lover and child. Leaving Agnes to get Marcelle and the child to safety, the Scarlet Pimpernel and Alminsky disappear from Moscow by magic. Their phantomlike elusiveness fills the people of Moscow with terror, and *Izvestia* gives their exploits major coverage, accusing them of hostile acts against the Soviet Union.

With Agnes's help Marcelle and her son escape from Moscow, passing through Poland to Marseille and thence to Paris. Semounov accompanies them. Ever since his meeting with the Scarlet Pimpernel in Siberia, Semounov has realized that he may well be the next to be purged, and he has decided to leave Russia. Thoroughly disillusioned with the intrigues, treachery, jealousies, and suspicions of politics, he decides to live in Paris, where he begins studying for a doctorate at the Sorbonne.

Having crossed the Caucasus Mountains into Georgia, the Scarlet Pimpernel evades the GPU at the border to enter Iran and make his way to Teheran. There he addresses a mass gathering of Shiite Muslims who have come together to commemorate the martyr al-Husayn. His call for a revival of the past glory of Iran is greeted with a roar of approval from the tens of thousands of people before him. Despite this, the Scarlet Pimpernel and Alminsky are arrested by the shah's police, who have been told by the GPU that the two are undercover agents sent by Moscow to foment unrest in Iran. After two weeks in prison, they are brought to trial. Eventually the GPU plot to discredit the Scarlet Pimpernel is discovered and they are released on condition that they leave Iran within forty-eight hours. At this point Alminsky receives a telegram from Marcelle reporting that she has escaped from the Soviet Union with Agnes and Semounov. Relieved to learn that his family is safe, Alminsky asks the Scarlet Pimpernel what he plans to do next.

The Scarlet Pimpernel suggests that they make a pilgrimage to Mecca and then go on to Palestine to join the holy war in defense of the great cause of Islam (*ke-Islaman*). Alminsky agrees enthusiastically to his urging that they sacrifice themselves for the cause of religion and humanism (*agama dan kemanusiaan*). For the Scarlet Pimpernel, this marks a return to the battle he interrupted to attend the Pan-Malay Congress in Jodhpur and then go to Russia. United by their vow of sacrifice, the two discard their Western dress for the garb of Muslim *fakir* (ascetics) and embark on their new and final pilgrimage.

Ibrahim el Molqa (the Scarlet Pimpernel) and Hadji Salehoeddin (Alminsky) lead a caravan of Kurdish traders across the desert. They hide in the shade of rocks during the day and travel by night, battling their way through sandstorms. They guide the Kurds to Palestine to join the battle of the Arabs against the British and the Jews. The Arabs welcome their support, but the British have also brought in reinforcements from Malta and Rhodes, and neither side can prevail.

One night, as they lie on the desert sand weary from battle, the Scarlet Pimpernel tells Alminsky that they may soon be parted forever. He recalls a dream he once had of losing a tooth. It is a prophecy, he says, that a dear friend will be taken from him. Alminsky has also dreamed of death and asks that should he fall in battle, he be buried in Palestine and the national song, "Indonesia Raya," be sung over his grave. He also asks that it be made known to one and all that he died a martyr (*syahid*). The Scarlet Pimpernel promises to fulfill Alminsky's requests.

That very night Alminsky is killed in a fierce battle sparked by a grenade attack on a British transport vehicle carrying explosives. The Scarlet Pimpernel is shot in the right shoulder and severely wounded. The unconscious hero is saved by Abdul Qadir Macdonald, an American journalist who happens to be a friend of the Scarlet Pimpernel and has joined the Arabs in their fight, and is taken to a hospital. Despite the severity of his wound, the Scarlet Pimpernel honors his final promise to his friend, attending Alminsky's funeral and asking Macdonald to tell the world of the martyr's death. The Scarlet Pimpernel's last words to Macdonald are "I myself have only one wish, and that is to be buried in the soil of Palestine."

Thus end the adventures of the Scarlet Pimpernel in the first two volumes of *Patjar Merah Indonesia*. The first story begins in 1930, while Marcelle's telegram to Alminsky toward the end of the second story is dated 1937. Together, the two books encompass the years between 1930 and 1937 or perhaps 1938.

In contrast to the global setting of the first two books, by Matu Mona, the action in the fourth and fifth books in the series, by Yusdja, is restricted to Sumatra, Java, Malaya, and Singapore. The period of the latter stories is not clear, but judging from the opening scene, in which troops are sent from Padang to suppress rebellions in Sawahlunto and Silungkang in West Sumatra, their events probably begin in early 1927, which would be shortly after the armed uprising in West Sumatra and Java orchestrated by the PKI.

Except for the Scarlet Pimpernel, Yusdja introduces an entirely new cast of young revolutionaries. His focus is on Yamin, a member of the Sarekat Rakjat who is wrongly accused of betraying the organization to the authorities and is forced to part from his beloved. Overcoming the obstacles set before him by a secret-police agent who has infiltrated the Sarekat Rakjat, Yamin proves his innocence, rebuilds the organization, and is reunited with his lover. The plot shows the typical progression of the popular novel, from love to interference to happy ending. The Scarlet Pimpernel encourages and guides the hero, watching over him from the sidelines and appearing like a *deus ex machina* to extricate him from trouble. Their relationship is portrayed as one of teacher and disciple (*guru* and *murid*). The "soiled pearl" of the fourth book's title is an allusion to the Scarlet Pimpernel's description of Yamin, who is "soiled" by the accusation of treachery but is finally revealed to be shining and clean, absolved of all wrongdoing.

Panggilan Tanah Air, the third book in the series, is apparently an adventure story with political overtones about two youths who flee Indonesia and end up in Egypt, where they become entangled in political intrigue involving women and espionage,[43] but the Scarlet Pimpernel's place in the tale is not clear.

IV. The Scarlet Pimpernel and the Legend of Tan Malaka

I will now examine the special characteristics of the *Patjar Merah Indonesia* books and consider the way in which they must have been read at the time they were published, after which I will identify the features of the fictional Scarlet Pimpernel that corre-

---

[43]See Teeuw, *Pokok dan Tokoh dalam Kesusasteraan Indonesia Baru*, 1: 68–69.

spond most closely to the image of Tan Malaka that prevailed around the time that Indonesia declared independence in 1945. Finally, I will trace the process by which the Scarlet Pimpernel was transformed into a symbol of Tan Malaka by referring to articles about Tan Malaka that appeared in the Indonesian press when the books were published.

1. INFORMATION AND UTOPIA

In his preface to the second book, the publisher states that the Scarlet Pimpernel does not correspond to any historical person but is purely the product of Matu Mona's imagination. Yet the Scarlet Pimpernel's personality, actions, and circumstances clearly point to Tan Malaka as the model. Of course, it cannot be expected that the story of the Scarlet Pimpernel, being a work of fiction, would correspond exactly to the historical facts regarding the revolutionary Tan Malaka. While the first book incorporates numerous real events and places associated with Tan Malaka, the second is mostly pure fantasy. The reader is persuaded, however, to suspend disbelief by the presence of many historical figures and a wealth of detail suggesting the author's deep interest in events in the real world. In fact, the first two books of the *Patjar Merah Indonesia* series are notable for the amount of factual information they offer readers. This can be attributed first and foremost to Matu Mona's own thirst for knowledge, but it also reflects the intense curiosity of contemporary readers.

A great deal of information on the history of the 1930s when Tan Malaka was active is provided. Among the world events incorporated into the books are the independence movements that dominated Asia at the time (in the Philippines, Thailand, French Indochina, and India); the Sino-Japanese war; the rise of fascism in Europe; the Spanish civil war; Stalin's purge of his opponents; and the war in Palestine. The cities that form the backdrops for these events—Calcutta, Shanghai, Paris, Madrid—are described in vivid detail. The verisimilitude of the descriptions is enhanced by more than twenty photographs of the Paris colonial exhibition, the Shanghai Incident, the Spanish civil war, Hitler and Mussolini, Lenin's tomb, and other relevant scenes, and a number of diagrams and maps. As the publisher notes, *Patjar Merah Indonesia* bears many characteristics of a documentary account or a travelogue, an allusion to the series' abundant information on actual events and places.

Naturally enough, the most voluminous data relate to the main character, the Scarlet Pimpernel/Tan Malaka. Included are details of Tan Malaka's personality and *modus operandi* and of the revolutionary movement to which he belonged, profiles of his fellow nationalists, and even facts about their web of relationships. What is most intriguing is the amount of information to which only intelligence agents or actual participants in the events discussed could have had access, such as Tan Malaka's relationship with the Comintern (in the novel it is the Scarlet Pimpernel and Moscow) and his break with the Comintern to establish his own organization, Pari (in the first book this is the underground organization formed in Bangkok).

The sailor Djalumin, who rescues the sick Scarlet Pimpernel early in the first book, is Djamaluddin Tamin, one of the three founders of Pari. Tamin remained loyal to Tan Malaka even after he was arrested in Singapore in 1932 and exiled to Boven Digul, and his fictional counterpart has the same kind of loyalty toward the Scarlet Pimpernel. Only Dutch intelligence agents or those directly involved could have known of Alimin's being sent from Moscow to Shanghai to persuade Tan Malaka to return to the Comintern's fold, or that secret messages to Pari activists were transmitted through the *North China Daily News*.[44] These facts are used to establish the setting and act as props for the first two *Patjar Merah Indonesia* books.

Matu Mona obviously had a reliable source of information among those close to Tan Malaka or in Pari. This is seen most clearly in the episode of the Scarlet Pimpernel's arrest in Manila. Tan Malaka's arrest in 1927 created quite a stir in the Philippine press, and it would have been simple to craft the fictional event from newspaper articles. But there are some things only Tan Malaka himself could have known: the exchange between him and a detective over the meals served in the detention center, or the incident in which a woman who claims to be his wife is not allowed to visit him in prison. These and other details in the fictional account closely resemble Tan Malaka's own recounting of events in his autobiography,[45] written some ten years after publication of the first two *Patjar Merah Indonesia* books. The source of information must have been Tan Malaka himself or someone very close to him.[46]

Judging from the extent and variety of information packed into them, these two volumes might be termed an "information novel." We are told of the world as it was in the 1930s, of the Scarlet Pimpernel/Tan Malaka and his exploits, of the movements of exiled nationalists, and of revolutionary know-how—disguise, the art of shaking a tail and otherwise evading the pursuit of the authorities, methods of spreading underground propaganda. This is not information that can be of immediate use to the reader, of course. Nor does it offer profound lessons of life. But we must remember that by the latter half of the 1930s the zeal that had characterized the nationalist movement in the preceding decade had ebbed considerably, and its remaining organizations had been co-opted by the colonial government. Given these circumstances, the information packed into the first two *Patjar Merah Indonesia* books introduced a new dimension of space and time divorced from the controlled reality of colonial life and opened up vistas of a new world that was sure to excite readers' imagination.

The elaborate disguises, methods of evading enemies, and systems for transporting secret documents described in the books provide glimpses of the real revolutionary movement. The overall effect was to turn the familiar upside down and send readers soaring into an exciting dream world. For a brief moment they could escape the reality of the here and now by participating in the fantasy of living in the same dimensions of space and time as the Scarlet Pimpernel.

This brings us to another characteristic of *Patjar Merah Indonesia*, its utopian aspect. When I speak of a utopian novel, I am referring to utopia not in the sense of an ideal realm but in the sense of "a place that is nowhere": the "place beyond" or the "antiworld" of the real world. In *Patjar Merah Indonesia*, this utopia is expressed through the travels, friendship, and camaraderie of the Scarlet Pimpernel and Alminsky. Since a utopia is nowhere, it is only natural that the heroes of the story, seeking to overturn the world, embark on a never-ending journey. The utopian concept is

---

[44]The intelligence agency knew of Pari's system of transmitting messages (see *Mailrapport* 509x/31). Since the confidential colonial government reports known as *Mailrapport* were not declassified until the latter half of the 1960s, it is highly unlikely that Matu Mona could have had access to such documents in 1938. I am indebted to Associate Professor Takashi Shiraishi of the University of Tokyo for pointing this out.

[45]Compare, for example, *Spionnage-Dienst*, 112–17, and Tan Malaka, *Rōgoku kara rōgoku e*, 1: 249–66.

[46]According to the preface to the second book in the series, Matu Mona conceived the plot while in Singapore's Raffles Museum. Tan Malaka was in Singapore at the time and often visited the museum. It is tempting to speculate that the two may have met.

fully realized in the context of the miniature universe created by the bond of comradeship between the two men.

The real Tan Malaka and Alimin actually had a hostile relationship, as is obvious from their confrontation over the 1926–1927 issue of whether the PKI should instigate an armed uprising and their differing attitudes toward the Comintern. They were neither the comrades nor the old friends (*kontjo-lawas*) portrayed in *Patjar Merah Indonesia*.[47] Thus such episodes as the clandestine trip to Russia to rescue Marcelle and Semounov and the do-or-die participation in the Palestinian war are totally fictional.[48]

At the time that the Scarlet Pimpernel and Alminsky were sacrificing themselves for the Palestinian cause, Tan Malaka was living secretly in Singapore's Chinese community and Alimin was in France, the Soviet Union, or China.[49] It is not really important to the utopian nature of the fictional story, however, whether the two men actually made the journeys described or were as close to each other as the tale would have it. In fact, the more elaborate the fiction, the more freedom the author has to give rein to his imagination and hence achieve greater verisimilitude in the story itself. (In any case, readers were not likely to have known the real relationship between Tan Malaka and Alimin.) The story goes beyond mere fabrication when it succeeds in drawing in readers so that they participate in the protagonists' adventures and fiction just for a moment becomes reality.

The Scarlet Pimpernel and Alminsky can never remain in one place for long. Something is always compelling them to move on. Because they are seeking "a place that is nowhere," the beyond, the antiworld, their story requires the element of fantasy, and by its very nature fantasy has the power to overturn reality. Sorcery and disguise are the tools that give the two access to the antiworld and allow them to move back and forth between reality and fantasy, thereby adding an element of freedom to their dangerous journeys.[50] The tale's fantastic aspects also furnish readers with the weapon of imagination, with which they too can transcend reality and win a momentary freedom. Through imagination they can accompany the Scarlet Pimper-

---

[47]For more on the conflict between the two, see Alimin, *Analysis* (Yogyakarta: Bintang Merah, 1947); Tan Malaka, *Rōgoku kara rōgoku e*, 1: chaps. 6, 8.

[48]The Scarlet Pimpernel's fantastic journey to Siberia to rescue Semounov reminds me of the stories of heroic adventure by the Japanese writer Shunrō Oshikawa (1876–1914), such as *Kaitei gunkan* [Battleship under the sea] and *Shin Nippontō* [The new Japanese islands], and four others. In Oshikawa's tales Saigō Takamori (1828–1877), a historical figure who was instrumental in the Meiji Restoration of 1868, is rescued from Siberian exile. The fictional Saigō is working behind the scenes in support of the Philippine nationalist movement. Of course, Oshikawa's books, published between 1900 and 1907, were written over thirty years before *Patjar Merah Indonesia*, but it would be an interesting project to compare the global environment surrounding Japan and Indonesia at the times Matu Mona and Oshikawa were writing (the nationalist movement in the Far East, colonialism, imperialism, Russia/the Soviet Union, and so on).

[49]See Poeze, *Tan Malaka*, p. 482.

[50]The Scarlet Pimpernel, Alminsky, Mussotte, and Darsonov are credited with having the power of "mysterious knowledge" (*ilmu gaib*), though Mussotte and Darsonov never use this power. The Scarlet Pimpernel paralyzes his enemies by reciting a spell while his adversaries are looking at his face or into his eyes. This "magic" may actually have been a form of hypnosis. Only the source of Mussotte's and Darsonov's power is explained: their ability to disappear was acquired in training with famous *kiyai* while they were in Java. See *Rol Patjar Merah Indonesia c.s.*, pp. 37–41.

nel and Alminsky on their travels and make use of their sorcery and disguises to fly with them beyond the horizon of reality.[51]

The fantastic qualities of *Patjar Merah Indonesia* exist because readers want a means of escape from the here and now. Of course they are aware of the absurdity of such exploits as the Scarlet Pimpernel's using magic to disappear from Moscow and cross the Caucasus mountains at a bound. Yet while fully aware of the story's unreality, they depend on *Patjar Merah Indonesia* to lend them wings on which to escape from the real world, from "the reality of a self for whom all things have been destined and for whom all is immovable."[52] With the Scarlet Pimpernel's help, they too can magically disappear from Moscow and fly across the Caucasus Mountains.

The appeal of *Patjar Merah Indonesia* is that it enables readers to experience in fiction what they cannot in reality. This allure stirs hopes for another, different kind of world that are transformed into a critical view of the real world. Thus the Scarlet Pimpernel's aspiration of overturning the world as he knows it also becomes the readers' aspiration. The quest for another world and criticism of the existing world are the factors that make *Patjar Merah Indonesia* utopian fiction.

In short, *Patjar Merah Indonesia* creates a fictional time and space based on historical events of the 1930s and on detailed information about the Tan Malaka who lived through those events. Having set the stage, the author goes on to relate the kaleidoscopic adventures of the Scarlet Pimpernel and his comrades.

2. A REVOLUTIONARY OF MANY GUISES: MUTABILITY AND STOICISM

How, precisely, did these tales meld the images of the Scarlet Pimpernel and Tan Malaka? The Scarlet Pimpernel is above all a nationalist and patriot, ever ready to sacrifice himself for his country. He is also described as a "great" and "outstanding" leader who is revered by his comrades and subordinates.[53] Nothing is more important to him than the liberation of his country. It is only natural, then, that he would resist Moscow's assumption that it could lay claim to all the world's independence movements in the name of internationalism. On this point there is no doubt in his mind. This is in sharp contrast to the uncertainty of the other nationalists—Darsonov, Mussotte, Semounov, and the Alminsky of the first book in the series—who comply with Moscow's instructions even though they question its authority.[54]

By denouncing both imperialism and Moscow's brand of communism, the Scarlet Pimpernel draws down upon himself the enmity of both camps and is constantly pursued by their intelligence agents and secret police. But his uncanny ability to appear and disappear at will leaves both friend and foe in a fog as to his whereabouts. Fluent in several languages, he may take on the guise of an old woman, a coolie, a Japanese or Chinese merchant, even an enemy policeman or soldier. When danger threatens, he uses sorcery and supernatural powers (*kesaktian*) to disappear. Mystic powers, including the ability to change form, are among the first attributes of the Scarlet Pimpernel that are brought to the reader's attention. Various appellations in

---

[51]I am indebted to Ikeda, *Taishū shōsetsu,* for the concept of dreams (or illusions) shared by the popular novel and its reader. The term "antiworld" is also borrowed from this book.

[52]Ibid., p. 123.

[53]Interestingly, the Scarlet Pimpernel is nowhere referred to as a communist (*orang komunis*).

[54]Scornfully referring to his own inability to defy Moscow's authority, Alminsky calls himself "a machine that can only carry out orders" (*mesin yang mesti menjalankan kewajiban saja*). See *Spionnage-Dienst,* p. 103.

both Matu Mona's and Yusdja's *Patjar Merah Indonesia* stories serve to reinforce this image: "mystery man" (*mysterieman, orang rahasia*), "miraculous protector" (*pembela yang ajaib*), "slippery as an eel" (*licin sebagai belut*).

The Scarlet Pimpernel always comes across enemies in his travels and is in constant danger. Yet there is an enviable quality of freedom in his adventures, a freedom he zealously maintains through the artifices of disguise and magical transformation. He possesses the supernatural ability to break out of the seemingly closed space of reality. His magical abilities are the Scarlet Pimpernel's most potent weapon and the source of his mystical aura.

Another attribute of the Scarlet Pimpernel is his stoic response to women. This quality emerges in his relationship with Ninon Phao in the first book and with Agnes Paloma in the second. Both women confess their love for him, but the Scarlet Pimpernel turns them aside, citing his responsibilities to his country or the need to rescue his comrades from Siberia. Such excuses are merely ways of persuading women. Rather than a Stoic, he may be perceived as an androgynous Scarlet Pimpernel, capable of moving back and forth between different dimensions at will, unable to perceive women as sexual objects. This is probably why he remains ever a protector in his relationships with women, though the frustrated women accuse him of having a heart of stone and of not knowing the meaning of love. He never suffers Alminsky's dilemma of being torn between yearning for his lover and his sense of duty to the revolution.[55]

The Scarlet Pimpernel's mutability and stoicism are echoed in Tan Malaka's rumored ability to fly and in his image of purity in regard to women.[56] I do not claim that everything in the legend of Tan Malaka during the revolutionary period stems from *Patjar Merah Indonesia*. Many aspects are based on reports in the Indonesian newspapers, which frequently published stories on Tan Malaka during his years as a fugitive. Some articles, for example, report that he smuggled himself into Sumatra disguised as a Chinese cloth vendor.[57] The Scarlet Pimpernel is probably a composite of the many facts and rumors about Tan Malaka. Matu Mona may simply have given coherent form to these in creating the character of the Scarlet Pimpernel. In any case, once the public becomes familiar with a novel's hero, whether factual or fictional, he steps out of its fabricated world and acquires an existence quite independent of the author. The newspaper articles on Tan Malaka that I discuss below show how the Scarlet Pimpernel, originally a fictional hero, was gradually transformed into a symbol.

---

[55]The lyrics of Josephine Baker's famous *chanson* "J'ai deux amours," quoted on page 83 of *Spionnage-Dienst*, eloquently express this dilemma.

[56]Rumors of Tan Malaka's magical abilities were widespread during the revolutionary years. In his memoirs, Adam Malik writes of Tan Malaka: "He was rumored to have the miraculous ability to disappear at will and to appear in two different places at the same time. Such fantastic rumors are what turned him into a superhuman being on an equal footing with the gods." See Adam Malik, *Kyōwakoku ni tsukaeru—Adamu Mariku kaisōroku* [Serving the republic: The memoirs of Adam Malik; original title *Mengabdi Republik*], trans. Keiji Omura (Tokyo: Shū ei Shobō, 1981), p. 179. The activist S. K. Trimurti, who knew Tan Malaka during the revolutionary period, has noted that one of his distinguishing characteristics was that he never treated women as sex objects and in this respect was "pure" (*bersih*). See her reminiscences in Bulletin Murba, ed., *Peringatan Sewindu Hilangnja Tan Malaka, Bapak Murba dan Republik Indonesia* (Jakarta: Bulletin Murba, 1957), p. 21; Anderson, *Java in a Time of Revolution*, p. 276.

[57]See Poeze, *Tan Malaka*, p. 482.

3. Reality and Fiction: The Scarlet Pimpernel in the Newspapers

The *Pewarta Deli*, published in Medan, was probably the first newspaper to refer to Tan Malaka as the Scarlet Pimpernel. A February 12, 1938, article headlined "Republic of Indonesia Party" (*Partai Republiek Indonesia*), written under the byline Tumasik, reports on Pari's activities. Appended to the article is a feature headed "Experiences of a Spy" (*Pengalaman seorang spion*), which purports to relate the experiences of a former Dutch intelligence agent identified only as L. The gist is as follows.

In 1934 L, who had been tracing the movements of the Scarlet Pimpernel, learned that he was staying in a Kuala Lumpur hotel under the alias Oesman. The Scarlet Pimpernel was on his way to the Punjab to preside over the Pari party congress. After ascertaining that the Scarlet Pimpernel had left the hotel and was on his way to Singapore, L telegraphed his superior in Singapore to report to him on the Scarlet Pimpernel's movements. He then checked into the same hotel to rest and wait for further instructions. By chance, he was given the very room in which the Scarlet Pimpernel had stayed. Late that night L was awakened by the Scarlet Pimpernel appearing at his bedside. He searched the room but found no one, and his door remained locked. For ten days thereafter, the Scarlet Pimpernel appeared nightly, tearing away his blanket and glaring at him. Worn down by fear and lack of sleep, L had a nervous breakdown and notified his superior of his wish to quit his job. For six months, L was plagued by the Scarlet Pimpernel's shade night and day. The feature concludes: "This is a true story told to us [the *Pewarta Deli*] by L himself, who calls the Scarlet Pimpernel a 'living miracle' [*keramat hidup*]."

The preface to the first *Patjar Merah Indonesia* book is dated March 1938, indicating that the *Pewarta Deli* article preceded publication of the book. However, for many years Matu Mona had been the editor of the *Pewarta Deli*, and since he had probably finished the first book by the time the article appeared, it is likely that the appellation of Scarlet Pimpernel for Tan Malaka was adopted from the book. After this the Scarlet Pimpernel was mentioned frequently in Indonesian newspapers. At some point the boundary between the Scarlet Pimpernel of fiction and the Tan Malaka of fact was crossed and the two merged.

The *Pemandangan*, published in Batavia [Jakarta], had one of the largest circulations of any newspaper during the colonial period. On April 8, 1938, this paper ran an article with the headline "The Scarlet Pimpernel of the Republic of Indonesia Party Arrested" (*Patjar Merah dari Party Republiek Indonesia tertangkap*) and the subhead "Tan Malaka and Alimin Are 100% Nationalists," reporting a story told to the paper's Cairo correspondent by two Indians, one a graduate of Oxford, the other a graduate of Aligarh Muslim University. They said they had arrived in Cairo from Teheran five days earlier. In Teheran they had been arrested because of passport irregularities and had spent several days in a detention center. There, they told the correspondent, they met two men detained as spies who looked like a Chinese and a Ceylonese. The two introduced themselves in Chinese and Javanese as Tan Malaka and Alimin, respectively, and said they had just entered Teheran after crossing the Soviet border by way of the Caspian Sea when they had been arrested by the Iranian police on suspicion of being secret agents of Moscow.

The article goes on to relate that a "love letter" was delivered to the two men, that they were released after it was proved in court that they were not Soviet agents, and that Tan Malaka made a speech before the people of Teheran. These events are exactly the same as those in chapter 12 of the second *Patjar Merah Indonesia* book.

The follow-up story in the same chapter appears exactly the same way in the article dated October 19, 1938, in the *Pewarta Deli*, supposedly dispatched from Cairo. The article is headed "Palestine Claims an Indonesian Martyr: The Death of the Right-Hand Man of the Scarlet Pimpernel of Indonesia" (*Korban yang dimintak oleh tanah Palestina didalam sejarah Indonesia atau meninggalnya tangan kanan dari Patjar Merah di Indonesia*). It reports the journal of the Scarlet Pimpernel and Alminsky to Palestine, the Scarlet Pimpernel's wounding, and Alminsky's death, as well as the existence of other characters, such as the American journalist Macdonald, as if these things were actually about the real-life Tan Malaka and Alimin. On December 29, the same paper featured the headline, also dispatched from Cairo, "The Role of the Scarlet Pimpernel of Indonesia" (*Rol Patjar Merah Indonesia*). The April 8 and October 19 articles, reporting the Scarlet Pimpernel's infiltration of Iran and his activities in Palestine, respectively, appeared before publication of the second book, "The role of the Scarlet Pimpernel of Indonesia and his company," whose preface is dated November 1938.

It is not clear whether the book derived its material from newspaper articles or whether the newspapers created articles on the basis of the book. In either case, the newspaper articles are definitely fictional. The questions of which is based on which and whether the stories are true are not important here, however. What is important is the indication that the character of the Scarlet Pimpernel assumed a life of its own and even infiltrated journalism, which is supposed to adhere to facts.

In the newspapers as in the books, the Scarlet Pimpernel was "slippery as an eel," always escaping danger at the last moment. No matter how tight a corner he was driven into, he remained the calm and steady leader, immune to panic and confusion (*tak hilang akal*).[58] He had become much more than the hero of a popular novel. Through the medium of the press he had won a broader readership and had been transformed into a symbol that was everyone's common property.

CONCLUSION: TWO BOOKS, TWO READINGS

During and after the Indonesian revolution, the tale of the Scarlet Pimpernel of Indonesia was related as though it were the story of Tan Malaka himself. Nearly all the biographies of Tan Malaka written by Indonesians during that period regard the Scarlet Pimpernel's personality, *modus operandi*, and circumstances to be those of Tan Malaka.[59] Undoubtedly, the Scarlet Pimpernel's image had an influence on Tan Malaka's own behavior.[60] One thing is sure: as noted above, the Scarlet Pimpernel

---

[58]Tan Malaka was repeatedly described this way in the newspapers.

[59]See Sakti Arga, *Tan Malaka Datang!!!* (Bukittinggi: Tjerdas, 1945?); Tamar Djaja, *Trio Komoenis Indonesia: Tan Malaka, Alimin, Semaoen berikoet Stalin dan Lenin* (Bukittinggi: Penjiaran Ilmoe, 1946); Ratu Sukma, *Tan Malaka* (Bukittinggi: Pustaka Rakyat, 1948); Tamar Djaja, *Orang-Orang Besar Indonesia*, vol. 3 (Jakarta: Pustaka Antara, 1975), pp. 26–37. *Orang-Orang Besar Indonesia*, a collection of biographies of great figures in Indonesian history written for elementary school children and published 26 years after Tan Malaka's death, still refers to him as "the Scarlet Pimpernel of Indonesia."

[60]In his December 13, 1945, article in the *Kedaulatan Rakjat* (see note 9), Tan Malaka refers to himself in the third person as "Tan Malaka" or "he" (*dia*) and denies that he entered Indonesia with the Japanese forces. His use of the third person indicates that he too thought of himself as a legendary figure and acted accordingly, as suggested by the article's opening statement that

escaped from the world of fiction, taking on a life of his own. It was not that Tan Malaka was the Scarlet Pimpernel; but the Scarlet Pimpernel had become Tan Malaka. This phenomenon can be traced to a function inherent in the popular novel as well as to the influence of the newspapers. In conclusion, I would like to consider this phenomenon while comparing the ways in which Takdir Alisjahbana's *Lajar Terkembang*, published in 1936,[61] and *Patjar Merah Indonesia* were read.

Alisjahbana is one of the founders of modern Indonesian literature. His novel *Lajar Terkembang*—a love story involving two sisters, Tuti and Maria, and Maria's fiancé, Jusuf, who marries Tuti after Maria's death—is considered to be a benchmark in Indonesian literature during the colonial period. The three protagonists are completely liberated from traditional social restrictions, particularly those relating to the feudalistic custom of forced marriage, which was a favorite theme of the writers of the 1920s.[62] The characters reflect Alisjahbana's central theme as a thinker, the search for a modern sense of self. His work must be read in terms of its characters' thoughts and feelings, in other words, of the theme imposed by the author. Even the settings are filtered through the modern consciousness of the characters, the author's alter egos. The readers are restricted by Alisjahbana's own design whether explicit or implicit, bound irrevocably by the meanings imparted to things by the work—which is to say, by the author.

The relationship between *Lajar Terkembang* and its readers flows only one way, from the work (author) to the reader. Not even critics of the novel can escape the constraints of this relationship. The author retains the prerogative of interpreting the reality he has created in the novel. This being the case, each reader is cut off from all other readers. Thus the novel's readers inhabit a doubly closed world. *Lajar Terkembang* will always be the work of Alisjahbana, seeker of a modern sense of self. The work can never be severed from his name.

In contrast, *Patjar Merah Indonesia* maintains an open relationship with its readers. This is due to more than the special characteristics of the popular novel (subscription-based publication, communication with readers through letters to the editor, and so on). The world of the Scarlet Pimpernel, the antiworld to which he gives readers access, is precisely that sought by readers, and they are free to interpret the story as they wish, regardless of the author's intent. The story is passive, adapting itself to the interpretations of individual readers. In this way the novel becomes independent of its author. Through its own momentum and its readers' input, it advances toward new horizons.

It does not really matter whether the Scarlet Pimpernel is a factual or a fictional character. When readers absorb the story and make it their own, the Scarlet Pimpernel becomes, for them, very real. The way in which *Patjar Merah Indonesia* was read, the relationship that developed between the work and its readers, is one reason the

---

Tan Malaka would appear according to the circumstances and capacity of the Indonesian people. Tan Malaka also knew of *Patjar Merah Indonesia* and its content. See Tan Malaka, *Rōgoku kara rōgoku e*, 2: 256.

[61]*Lajar Terkembang* has been translated into Japanese by Misao Kimura as *Kaenju—Indoneshia josei, ai no seisatsu* [The flame tree: Indonesian women's reflections on love] (Tokyo: Gakuensha, 1978).

[62]A typical example is the novel *Sitti Nurbaya* by Marah Rusli (Weltevreden: Balai Pustaka, 1922).

story of the Scarlet Pimpernel merged with the story of Tan Malaka and grew into a revolutionary legend.[63]

The Scarlet Pimpernel fulfills the readers' wish to assume a new identity. To them he must have represented the fulfillment of dreams impossible to realize in the real world. To this day there are those in Minangkabau in western Sumatra, Tan Malaka's birthplace, who believe that he still lives and will reappear when his country needs him, as he did at the time of the independence revolution of 1945. Some people even claim to have seen him in the guise of a Chinese fruit vendor.[64] (For some reason, people most often see Tan Malaka disguised as a Chinese. In *Patjar Merah Indonesia* the Scarlet Pimpernel, too, most often assumes the disguise of a Chinese.) Here we are truly in the world of the Scarlet Pimpernel.

Of course, Tan Malaka has long since departed this world forever. And the Scarlet Pimpernel's world is, after all, only a fictional one. Yet it would be simplistic to dismiss the sightings of the people of Minangkabau as mere fantasy. For those who remember the independence revolution of 1945 and hope for Tan Malaka's return, the world they share with the Scarlet Pimpernel/Tan Malaka is the real world and the world in which they live is not genuine. The Scarlet Pimpernel's hopes and dreams of overturning reality continue to live in their hopes and dreams. As long as people continue to believe that the present reality is not the true reality, for them the legend of Tan Malaka will live on.

This paper, originally published under the title *"Indoneshia no benihakobe to Tan Maraka: Taishū shōsetsu to kakumeika densetsu"* [Patjar Merah Indonesia and Tan Malaka: A popular novel and a revolutionary legend] in the *Journal of Sophia Asian Studies* 4 (1986), 121–55, is a revised and expanded version of a paper presented on March 29, 1986, at a monthly meeting of the Kantō (East Japan) chapter of the Japan Society for Southeast Asian History held at Sophia University, Tokyo. After its presentation I received very helpful comments from Associate Professor Takashi Shiraishi of the University of Tokyo, Associate Professor Kenji Tsuchiya of Kyoto University's Center for Southeast Asian Studies, and many others. I would also like to take this opportunity to thank Ms. Yuri Satō, an overseas researcher of the Institute of Developing Economies in Jakarta, for her invaluable help in gathering material on *Patjar Merah Indonesia*.

Finally, I should like to note that modern Indonesian spelling has been used in this paper except in the case of book titles, names of magazines and newspapers, and personal names for which older forms are customary.

---

[63]The same can be said of *Tjerita Njai Dasima*.

[64]See Helen Jarvis, "From Jail to Jail: The Autobiography of Tan Malaka" (unpublished MS), pp. 92–93.

BIBLIOGRAPHY

Aeusrivongse, Nidhi. "Fiction as History: A Study of Pre-war Indonesian Novels and Novelists (1920–1940)." PhD dissertation, University of Michigan, 1976.

Alfian. "Ama kakeru kakumei no shisō—densetsu no kyōsanshugisha Tan Maraka" [A soaring revolutionary philosophy: The legendary communist Tan Malaka]. In *Shinjitsu no Indoneshia* [The true Indonesia; original title Manusia dalam Kemelut Sejarah], edited by Taufik Abdullah. Translated by Masahide Shibusawa and Kenji Tsuchiya. Tokyo: Simul Shuppankai, 1978.

Alimin. *Analysis*. Yogyakarta: Bintang Merah, 1947.

Alisjahbana, Takdir. *Kaenju—Indoneshia josei, ai no seisatsu* [The flame tree: Indonesian women's reflections on love; original title Lajar Terkembang]. Translated by Misao Kimura. Tokyo: Gakuensha, 1978.

Anderson, Benedict. *Java in a Time of Revolution: Occupation and Resistance, 1944–1946*. Ithaca, NY: Cornell University Press, 1972.

———. *Imagined Communities: Reflections on the Origin and Spread of Nationalism*. London: Verso, 1983.

Ardan, S. M. *Njai Dasima*. Jakarta: Pustaka Jaya, 1965.

Arga, Sakti. *Tan Malaka Datang!!!* Bukittinggi: Tjerdas, 1945?.

Djaja, Tamar. *Trio Komoenis Indonesia: Tan Malaka, Alimin, Semaoen berikoet Stalin dan Lenin*. Bukittinggi: Penjiaran Ilmoe, 1946.

———. *Orang-Orang Besar Indonesia*, vol. 3. Jakarta: Pustaka Antara, 1975.

Emnast [Nasution, Muchtar]. *Tan Malaka di Medan*. Doenia Pengalaman 9. Medan: 1940.

Escarpit, Robert. *Bungaku no shakaigaku* [The sociology of literature; original title *Sociologie de la Littérature*]. Translated by Yukio Ōtsuka. Tokyo: Hakusuisha, 1980.

Ikeda, Hiroshi. *Taishū shōsetsu no sekai to hansekai* [The world and antiworld of popular novels]. Tokyo: Gendai Shokan, 1983.

Isa, Zubaidah. "Printing and Publishing in Indonesia: 1602–1970." PhD dissertation, Indiana University, 1972.

Jassin, H. B. *Kesusastraan Indonesia Modern dalam Kritik dan Esei*. 4 vols. Jakarta: Gunung Agung, 1967.

Jauss, Hans Robert. *Chōhatsu to shite no bungaku shi* [The history of literature as provocation; original title *Literaturgeschichte als Provokation*]. Translated by Osamu Kutsuwada. Tokyo: Iwanami Shoten, 1976.

Maeda, Ai. *Kindai dokusha no seiritsu* [The formation of the modern reader]. Tokyo: Yūseidō, 1973.

Malik, Adam. *Kyōwakoku ni tsukaeru—Adamu Mariku kaisōroku* [Serving the republic: The memoirs of Adam Malik; original title *Mengabdi Republik*]. Translated by Keiji Omura. Tokyo: Shūei Shobō, 1981.

McVey, Ruth T. *The Rise of Indonesian Communism*. Ithaca, NY: Cornell University Press, 1965.

Miyatake, Seidō. *Nan'yō no gengo to bungaku* [The languages and literatures of the South Seas]. Osaka: Yukawa Kōbunsha, 1943.

Mrazek, Rudolf. "Tan Malaka: A Political Personality's Structure of Experience." *Indonesia* 14 (October 1972).

Nio Joe Lan. *Sastera Indonesia-Tionghoa*. Jakarta: Gunung Agung, 1962.

Poeze, Harry A. *Tan Malaka: Strijder voor Indonesie's Vrijheid, Levensloop van 1897 tot 1945*. The Hague: Nijhoff, 1976.

Pramoedya Ananta Toer, ed. *Tempo Doeloe: Antologi Sastra Pra-Indonesia*. Jakarta: Hasta Mitra, 1982.

Roolvink, R. "Roman Pitjisan Bahasa Indonesia." In A. Teeuw, *Pokok dan Tokoh dalam Kesusasteraan Indonesia Baru*, vol. 2. Jakarta: Pembangunan, 1955.

Rosidi, Ajip. *Ikhtisar Sejarah Sastra Indonesia*. Bandung: Binacipta, 1976.

———. *Pembinaan Minat Baca, Bahasa Dan Sastera*. Surabaya: Bina Ilmu, 1983.

Salmon, Claudine. *Literature in Malay by the Chinese of Indonesia: A Provisional Annotated Bibliography*. Paris: Editions de la Maison des Sciences de l'Homme, 1981.

Shiraishi, Takashi. "Oranda Higashi Indo Kokka to Indoneshia nashonarizumu—pergerakan (undō) no rekishi jojutsu o megutte" [The Netherlands East Indies State and Indonesian nationalism: On historical accounts of the *pergerakan* (movement)]. In *Oranda to Indo-*

neshia—rekishi to shakai [The Netherlands and Indonesia: History and society], edited by Nichi-Ran Gakkai (Japan-Netherlands Society). Tokyo: Yamakawa Shuppansha, 1986.

Siregar, Bakri. *Sedjarah Sastera Indonesia Modern*. Jakarta: Akademi Sastera dan Bahasa "Multatuli," 1964.

Soenoto, Faizah. "Tinjauan Bahasa Roman Indonesia Sebelum Perang." *Archipel* 20 (1980).

Sukma, Ratu. *Tan Malaka*. Bukittinggi: Pustaka Rakyat, 1948.

Sumarjo, Jakob. "Tradisi Novel Pop Indonesia." *Pikiran Rakyat*, May 25 and 26, 1977.

———. *Novel Populer Indonesia*. Yogyakarta: Nur Cahaya, 1982.Sykorsky, W. V. "Some Additional Remarks on the Antecedents of Modern Indonesian Literature." *Bijdragen tot de Taal-, Land- en Volkenkunde* 136, no. 4 (1980).

Tan Malaka. *Rōgoku kara rōgoku e—Tan Maraka jiden* [From jail to jail: The autobiography of Tan Malaka; original title *Dari Pendjara ke Pendjara*]. 3 vols. Translated by Noriaki Oshikawa. Tokyo: Rokusaisha, vol. 1, 1979; vol. 2, 1981; vol. 3, forthcoming.

Teeuw, A. *Pokok dan Tokoh dalam Kesusasteraan Indonesia Baru*. 2 vols. Jakarta: Pembangunan, 1955.

———. *Modern Indonesian Literature*. The Hague: Nijhoff, 1967.

———. *Modern Indonesian Literature*, vol. 2. The Hague: Nijhoff, 1979.

Tio Ie Soei. *Lie Kimhok: 1853–1912*. Bandung: Good Luck, 1959.

Tsuchiya, Kenji. "'Jawa' kara 'Indoneshia' e—Indoneshia nashonarizumu sairon" [From Java to Indonesia: Indonesian nationalism reconsidered]. In *Tōnan Ajia sekai no kōzō to hen'yō* [The structure and transformation of the Southeast Asian world], edited by Yoneo Ishii. Tokyo: Sōbunsha, 1986.

———. "Karutini sairon—19 seiki Jawa bunka ron e no ichi shikaku" [Kartini reconsidered: Toward a view of nineteenth-century Javanese culture). In *Oranda to Indoneshia—rekishi to shakai* [The Netherlands and Indonesia: History and society], edited by Nichi-Ran Gakkai (Japan-Netherlands Society). Tokyo: Yamakawa Shuppansha, 1986.

———. "Nyai Dashima" [*Njai Dasima*]. *Hon'yaku no sekai*, June 1986.

———. "Nyai Dashima monogatari ron" [On *Tjerita Njai Dasima*]. *Tōyō bunka* 67 (1987).

Tsurumi, Shunsuke. *Taishū bungaku ron* [On popular literature]. Tokyo: Rokkō Shuppan, 1985.

Watson, C. W. "Some Preliminary Remarks on the Antecedents of Modern Indonesian Literature." *Bijdragen tot de Taal-, Land- en Volkenkunde* 127, no. 4 (1971).

2

A STUDY OF *BUSTANU'S-SALATIN* (THE GARDEN OF THE KINGS)

Saya Shiraishi

I. INTRODUCTION

Bustanu's-Salatin [The garden of the kings] was written around the middle of the seventeenth century as the golden age of the kingdom of Aceh was drawing to a close. In this paper I will attempt to read and understand the way in which the culture and history of the kingdom are presented in this work in comparison with *Hikajat Atjéh*, another major historical literary work of seventeenth-century Aceh. I will begin by reviewing the historical context in which the text was produced and will provide a brief summary of the chapter that concerns the kingdom of Aceh, relying on Dr. Teuku Iskandar's edition of the text.[1] I will then examine its main themes, the construction of the garden and the funeral ceremony that follows, through which the nature of kingship in Aceh is expressed.

II. BACKGROUND AND CONTENTS

The greatest king in Aceh's history, who ruled at the peak of the kingdom's power, was Sultan Iskandar Muda (r. 1607-1636). *Hikajat Atjéh* was compiled during his reign.[2] His successor, Sultan Iskandar Thani (r. 1636-1641), commissioned the writing of *Bustanu's-Salatin*, which was begun in 1638. Its main portion was completed by the early years of the reign of the next ruler, Sultan Taju'l-'Alam (r. 1641-1675).[3] Taju'l-'Alam, Aceh's first female ruler, was the daughter of Iskandar Muda and the wife of Iskandar Thani. Three other queens followed her. The final portion of *Bustanu's-Salatin* (hereafter referred to as *Bustan*) records that everything that symbolized the glory of the kingdom of Aceh was destroyed by fire during the rule of the second of those queens.

Today, Aceh is merely a special autonomous region of the Republic of Indonesia located in northern Sumatra. After the Portuguese seizure of Malacca in 1511, however, Aceh had been a major base for Muslim traders. By the early seventeenth century, when *Hikajat Atjéh* and *Bustan* were compiled, Aceh not only was an important

---

[1]My primary source is Nuru'd-Din ar-Raniri, *Bustanu's-Salatin, bab 2, fasal* 13, ed. Teuku Iskandar (Kuala Lumpur: Dewan Bahasa dan Pustaka, 1966). For the most part, the spellings of Indonesian words follow the spellings in the respective sources.

[2]Teuku Iskandar, ed., *De Hikajat Atjéh*, Verhandelingen van het Koninklijk Instituut voor Taal-, Land- en Volkenkunde van Nederlandsch-Indië 26 (The Hague: Nijhoff, 1958): 17–18.

[3]Raniri, *Bustanu's-Salatin*, pp. 4–10.

entrepôt of Muslim trade, linking India with the Red Sea to the west and the Spice Islands to the east, but also flourished as a center for Muslim scholars and writers in the Malay world.[4]

Sheik Nuru'd-Din Muhammad ibn Ali Hamid ar-Raniri, the author of *Bustan*, was born in Ranir, Gujarat. In 1628, after studying Sufism in Arabia, he began to pursue an active career as a writer and translator in Arabic and Malay.[5] In those days relations between Gujarat and the various Malay kingdoms on the Strait of Malacca were very close, and even closer with Aceh, since its markets were dominated by Gujarati cotton merchants. Raniri's uncle traveled to Aceh twice, in 1580 and 1583, to establish Islamic studies there. In addition, Raniri's mother was Malay, so his ties to the Malay world were strong.

Raniri arrived in Aceh on May 31, 1637, and soon came under the patronage of its new king, Iskandar Thani, a native of Pahang, on the east coast of the Malay Peninsula, who had acceded to the throne the previous year. In Aceh, Raniri wrote numerous books on Islamic theology, including *Bustan*. This work, commissioned by Iskandar Thani in 1638 and continued under Taju'l-'Alam after Iskandar Thani's death in 1641, became Raniri's best-known writing. Raniri left Aceh in 1644 and returned to Ranir.

Bustan, aptly described as an "encyclopedia of world history,"[6] includes seven chapters, the contents of which are outlined below.

I. The Creation of Heaven and Earth
II. Prophets and Kings
   1. The Prophets from Adam to Muhammad
   2. Persian Kings to the 'Umar Period
   3. Byzantine Kings to the Time of the Prophet Muhammad
   4. Egyptian Kings to the Time of Alexander the Great
   5. Arab Kings before Islam
   6. Nedjd Kings to the Time of the Prophet Muhammad
   7. Hidjaz Kings to the Time of the Prophet Muhammad
   8. History of the Prophet Muhammad and the Four Early chalifah
   9. Arab History under the House of 'Umajja
   10. Arab History under the House of Abbas
   11. History of the Islam Delhi Kings
   12. History of the Kings of Malacca and Pahang
   13. History of the Kings of Aceh
III. Just Kings and Able Officials
IV. Pious Kings and Saints

---

[4]B. J. O. Schrieke, "The Penetration of Islam in the Archipelago," in *Indonesian Sociological Studies*, vol. 2 (The Hague and Bandung: Van Hoeve, 1957): 230–67; Anthony Reid, "Trade and the Problem of Royal Power in Aceh. c. 1550–1700," in *Pre-Colonial State Systems in Southeast Asia*, ed. Anthony Reid and Lance Castles, Monographs of the Malaysian Branch of the Royal Asiatic Society 6 (Kuala Lumpur: Royal Asiatic Society, 1975), pp. 45–55.

[5]For references to Raniri, see Syed Muhammad Naguib Al-Attas, *Rānīrī and the Wuj ūdiyyah of 17th Century Acheh*, Monographs of the Malaysian Branch of the Royal Asiatic Society 3 (Singapore: Royal Asiatic Society, 1966), pp. 12-17; Teuku Iskandar, ed., *Bustanu's-Salatin*, pp. 2-10.

[6]Richard Windstedt, *A History of Classical Malay Literature, Oxford in Asia Historical Reprints* (Kuala Lumpur: Oxford University Press, 1969), p. 90.

V. Unjust Kings and Ignorant and Dishonest Officials
VI. Noble and Compassionate Personages and Dashing and Daring Heroes
VII. Intelligence and Various Sciences.[7]

As the organization of the work indicates, the kingdom of Aceh is located within the context of the history of the Islamic world as a whole. In this paper I will discuss chapter 2, section 13, "History of the Kings of Aceh," as edited and transliterated into the Latin alphabet by Iskandar. Taking the sentences that begin "Kata yang" (It is said that) as markers, the contents of the section can be summarized as follows:

1. The thirteen kings from the early kingdom to Iskandar Thani are discussed (about twenty pages).
2. The layout of the garden constructed by Iskandar Thani is described (about five pages).
3. Iskandar Thani decides to go on a pilgrimage to Pasai after the rice harvest (one page).
4. He travels with emissaries from Johor, hunts deer and wild cattle along the way, captures elephants, and concludes his pilgrimage with visits to the tombs of saints and royalty in Pasai and Samudra (about four pages).
5. Iskandar Thani visits Pahang by sea and erects a tombstone to his father (four pages).
6. Taju'l-'Alam becomes queen after the death of her husband, Iskandar Thani (about one page).
7. Taju'l-'Alam expresses her will to honor the late Iskandar Thani's words to the emissary from Gujarat (one page).
8. Taju'l-'Alam has a tombstone made for Iskandar Thani (about seven pages).
9. The funeral procession and the golden float bearing the tombstone are described (about three pages).
10. The tombstone is erected at the royal abode (four pages).
11. The tombstone is described (one page).
12. Taju'l-'Alam's death and the two succeeding queens are touched on (about one page; this portion is said to have been written by someone other than Raniri).

As is evident from this summary, the main characters in *Bustan*'s account of Aceh's rulers are Iskandar Thani and Taju'l-'Alam. The theme employing the most pages is the funeral of Iskandar Thani, presided over by Taju'l-'Alam. The other major themes are Iskandar Thani's construction of the garden, pilgrimage to Pasai, and visit to Pahang. However, the funeral, pilgrimage to Pasai, and visit to Pahang can be regarded as a single theme, because all these episodes are tombstone rites. In part three of this paper I will discuss the meaning of Iskandar Thani's garden, and in part four, that of the tombstone rites.

III. THE GARDEN OF THE KINGS

The main stone portions of the garden described in *Bustan* still exist, as the only remnants of the flourishing seventeenth-century kingdom of Aceh. They are located at Kuala Aceh, at the confluence of the Aceh and Darul-'Ishki rivers, where the royal

---

[7]Denys Lombard, *Le Sultanat d'Atjéh au temps d'Iskandar Muda (1607-1636)* (Paris: École Française d'Extrême-Orient, 1967), pp. 152-54.

palace and the Great Mosque were once located. Recent books on Aceh's history published in Indonesia invariably include photos of the remains and generally explain that the garden was built by Iskandar Thani for his wife.[8] L. F. Brakel, writing on the meaning of the garden's design, points out that it expresses in concrete form the concept of kingship in Aceh, yet he is content to relocate it from the context of Muslim Aceh to the general context of the "Hinduised States of Southeast Asia."[9] The purpose of the present study is to place it in the context of *Bustan* itself.

The garden described in *Bustan* has a width of one thousand *depa* (equivalent to fathoms) and is planted with various kinds of flowers and fruit trees. The garden is surrounded by a stone wall painted a pure milky white. Facing the palace, which is next to the garden, is a stone gate (*pintu*) named Pintu Biram Indra Bangsa; on the upper part of its domed roof is carved a *biram*, a snake with a head at either end of its body. The Darul-'Ishki flows through the center of the garden, its clear, cool waters springing from a black stone in the mountains to the west. In the center of the open field on the right bank of the river is a stone mountain with a seat atop it and a cave (*guha*) in its lower portion. On one side of this mountain (*gegunongan* in the text, but I will use the common term *gunongan* in this paper) is a cemetery; on the other, a pedestal facing the river. Remains of these stone structures can still be seen today. Furthermore, according to *Bustan*, the garden contains various topographical features--ponds, inlets, islands, and rapids--bearing imaginative names, such as Pond of Sensual Love and Shore of Bright Jewels. *Bustan* records the names of over one hundred flowers and trees.

This description of the garden and the names of its main features bring to mind the part of *Hikayat Atjéh* in which Mansur Sjah, the father of Iskandar Muda, has a dream after the magnificent celebration of his marriage to Indera Bangsa.[10] This marriage and the dream, as I pointed out in an earlier study on *Hikajat Atjéh*,[11] form the focal point of the text that deals with the preceding period of the kingdom. In the dream Mansur Sjah, seated atop a large stone in the place named Kota Biram, urinates. The liquid fills Aceh and flows through the Aceh River out to sea. This dream is held to presage the birth of the great king, and in due course Indera Bangsa gives birth to Iskandar Muda.

The dream in *Hikajat Atjéh* and the garden in *Bustan* correspond in the following three points. The first is that the names of Mansur Sjah's bride, Indera Bangsa, and of the stone upon which Mansur Sjah sits, Biram, form the name of the stone gate in the garden, Pintu Biram Indra Bangsa. The liquid released by Mansur Sjah in his dream is clearly semen, and the name Biram, meaning a snake with a head at either end of its body, can be taken to symbolize the union of Mansur Sjah and Indera Bangsa. The gate of the garden in *Bustan*, by the carving of a *biram* and by its name, Pintu Biram Indra Bangsa, suggests that it is to represent the site of the dream in *Hikajat Atjéh*.

---

[8]Mohammad Said, *Atjeh Sepandjang Abad* (privately published, 1961); H. M. Zainuddin, *Djeumpa Atjéh* (Medan: Pustaka Iskandar Muda, 1958), and *Tarich Atjeh dan Nusantara* (Medan: Pustaka Iskandar Muda, 1961).

[9]L. F. Brakel, "State and Statecraft in 17th Century Aceh," in *Pre-Colonial State Systems in Southeast Asia*, ed. Reid and Castles, pp. 56-66.

[10]Iskandar, ed., *De Hikajat Atjéh*, pp. 115-16.

[11]Saya Shiraishi, "Hikayatto Ache ni tsuite no ichi kōsatsu" [A study of *Hikajat Atjéh*], in *Yamamoto Tatsurō hakase koki kinen: Tōnan Ajia, Indo no shakai to bunka* [In commemoration of Dr. Tatsurō Yamamoto's seventieth birthday: The societies and cultures of Southeast Asia and India] (Tokyo: Yamakawa Shuppansha, 1980), pp. 487-508.

The second point of correspondence between the dream and the garden is the Darul-'Ishki. This river, whose name means "abode of love," is in *Hikajat Atjéh* to represent the "white blood" that flows into Mansur Sjah and the semen that flows out of him.[12] The river that flows through the garden in *Bustan* is also the Darul-'Ishki.

The third point of correspondence is the symbolic meaning of the central structure in the garden, the *gunongan*, or stone mountain, of *Bustan*. The *gunongan* has a cave in it and a seat on top. In *Hikajat Atjéh* the term *guha batu*, "stone cave," appears in reference to the source of the waters of the Darul-'Ishki, and the seat atop a large stone designates the place where Mansur Sjah urinates in his dream. Therefore the *gunongan* in *Bustan* is designed to represent the source of the Darul-'Ishki's waters, that is, the royal white blood, or the royal semen.

These parallels indicate that the garden described in *Bustan* is the concrete manifestation or the emblem of the imagery of the dream in *Hikajat Atjéh*. The dream in *Hikajat Atjéh*, expressing the significance of the birth of Iskandar Muda, is given a stage--the garden--by Iskandar Muda's successor, Iskandar Thani, who thus makes it possible to re-create the dream. *The Achehnese*, the classic study of nineteenth-century Aceh by Christiaan Snouck Hurgronje, records that the king's coronation ceremony was held in a square enclosure bounded by low walls that was adjacent to the royal palace. The new king sat on a seat atop a roughly arranged pile of stones that was called *"pra'na seumah"* (the royal sitting mat of obeisance) and received pledges of loyalty with the word *dèëlat*, meaning "sovereignty" in Achehnese. Snouck Hurgronje also notes that the coronation ceremony was treated as the marriage between the new king and Aceh, the eternal bride.[13]

The site of the coronation ceremony described by Snouck Hurgronje clearly corresponds to the garden in *Bustan*, and the new king's seat, judging from its structure, was most likely the *gunongan*. The garden that represents the site of the union of Mansur Sjah and Indera Bangsa in *Hikajat Atjéh* was thus used as the site of the marriage of the new king and the eternal bride--in other words, the coronation ceremony; thus Aceh's kingship came to be renewed and re-created in the Garden of the Kings.

What is the meaning of this kingship that is institutionalized so as to renew itself through the marriage ceremony? To answer this question, we must consider the significance of the marriage ceremony itself. According to Walter William Skeat, the principal stage setting in Malay weddings was the *pĕtărana*, a ceremonial wedding couch or bed piled with a number of pillows and called *gunong-gunongan*; he names the seat "marriage throne." No matter how poor the bridegroom was or how low his social status, on his wedding day he was called *raja sa-hari*, "one-day king." Dressed in a king's garments, he was treated as the sovereign, and all were obliged to obey his commands.[14]

In Acehnese weddings the *prataih*, a bedstead with a "vast pile of cushions," was set up in an inner chamber called a *jurèë*, which was considered the most sacred place

---

[12]The Darul-'Ishki is known today as the Krueng Daroy or the Ika' Daroy, meaning "rope of love" in Acehnese.

[13]Christiaan Snouck Hurgronje, *The Achehnese*, trans. A. W. S. O'Sullivan, 2 vols. (Leiden: Brill, 1906), 1: 132-40.

[14]Walter William Skeat, *Malay Magic: Being an Introduction to the Folklore and Popular Religion of the Malay Peninsula* (New York: Dover, 1967; orig. pub. London: Macmillan, 1900), pp. 368-96.

in the Acehnese house.[15] This inner chamber contained the two main pillars of the house, which were called *raja* and *putròë*, prince and princess. The walls and ceiling of the chamber were always covered with white cloth, unlike the walls and ceilings of the other rooms in the house, which were covered with white cloth only on ceremonial occasions. This chamber was where the bride received the groom on the wedding day. It was also the couple's bedchamber and the room in which bodies were laid out to be washed and purified for funerals. Usually only members of the household entered the *jurèë*, but on wedding days the guests were allowed to peer through the walls at the couple within.[16]

The function of the *jurèë* at weddings was similar to that of the garden in which the king's coronation took place. The piled-up stones of the *gunongan* corresponded to the bedstead with its piled-up pillows. Just as onlookers gathered outside the chamber to see the bride and groom, so the coronation ceremony could be observed from outside the low wall surrounding the garden. In addition, the cemetery on the other side of the *gunongan* corresponded to the use of the *jurèë* not only for weddings but also for funerals.

The basic layout of the garden built in the seventeenth century and of the *jurèë* of nineteenth-century Aceh were thus similar, though it is unclear which came first. Did the form and function of the *jurèë* already exist in the seventeenth century, so that the garden was modeled after it, or was the *jurèë* patterned on the garden, adopting its significance? The Acehnese themselves believed that their unique customs, *adat Aceh*, were developed by the great kings, especially those of the seventeenth century, Aceh's golden age.[17] Rules for the construction and materials of the Acehnese house, or *rumah Aceh*, were also laid down at that time: commoners' houses had to be built of wood; only the king and his relatives were allowed stone houses. We may assume here rather that it was in the name of the royal customs, or *adat Meukuta Alam*, that the form and function of the garden built by the king and those of the *jurèë* were provided with the conceptual framework that gave them a unified meaning.

The new king who sits on the royal seat atop the *gunongan* in the Garden of the Kings at his coronation ceremony is, as we already know, the bridegroom who is marrying the eternal bride, Aceh. At the same time, as we have just learned, any bridegroom who sits on the marriage throne at his wedding is a "one-day king." The king and the bridegroom are, thus, interchangeable.

The bridegroom on his wedding day is neither an unmarried youth nor yet a husband. He is between these two categories and belongs to neither. The bridegroom is released from his social position and role as an unmarried youth, but is not yet bound by his position and role as a husband. He transcends any given social relations. He is to obey no one, because there is no one above him. On the other hand, it is the existence of the bridegroom that creates partitions in society by separating unmarried youths and husbands. It is the bridegroom, therefore, who tells the members of his society who they are and, consequently, what their obligations are. The nature

---

[15] Snouck Hurgronje, *The Achehnese*, 1: 41.

[16] Ibid., pp. 319-20.

[17] Ibid., pp. 4-16.

of the sovereignty of the one-day king, or the bridegroom, is, thus, his command of social classifications.[18]

With this in mind, let us again examine the layout of the Garden of the Kings described in *Bustan*. The flow of the Darul-'Ishki in the garden is the source of the topographical features (rapids, islands, ponds, waterfalls, and so on) in *Bustan*'s garden, and gives life to the various flowers and fruit trees growing there. These topographical features and plants, moreover, have their names given in *Bustan*. They are not merely ponds or flowers. They are the Pond of Sensual Love and the Shore of Bright Jewels; they are *chempaka, manggista, jambu, nyior, tempoi,* and many, many more names. The garden consists of names, the names of all the topographical features and the names of all the flowers and fruit trees. The Darul-'Ishki, which flows through the center of the Garden of the Names, is, therefore, the source of, and gives life to, all these names and categories.

In discussing the dream in *Hikajat Atjêh*, I mentioned that the Darul-'Ishki symbolizes the "white blood" of Aceh's kingship, which gave birth to the King of Kings in Aceh, Iskandar Muda, the ultimate sovereign, who centuries after his death still monopolized fame as the source of all the laws and customs of the people of Aceh.

The garden constructed by Iskandar Thani, Iskandar Muda's successor, and the book titled *The Garden of the Kings*, which was commissioned from Raniri at the same time, together embodied and expressed the concept of kingship in Aceh as the source from which all the names of classification, that is to say, the laws of the land, originate.

Just as naming the stone gate of the garden Pintu Biram Indra Bangsa made the garden the emblem of the dream in *Hikajat Atjêh*, so the garden as a whole was made complete by being ascribed to *Bustanu's-Salatin*. In other words, giving existence to things that have names, which is to say things that are categorized, creates categories themselves. Snouck Hurgronje writes that, although Aceh's kings lacked actual power and the means to enforce it, they were held in awe as the creators of all laws and were thought of as those who transcended law.[19] The relationship between the Darul-'Ishki and the garden expressed the same notion of the creator and his creature: the king as creator of laws, that is, creator of the structure of names and categories in Aceh, and his book, *The Garden of the Kings*.

The king as the eternal bridegroom is thus the counterstructural existence that is the source of the social structure and of all categories, just as water is the source of topography, flowers, and trees. He is the one who resides permanently on an extraordinary (out-of-the-ordinary) plane that the common people can glimpse or experience only on the occasion of their weddings. The Garden of the Kings embodied and expressed the concept of kingship as the source of all topographical features and living beings in Aceh, or rather, of their names and their meanings, through both the garden itself and through *Bustan*, the written record of the Garden of the Names.

IV. THE SEASON OF PLANTING STONES

Let us now examine what royal tombstone rites further reveal about the concept of kingship in Aceh. Following the description of the garden, *Bustan* deals almost en-

---

[18]This phenomenon is best explained in terms of the anthropological concept of liminality. For a discussion of this concept and its theoretical meaning in the ritual process, see Victor W. Turner, *The Ritual Process* (Chicago: Aldine, 1966).

[19]Snouck Hurgronje, *The Achehnese*, 1: 140-45.

tirely with rites related to tombstones. Iskandar Thani's first act after constructing the garden was to embark on a pilgrimage to Pasai and Samudra[20] to pay his respects to the tombs of saints and royalty there, after which he visited Pahang, his birthplace, to erect a tombstone for his father.[21] These episodes, together with the detailed description of the elaborate ceremonies in connection with Iskandar Thani's own tombstone that were presided over by his widow and successor, Taju'l-'Alam, make it evident that tombstone rites are another major theme of *Bustan*, the Garden of the Kings. This is also where *Bustan* departs most markedly from *Hikajat Atjéh*, whose central theme is the wedding of Iskandar Muda's parents, Mansur Sjah and Indera Bangsa.[22]

---

[20]Pasai and Samudra, twin kingdoms on opposite banks of a river, were both founded by Sultan Malikul Saleh. Among the earliest of the kingdoms in the northern Sumatra estuaries to be Islamized, they conducted a flourishing inter-island trade in Southeast Asia and were also known as centers of Islamic learning. Malikul Saleh's tombstone, still extant, came from Cambay in India; the date inscribed on it is AH 696 (AD 1297). The oldest classic of historical literature in the Malay world, *Hikayat Raja-Raja Pasai*, is a record of these twin kingdoms. Its form, techniques, and content are echoed in the later *Sejarah Melayu*, the greatest work of Malay literature. The kingdom of Malacca, which bequeathed us *Sejarah Melayu*, received its queen, its position as a political, economic, and religious center, and its cultural tradition from Pasai. Furthermore, chapter 2, section 12, of *Bustanu's-Salatin*, "History of the Kings of Malacca and Pahang," reflects the account in *Sejarah Melayu*. Iskandar Thani, believed to have been a legitimate heir of the Malaccan royal family, was accompanied on his pilgrimage to Pasai by Bendahara Paduka Raja, reputed to have been the author of *Sejarah Melayu*, who was the emissary of the king of Johor. This may also be taken as indicating the line of succession of the leading Islamic centers in the Malay world. See Schrieke, "The Penetration of Islam in the Archipelago"; J. P. Mead, ed., "Hikayat Raja-Raja Pasai" (romanized), *Journal of the Straits Branch of the Royal Asiatic Society*, no. 66 (1914); *Sejarah Melayu: "Malay Annals,"* trans. C. C. Brown, intro. R. O. Roolvink, Oxford in Asia Historical Reprints (Kuala Lumpur: Oxford University Press, 1970); Winstedt, *Classical Malay Literature*, pp. 155-62.

[21]Iskandar Thani was born in Pahang and lived there until the age of seven, when he was taken to Aceh by Iskandar Muda. The royal family of Pahang linked Iskandar Thani to the Malaccan royal family genealogically. Aceh's domination of Pahang, which was situated on the east coast of the Malay Peninsula, had a bearing on Aceh's control of the Strait of Malacca. After Iskandar Thani's death Pahang came under the control of Johor. See Leonard Y. Andaya, *The Kingdom of Johor: 1641-1728* (Kuala Lumpur: Oxford University Press, 1975), pp. 55-65.

[22]Here I would like to make a simple comparison of the genealogies of the kings of Aceh recorded in *Hikajat Atjéh* and *Bustan*. While both works appear to use the same format, close examination reveals that the names of the kings in the two texts do not always agree and that there are discrepancies in the reign dates given. There are also basic differences in the form and content of the accounts in the two works. This results in shorter and simpler genealogical accounts in *Bustan* than in *Hikajat Atjéh*. The core of the genealogical narrative in *Bustan* consists of the king's titles, year of accession, length of reign, and year of death or abdication. When the relationship of a particular king to the preceding and/or following rulers is discussed or the characteristics and achievements of individual kings are described, there is no attempt to link them directly to the issue of kingship itself. That a particular king was pious and just, that he expanded the kingdom, or that he encouraged Islamization is not seen as having any connection with his being assassinated or the throne's being usurped. *Hikajat Atjéh*, by contrast, invariably relates episodes illustrating the character of the king and points out their bearing on the succession, and thus closely links the characteristics of individual kings with kingship itself. *Bustan* records the period that each king spent as a resident of the Garden of the Kings and verifies that there was always a king residing there. In a sense, it is a record of the names of residents.

The practice of erecting tombstones has left tombstone inscriptions that are important sources for the study of the Islamization of the Malay world.[23] This practice itself, however, is referred to as "planting stones" (*menanam batu*; Acehnese, *pula batëë*), as if stones were a species of flower or rice plant.

According to Snouck Hurgronje, the Acehnese year was divided into the "season when the land is closed" (*musém pichë' blang*) and the "season when the land is open" (*musém luaih blang*). "Planting stones" could only be carried out in the latter season. The "season when the land is closed" referred to the eight months of the rice-growing period. During that time villagers tilled their own fields, to which they had ownership rights. The "season when the land is open" referred to the remaining four months, when rice was not grown. After the rice harvest the land became more or less the common property of the village (*gampōng*) and was used to graze the villagers' cattle. Intermediary crops could be grown, but no attention would be paid to individuals' rights over the land; they had to take their own measures to protect their crops from the grazing herds.[24]

In other words, the Acehnese year consisted of the rice-planting season, when villagers grew rice in individually divided plots, and the stone-planting season, when the land was held in common. It was generally believed that if a stone was planted—that is, a tombstone erected—while rice was growing, the rice in the surrounding area would be spoiled. Accordingly, if someone died during the rice-growing season, a temporary wooden marker was erected, to be replaced by a permanent tombstone only after the harvest. This taboo was the most rigorously observed custom in Aceh.[25]

The distinction between the seasons for planting rice and for planting stones is found in *Bustan*, as well. When Iskandar Thani first said that he wished to go on a pilgrimage to Pasai and Samudra, one of the *orang kaya* reminded him that it was the rice-growing season, too busy a time for the people to cater a royal pilgrimage. The journey finally took place after the harvest.[26] The party that set out on the pilgrimage included not only *orang kaya* and *uleebalang* but also common people who had finished harvesting their rice. On the way to Pasai they hunted deer and wild cattle and captured elephants. Thus, during the rice-planting season all the people were busy tending their own plots. During the stone-planting season, when private plots disappeared and the land belonged to all, people erected tombstones, visited graves, and hunted in the fields and mountains.

After rice seedlings are planted, rice is harvested. What do stones yield after they are planted? The following passage in Skeat's record of Malay proverbs and incantations provides a clue: "*Tepong tawar*, the true *tepong*, just like *kerakap*, grows on a stone."[27] *Tepong tawar* (Acehnese, *teupōng taweuë*), or "neutralizing rice flour (water)," refers to a white pasty liquid made by mixing rice flour with water. It is to neutralize poisons and pacify evil spirits, and is used in most purification ceremonies. Skeat also recorded another charm that often accompanied the ceremony:

---

[23]For information on the numerous tombstones and their inscriptions still to be found in Aceh, Pasai, and Samudra, see Zainuddin, *Tarich Atjeh*, pp. 44-96.

[24]Snouck Hurgronje, *The Achehnese*, 1: 254-60.

[25]Ibid., pp. 430-31.

[26]Raniri, *Bustanu's-Salatin*, pp. 52-53.

[27]"Tepong tawar, tepong jati, / [bagai] kerakap tumboh di batu." Skeat, *Malay Magic*, pp. 588.

"Tepong tawar, the true *tepong . . .*

. . . .

Keep me from sickness, keep me from death,
Keep me from injury and ruin."[28]

In Aceh, according to Snouck Hurgronje, purification was called "cooling" (*peusijuë*)
and was performed at all kinds of ceremonies and on the occasion of significant
events: birth, marriage, death, building a new house, launching a new boat, planting
rice, returning from a long journey, a youth's finishing his first complete recitation of
the Koran, losing one's footing on stairs, and so on.[29] Though the cooling ceremony
differed somewhat in each case, the most common ceremony involved strewing
husked and unhusked rice (in Acehnese the two were considered a pair and were
called *breuëh-padé*) over the person or thing to be cooled, and also sprinkling this person or thing with *tepong tawar*. Husked and unhusked rice, of course, are the product
of rice seedlings, while *tepong tawar* can be considered the product of stone.

Tepong tawar, white water that springs from a stone and is used for cooling,
brings to mind the Darul-'Ishki, which *Bustan* describes as follows:

And in the middle of the garden there is a river named Darul-'Ishki [Abode of
Love] which is plastered with stones. Its water is extremely clear as well as intensely cool. Whoever drinks the water becomes healthy. And the river originates
in the west at the foot of Mount Jabalu'l-A'la, springing out of the black stone.[30]

A similar passage is found in Hikajat Atjéh. After discussing the Aceh River, the text
describes the Darul-'Ishki:

And there is another river, which springs out of a stone cave. Its water is extremely cool and also intensely sweet. The name of the river is Darul-'Ishki. All
the kings drink its water.[31]

Let me employ the hypothesis at this point that the water of the Darul-'Ishki is not
only white blood, or royal semen, but also *tepong tawar*, "cooling water." Considering
that the Darul-'Ishki symbolizes Acehnese kingship, this hypothesis leads us to see
that another significance of the kingship of Aceh, that is to say, the nature of the
kingship of Aceh, was to cool, or purify, like *tepong tawar*, the active potentialities of
evil spirits.

This may be well illustrated by an episode recorded by Snouck Hurgronje in the
late nineteenth century. Toward the end of the Aceh War, when some Acehnese leaders who had sided with the Dutch were sent to induce the sultan of Aceh to surrender, they were nevertheless implored by their friends and relatives to bring back water in which the sultan's feet had been washed.[32] As Snouck Hurgronje himself
concluded from this event, losing the war did not in itself weaken reverence for their

---

[28]Ibid., pp. 77-81.

[29]For information on the cooling ceremony, see Snouck Hurgronje, *The Achehnese*, 1: 305-7, and
also his discussion of individual topics (weddings, houses, farming, and so on).

[30]Raniri, *Bustanu's-Salatin*, p. 48.

[31]Iskandar, ed., *De Hikajat Atjéh*, p. 165.

[32]Snouck Hurgronje, *The Achehnese*, 1: 141.

sultan in the minds of the Acehnese. Rather, it was the collapse of the concept of kingship itself, which had been established in seventeenth-century Aceh and expressed in *Hikajat Atjéh* and *Bustan*, that deprived the kings of Aceh of their raison d'être.

When a stone is planted—that is, when a tombstone is erected—*tepong tawar*, "cooling water," is to be harvested. And if that *tepong tawar* is analogous to the white blood, or royal semen, that is produced from the marriage of Mansur Sjah and Indera Bangsa, Acehnese kingship can be expressed not only through the marriage ceremony but also through the erection of a tombstone. The Darul-'Ishki, whose clear, cool waters people actually see, can very well link the two. As I have already discussed, not only was the garden the embodiment of the site of the dream in *Hikajat Atjéh*, but also there was a cemetery to one side of the *gunongan*. The main theme of *Hikajat Atjéh* is the marriage ceremony, which signified Acehnese kingship in Iskandar Muda's time. By contrast, the main theme of *Bustan* is the ceremony surrounding the erection of the tombstone, which also signified Acehnese kingship. When Taju'l-'Alam, Iskandar Thani's widow, succeeded her husband, possibly it was anomalous for her to assume the role of bridegroom in the coronation ceremony.

Let us now examine the tombstone ceremony as the seal of the kingship's legitimacy, referring to the account in *Bustan* of the ceremony presided over by Taju'l-'Alam. The ceremony begins with all the *uleebalang* pledging loyalty through the oath of *dèëlat* to the new ruler, Taju'l-'Alam, who is seated on the seat of obeisance, the *Peratna Sembah*, atop the *gunongan*. This procedure is identical to Snouck Hurgronje's record of the king's coronation ceremony. After a feast, Taju'l-'Alam orders the *orang kaya* and *uleebalang* to prepare the ceremonial floats for the funeral procession. With the tombstone ceremony thus begun, Iskandar Thani's tombstone, initially brought to the *Peratna Sembah*, is placed atop a golden float. The procession, with the golden float in the center, leaves the garden, goes through the palace, and appears before the waiting crowd in the Medan Khayali (Plaza of Intoxication), in front of the main gate. Both sides of the procession's route from the plaza to the Great Mosque are lined with flags, banners, and parasols.

The major features of the tombstone ceremony recorded in *Bustan* closely resemble those of Acehnese funeral ceremonies in general, which are also recorded by Snouck Hurgronje. At a funeral, the body of the deceased is taken to the *jurèë*, the inner chamber that is the most sacred area of the house, and laid on the bedstead (*prataih*) there. After the body has been washed and purified (the floor of the chamber is equipped with a drain), it is moved from the bedstead into a coffin. Then the bier is taken from the *jurèë*, through the living quarters and down the stairs, and is laid in the front yard. There friends and relatives take their leave of the deceased. The bier, covered in beautiful fabric "such as a bride would wear," is then carried through the village to the cemetery. Poles with long white cloths attached to them are erected on either side of the route, forming a "bridge" (*tutuë*). The funeral procession, with the bier at the center, crosses this figurative bridge to the "other shore," that is, the world of the dead.[33]

Comparing these funeral ceremonies with the tombstone ceremony over which Taju'l-'Alam presided, we see that the *jurèë* corresponds to the garden, the bedstead, or *prataih*, to the *Peratna Sembah* atop the *gunongan*, the bier to the golden float, the front yard to the plaza facing the royal palace, and the "bridge" to the banner- and

---

[33]Ibid., pp. 418-26.

flag-lined route of the procession. The tombstone ceremony described in *Bustan* can be thought of as the funeral ceremony itself, with the tombstone replacing the king's body.

What merits special attention, in the case of the account in *Bustan*, is the composition of the procession and the attire and behavior of the spectators. The funeral procession is led by eighty wild elephants and eighty domesticated elephants, each ridden by a hero armed and attired for hunting. They are followed by war horses, then *raksasa* (giants) with bared teeth. Next comes a *naga*, a creature with the head of a lion and the body of a lizard. At its sight the people nearby cry out and flee, being jeered by onlookers farther away. The *naga* is followed by pairs of all sorts of beasts, each pair consisting of one wild and one domesticated animal. People enjoy watching this procession of elephants, horses, lions, tigers, rhinoceroses, water buffalo, deer, and so on. Then come fabulous creatures: some have the body of a lion, the head of a bird, the wings of a *garuda* (a mythical bird), and the feet of a *naga*; others have the body of a horse, the head of a *naga*, the horn of a rhinoceros, and the tusks of an elephant. Next are silver floats bearing singers from Java, Pahang, and Johor. Finally comes a resplendent seven-tiered golden float topped by the tombstone, which is guarded by maidens bearing the king's regalia and the royal drinking water.

The funeral procession described in *Bustan* is the allegory of kingship itself. Kingship is both wild and domesticated, and at the same time neither wild nor domesticated. Because kingship belongs to no category, it belongs to all categories simultaneously. It swims in the water, dwells in the forest, and flies in the air. It presides over extraordinary powers, wages war, and commands music. People enjoy and admire it from a respectful distance, fearful of approaching too close. At a funeral, as at a marriage ceremony, a person transcends his or her category and name. The person is no longer living but has not yet been buried as a deceased person. The person's name in life is lost, but a posthumous name is not yet appropriate, either. The funeral procession represents the extraordinary nature of the funeral and thus symbolizes kingship itself, as is apparent from the onlookers' praise of the king or queen and his or her ceremony.

The people, who have gathered to watch the procession cross the bridge between the worlds of the living and the dead, also represent the extraordinary nature of the occasion. All the descriptions of their appearance in *Bustan* use the word *sa-tengah*, which means "between," "half," "center," "during," or "halfway." The spectators consist of people who have applied only half their makeup, who have only half-dressed their hair, who are in the midst of laundering, who have only put on half their earrings, bracelets, anklets, and rings, who have only half-applied their tooth black. Among them are also people kicking each other and a woman who has given birth during the long journey to see the procession.

People who have applied only half their makeup belong neither to the category of people fully made up nor to that of people wearing no cosmetics at all. They are in a state of transition similar to that of the bride and groom during the wedding ceremony or of the deceased during the funeral, an extraordinary plane transcending categories. The same can be said of the spectators in the process of dressing their hair, staining their teeth, or putting on ornaments. Laundering describes a similar state, with soiled clothing in the process of becoming clean. Childbirth can also be thought of as a transitional state. The significance of the people kicking each other is not so clear. The symbolic significance of the people wearing only half their makeup and those kicking each other may in fact be the same as that of childbirth. Before considering this correspondence, however, I would like to discuss the sacrificial ceremony that took place in Aceh in the pilgrimage month, because the terms *cosmetics, hairdressing,* and *tooth black* bring to mind the appurtenances of that ceremony.

In Aceh, the sacrificial ceremony in the pilgrimage month used to take place in the village of Bitay, the site of the tomb of Tuan di Bitay, who is said to have been sent by the king of Rum (Turkey) to teach, among other things, the art of casting cannons. The gravekeepers, who were the saint's descendants, conducted the sacrificial ceremony. On this occasion they received raw eggs, husked and unhusked rice, fragrant oil, black powder with which to line the eyes, tooth black, a comb, a razor, a piece of white cotton cloth, and a mirror.[34]

Snouck Hurgronje, who spent over half a year in Mecca, comments that the teaching of Islam contains nothing of this kind. These articles do indicate the meaning of the sacrificial ceremony in Aceh, however. The sacrifice establishes the separation of those who receive the sacrifice from those who offer it, and thus creates distinct categories. At the same time, the sacrifice mediates between the two categories. The articles received by the gravekeepers also serve the same function as the sacrifice. Cosmetics separate faces that are made up from faces that are not and, at the same time, unite the two. Similarly, a comb separates and unites hair that is dressed and hair that is not, while a razor separates and unites faces that are shaved and those that are not. A raw egg stands between hen and chick, while a mirror both differentiates an object from its reflection and relates one to the other.

What is the significance of white cloth? The walls and ceiling of the *jurèë* are covered with white cloth, the Garden of the Kings is surrounded by a white wall, and the "bridge" a funeral procession crosses is made of white cloths. The *jurèë,* a newly married couple's bedchamber, not only is laid out similarly to the garden, which is the site which appears in the dream in *Hikajat Atjéh,* but is also itself the site for dreaming. The dream is neither sleep nor wakefulness. The *jurèë* is the site of dreams, marriages, and funerals. It is white cloths that create an extraordinary space. White belongs to no category of color, and like *tepong,* which means "to neutralize," achromatizes colors.

Let us examine further the significance of the combination of *tepong tawar* on the one hand and husked and unhusked rice on the other. Returning to the terminology we used in discussing the sacrifice ceremony, husked rice and unhusked rice are differentiated from each other and at the same time bound together by the process of husking. On the other hand, *tepong tawar,* like the sacrificial animal, the cosmetics, and the process of husking, differentiates purified objects from unpurified objects and unites the two, because it is a neutralizing agent. As suggested above, *tepong tawar* and the white blood that is royal semen are to be taken as one and the same; this white blood differentiates man from woman and unites the two. Thus its role becomes still clearer. Husked and unhusked rice are objects that are both differentiated and united, while *tepong tawar* is the differentiating and uniting subject. This combination of differentiating and uniting subject and differentiated and united object rep-

---

[34]Ibid., pp. 243-45.

resents in its simplest form the cooling power and the conceptual framework of the extraordinary plane that generates this power.[35]

Let us now read the description of the king's funeral procession in the light of this concept of the differentiating and uniting subject and the differentiated and united object. The wild and domesticated animals in the procession represent objects, while hunting is the subject. The episode of childbirth among the spectators represents both the differentiation of the bodies of mother and child through birth and their union through the mother-child bond. The pain caused by kicking differentiates the one who is kicked from the one who kicks and also mediates between the two. War serves the same function.[36] Finally, the tombstone at the center of the procession appears as the core of this conceptual framework. It represents sovereignty. The king is the hunter, the sacrifice, the cosmetics. Sovereignty, which transcends categories, which both creates and neutralizes them, is symbolized most vividly by the fabulous creatures in the procession. The mysterious creature with the body of a horse, the head of a *naga*, the horn of a rhinoceros, and the tusks of an elephant, for example, can only appear because of the presence of the power that can both create and destroy the categories of horse, *naga*, rhinoceros, and elephant.

The villagers in Aceh are bound to their own small plots of land during the rice-growing season, when they produce rice. It is in this season that people are categorized and differentiated. Social status, wealth, family relationships, and gender roles separate them into a myriad of categories. However, the situation changes completely once the harvest is over and the land is held in common. It is the season of planting stones that expunges all categories. By erasing the boundaries between plots of land, the elements that differentiate people from one another are also erased; now they belong nowhere but to the sphere of the sovereignty of Aceh. Stones are to be planted in the open land, and the white blood of kingship springs from these stones.

The season of planting stones is truly the season of kingship. The king leads his people on pilgrimages, spends his days hunting, or officiates at tombstone ceremonies. During this season all of Aceh is draped in white, so to speak, to be incorporated into the Garden of the Kings. This is eloquently narrated in *Bustan*'s description of the "halfway" state of the people—whose ornaments, clothing, and cosmetics have lost their function as indicators of social position or wealth—as they rush forward to watch the royal tombstone on its golden float pass from the garden to the palace plaza.

If Aceh is filled with the royal white blood and the gold of a marriage ceremony in *Hikajat Atjéh*, in *Bustan* Aceh is draped in white cloth and filled with the gold of the

---

[35]In Aceh a triangular winnow called a *jeu'èë* was used to separate the rice kernels from the husks. The Acehnese liked to compare Aceh itself to a *jeu'èë*, with Kuala Aceh, situated at the confluence of the Aceh and Darul-'Ishki rivers, as the apex of the triangle. This image probably belongs to the same conceptual framework. See Snouck Hurgronje, *The Achehnese*, 1: 1-2, 272.

[36]A good example is the holy war that both separates and neutralizes Muslim and infidel. In this case, martyrs correspond to the bridegroom. In *Hikajat Prang Sabil* [Song of the holy war], compiled in the late nineteenth century during the Aceh War, the young protagonist, who is later martyred, dreams that he walks along a sacred river and meets his bride, who is awaiting him on a marriage throne in a flower-filled garden. Heavenly maidens sing, "The king, the husband, has returned to the bride on the marriage throne." When the Garden of the Kings became a paradise that was accessible not only to kings but to all martyrs, the significance of Aceh's kingship probably reached a transition. For *Hikajat Prang Sabil*, see James Siegel, *Shadow and Sound: The Historical Thought of a Sumatran People* (Chicago: University of Chicago Press, 1979), pp. 229-51.

funeral ceremony. One cannot help admiring the brilliance and the beauty of organization of *Bustanu's-Salatin* in this regard.

V. CONCLUSION

Bustan illustrates Acehnese kingship as the source of Aceh's cultural and social categories. This kingship is represented by the king's tombstone, which both separates and unites the worlds of the living and of the dead. Is the kingship expressed through the funeral ceremony described in *Bustan* the same as that expressed through the marriage ceremony described in *Hikajat Atjéh?* As I have discussed above, the logical structure of the two ceremonies--the creation and neutralization of categories by a category-transcending presence--is the same. As the *gunongan* in the garden has a pedestal on one side and a cemetery on the other, sovereignty as marriage ceremony and sovereignty as funeral ceremony are the two sides of a coin. Nevertheless, the weddings and funerals we experience in life are not at all the same. A wedding is associated with a new step toward the future, a funeral with the end of a life. In fact, in 1636, the year Iskandar Thani acceded to the throne, a fleet from Aceh bound for Pahang was defeated for the first time by a naval force from Johor in the Strait of Malacca. In 1641, when Taju'l-'Alam became the ruler of Aceh, the allied Netherlands-Johor forces defeated Portuguese Malacca and established their control over the strait.

   Bustan was composed as the golden age of Aceh was ending. The appended final portion of the work records that the palace, its numerous villas, the Great Mosque, and all the treasures that symbolized the kingdom's prosperity were destroyed by fire during the rule of Nuru'l-'Alam, the second successor to Taju'l-'Alam. *Hikajat Atjéh* records the morning glory of the kingdom of Aceh; *Bustanu's-Salatin*, its evening glow.

This paper was originally published in Japanese under the title "Busutanusu Saratin (Ōja no teien) ni tsuite no ichi kōsatsu" [An interpretation of Bustanu's-Salatin] in *Asian Cultural Studies* [Tokyo] 13 (November 1981), 101–16.

3

STATE RITUAL AND THE VILLAGE: AN INDONESIAN CASE STUDY

Teruo Sekimoto

I. INTRODUCTION

Modern English history provides a pertinent example for the study of state ritual. The historian David Cannadine describes a remarkable shift in attitudes toward royal rituals in late-nineteenth-century England. In the first three-quarters of the century, such rituals were generally regarded as ridiculous and "nothing more than primitive magic, a hollow sham."[1] Enthusiastic involvement in ostentatious ceremonials was considered an aptitude "confined to the people of southern climate"[2] from which the English were exempt. Royal rituals were unimpressive, inconspicuous affairs that the general public viewed with disdain and indifference. After 1877, however, when Queen Victoria was made empress of India, a substantial change occurred. Royal rituals took on an unrivaled scale, grandeur, and national fervor, and the English began to believe that they were endowed with an innate sense of ceremonial grandeur unparalleled by any other people.[3]

Cannadine studies the historical background of this change in attitude from two angles: changes occurring within England at the time and international changes. In the first three-quarters of the nineteenth century, he writes, the prevailing conditions of society served to "contain the monarchy within society rather than elevate it above."[4] In other words, although the monarchy wielded real, effective political power, it "was neither impartial and above politics nor Olympian and above society, as it was later to become."[5] While its activities were the center of the cosmopolitan society of London, most people belonged to discrete local societies composed of those with whom they lived and interacted on a daily basis. The concept of belonging to a unified national entity had not yet fully developed. In the last quarter of the century, however, society grew more homogeneous and uniform owing to the spread of

---

[1]David Cannadine, "The Context, Performance and Meaning of Ritual: The British Monarchy and the 'Invention of Tradition', c. 1820–1977," in *The Invention of Tradition*, ed. E. J. Hobsbawm (Cambridge: Cambridge University Press, 1983), p. 102.

[2]Ibid., p. 101.

[3]"All the pageantry and grandeur of a thousand-year-old tradition" and "the English are particularly good at ceremonial" are phrases Cannadine quotes from present-day English commentators and journalists. Ibid., p. 102.

[4]Ibid., p. 111.

[5]Ibid., p. 110.

industrialization and urbanization, improvements in transportation and communications systems, and the development of mass media. At the same time, internationally, England faced a struggle for supremacy among the imperialist powers that threatened its position as "the workshop of the world." In response, the royal family took on a stronger role as the symbolic center of the nation and royal rituals became major national events.

Three important points are suggested by the above example. First, it is insufficient to view ritual as a characteristic of traditional societies that loses its importance in modern society. Second, the relationship between the state and society fluctuates; sometimes society exerts more influence, sometimes the state. Third, when the state's influence is stronger, this is manifested in the increased importance accorded to state rituals. These three points are helpful in studying state rituals in present-day Indonesia.

II. THE STATE AS EXTERNAL TO SOCIETY

Although historical analogies have limitations, there are some interesting similarities between the conditions that the Indonesian state is facing today and the changes described by Cannadine in the relationship between English society and the monarchy in the late nineteenth century. The state of Indonesia, which became independent some forty years ago, is based in the cosmopolitan society of Jakarta, the capital. Most citizens, however, identify with their own local society rather than with Jakarta, which they regard as external to their society. When I first visited the village of Darman (not its real name) in Central Java in 1975, the villagers looked at me curiously and whispered to one another, "He's from Jakarta. Jakarta." To them Jakarta represented the unknown world outside their village.

Unlike England at the end of the last century, Indonesia today does not face the imminent prospect of universal industrialization and urbanization. There is still a large gap between the world of the elite class of Jakarta and that of the urban and rural masses. However, people are not contained self-sufficiently within their own local societies; no one is in a position to ignore the existence of the state, which monopolizes wealth and authority. While the state and society do not yet sufficiently penetrate each other, neither is society turning its back on the state and functioning independently. Rather, society is constrained by the state's overwhelming presence.

Discussing the concept of the nation-state, Benedict Anderson, a leading figure in the study of modern Indonesian politics during the past decade, maintains that the concepts of nation and state represent "very different entities with distinct histories, constituents, and 'interests.'"[6] A tiny hyphen links these separate entities and engenders the new concept of the nation-state. The state, like the church, the university, and the modern corporation, is an autonomous institution with its own interests, which differ from those of society. If participation is the basic interest of the nation, then representation is the basic interest of the state.[7]

According to Anderson, "the policy outcomes of nation-states under unexceptional circumstances will typically represent a shifting balance between the two interests."[8] Indonesia's New Order, the system established by Suharto after the collapse

---

[6]Benedict R. O'G. Anderson, "Old State, New Society: Indonesia's New Order in Comparative Historical Perspective," *Journal of Asian Studies* 42, 3 (1983): 477.

[7]Ibid., p. 478.

[8]Ibid.

of Sukarno's regime in 1966, represents the maximal expression of state interests; during the twenty-year period from the declaration of independence until 1965, by contrast, society was in the ascendant and penetrated the state. He also argues that the Indonesian state is much older than the Indonesian society now in the process of formation, having come into existence in the seventeenth century with the establishment of the fortress of Batavia by the Vereenigde Oostindische Compagnie (VOC; the Dutch East India Company). In Anderson's view, the Republic of Indonesia is the successor of the Dutch Indies State, and the special characteristics of modern Indonesian politics can best be understood if one sees the continuity between the old and the new states.

As already pointed out, the state and society in Indonesia have not been sufficiently amalgamated, and at present the balance is tipped toward the state. Accordingly, I agree with many points of Anderson's argument. Rather than become entangled in the concept of the ideal nation-state and condemn the present Indonesian government for not fully representing the interests of the people, we will understand the actual workings of present-day Indonesian politics much more clearly if we view the state as an autonomous institution having a history and interests separate from those of society. However, this is the age of the nation-state. No state can justify its existence unless it endorses the principle of representing all the people within its borders by virtue of some internal tie between state and people. This tie need not be the parliamentary democracy of the West European model; but the people must have internalized the state order in one way or another.

Ever since Hobbes and Locke, society has been believed to precede the state. Marx's and Engels's theories of the formation of the state through class conflict rely on the same concept. The idea that the internal development of society gives birth to the state is generally accepted as correct and is used to explain history. Thus in Cannadine's exposition of nineteenth-century England society already exists, developing according to internal principles, and as a consequence of this development a new, more uniform and centripetal nation-state emerges. If we accept this argument, the "centrality" and "representativeness" that the state claims must be imparted to it by society. The Dutch Indies State, however, was imposed from without and spread over society like a cancer. That this is viewed as exceptional, that such a state is considered to be the result of the abnormal condition of colonialism, is a prejudice of modern social theory. Both the Portuguese state of Malacca and the state established by the VOC were modeled on and adapted to the forms of states already existing in Southeast Asia. According to M. C. Ricklefs's study of eighteenth-century Java, Javanese rulers regarded the VOC as a peer; local princes either allied themselves with or opposed the Dutch as a politico-military force of the same kind that they themselves were. The VOC "was not seen as dangerous simply because it was foreign."[9] What was external and alien to local societies was not Europeans as such but monarchs and their states, whatever their cultural origins might be.

The type of society that Cannadine characterizes as "localized, provincial, face-to-face"[10] has long been the customary subject of anthropological research. Accordingly, the state has been treated consistently as an external, alien entity. This approach has been criticized frequently by other disciplines for tending to represent

---

[9]M. C. Ricklefs, *Jogjakarta Under Sultan Mangkubumi, 1749–1792: A History of the Division of Java* (Oxford: Oxford University Press, 1974), pp. 35–36.

[10]Cannadine, "The Context, Performance and Meaning of Ritual," p. 110.

the small subject community as a microcosm divorced from the outside world. This criticism is particularly apt when the community is viewed from the perspective of functionalism, which tends to regard society as a monolithic, total system.

The state, however, always has characteristics that are external and alien to society. It does not arise as an extension of the endogenous development of an individual community, nor is it one of the various systems that make up a society. To give a comprehensive meaning to their everyday world, people collectively develop concepts of realms beyond their immediate experience, such as the "other world," heaven, and the macrocosm. In the same way, the state provides a comprehensive entity that is fundamentally different from and transcendent to the society comprising people's collective daily social relationships. For this reason the state is surrounded by myths, rituals, and religious symbols that cannot be explained in technical-rational terms.

The major point to be made here is that the state cannot be treated simply as one functional element of a particular social system. On the contrary, the state and society are alien, almost diametrically opposed, entities that exist in conjunction. This cannot be presented merely as a fixed proposition, however; to apply it to actual social analysis, two points must be added. First, as Anderson states, actual politics is an expression of the shifting balance of power between the state and society. Just as the mythic, ritualistic nature of the state was hidden behind the mundane rationale of society in nineteenth-century England and probably is in present-day Japan, so the opposite can occur. Second, the concept of the state as alien and external loses its impact when understood too mechanically and schematically. For the state to survive, it must absorb and embody the images of the alien and the external that people hold collectively, which are then forged into state symbols—myths, rituals, and so on—and thereby internalized by the people. Anderson's theory, though extremely useful for the analysis of modern Indonesian politics, does not take into account the interaction between the state and society through shared symbols and images. Ultimately, the tiny hyphen linking the words *nation* and *state* poses the largest question.

III. Indonesia's Independence Day Ritual

Below, I present a case study from a farm village in Central Java as a clue to the significance of that tiny hyphen. The study focuses on the Independence Day celebration that takes place every year on August 17 throughout Indonesia. Despite numerous anthropological studies of rituals, the theme of modern state rituals has only recently been given attention and is still relatively unexplored. Most studies of state rituals so far have concentrated on large-scale ceremonies performed at the state center, as recently surveyed and reviewed by Tamotsu Aoki.[11] My case study, by contrast, focuses on ceremonies on the level of the village, which is at the opposite end of the organizational scale. Though the ceremonies themselves are modest, considerable labor and resources are poured into preparations for the various events connected with the Independence Day celebration. It is therefore appropriate material for observing the way in which people are mobilized in state rituals, and, through this mobilization, how the state organizes people into a nation.

---

[11]Tamotsu Aoki, *Girei no shōchōsei* [The symbolism of ritual] (Tokyo: Iwanami Shoten, 1984).

I observed the Independence Day celebration in the village of Darman in Central Java in 1975, 1978, and 1980.[12] Over this six-year period the form of the ritual changed greatly. In general, family and other community rituals studied by anthropologists must also undergo changes with the passage of time. Usually, however, the people themselves are not fully aware of these changes, and the studies on these changes are hampered by the vagueness of people's memories and the lack of written records. The meanings of the rituals are often buried in the consciousness of people, who, consequently, explain their actions simply as part of immemorial custom or tradition. The meaning and purpose of most state rituals, on the other hand, are clearly stated, and people generally understand and can explain them through language. Thus, because those who design and direct ritual performances, and their purposes, are clearly defined, the process of trial and error, and of change itself, is clearly visible to the people involved in the rituals.

Accordingly, as Cannadine argues, it is essential to consider the historical context when studying modern state rituals.[13] Through the following case study, I will discuss changes in the form and intent of the Independence Day ritual in the historical context of the Republic of Indonesia over the forty years since independence. The material for this study is provided by only one village, and the time span is only six years. Nevertheless, it is possible to see therein the overall situation faced by the larger society and the state of Indonesia.

IV. From a Ritual of Society to a Ritual of the State

The first Independence Day celebration I witnessed in Darman, in 1975, was made up of three parts. The first part consisted of communal labor undertaken by the villagers, the second of the ceremony on August 17, and the third of entertainment on the evening of Independence Day and several evenings thereafter.

Communal labor was carried out by each of the hamlets (*dukuh*) that make up the village (*kelurahan*) under the direction of the village officials. Every year, two months before the celebration, the officials from the fourteen villages in the subdistrict are called to the subdistrict office and instructed by the *camat* (subdistrict head) about the Independence Day program, which is passed down from the provincial government through the regency, the subdistrict, and the village to the level of neighborhood associations (*rukun tetangga*), and is implemented in accordance with the actual conditions in each locality. Since the content of the program has already been determined by the subdistrict and village officials, at neighborhood-association meetings the villagers discuss only the details of implementation. In 1975 the *camat* focused on construction projects of a practical nature, such as maintenance of roads, bridges, and irrigation canals. Each neighborhood association set the days on which it would widen roads and repair bridges, and everyone in the neighborhood carried out the work together. In addition, each village and hamlet made a bamboo gate to decorate its entrance and fashioned other decorations for the celebration.

---

[12]The village of Darman (not its real name), in Sukoharjo Regency, Central Java, is situated in the well-irrigated and densely populated plain surrounding the city of Surakarta. I stayed in the village for seven months in 1975 and another nine months in 1978–1979 with the permission and sponsorship of Lembaga Ilmu Pengetahuan Indonesia. I had a chance to revisit the village for a few days in 1980 while I was at Sekolah Tinggi Seni Rupa Indonesia, Yogyakarta, upon invitation. I am indebted to these institutions for their generous hospitality and assistance.

[13]Cannadine, "The Context, Performance and Meaning of Ritual," pp. 104–5.

Mobilization of Javanese villagers in communal labor for public works dates back to the Dutch colonial period. After independence, communal labor was designated as the ideology of *gotong royong* (mutual assistance) to become the pivot of the Indonesian national spirit. Publicly, such labor was hailed as an expression of the sovereignty of the people, signifying that the people would build their society themselves. After Suharto's New Order stabilized, however, and the separation of the state from the masses became obvious, people tended to regard communal labor as a kind of corvée.

This contradiction in the concept of communal labor was already evident in 1975; when communal labor had barely survived by being linked with the Independence Day celebration. As public works would have become increasingly dependent on government subsidies, villagers' donations, and the use of paid labor, fewer substantive projects were to be planned for Independence Day. The meaning of communal labor was sought not in the substance of work but in the form of the act: meeting and working together on predetermined days. The contradiction was resolved by shifting the emphasis from public works with a practical purpose to decorative construction. In other words, communal labor as a part of the ritual was refined to the point of ritualizing labor itself.

A major feature of the Independence Day celebration in 1975 was the ceremony held on August 17 on the soccer field in front of the subdistrict office. This ceremony was later discontinued, and instead the village officials and other village leaders traveled by motorcycle to a ceremony held at the regency office, some distance away. When the ceremony took place at the subdistrict office, which was within the sphere of the villagers' daily lives, far more people participated. Even then, however, participation was limited to village officials, leaders of the civil defense corps (*hansip*) and youth group, and schoolteachers and pupils, and thus was not a spontaneous mobilization of the people. The ceremony in 1975 represented a transition from the mass ceremonies of the Sukarno period to the more strongly state-regulated ceremonies of the present system.

As is typical of modern state rituals, the ceremony in front of the subdistrict office was characterized by order and discipline which accorded with the authority of the center. The national flag—the Sang Merah Putih—and the *camat* as the highest state official in the subdistrict represented the central authority. The total concentration on this center was manifest in the almost military discipline evident throughout the ceremony. All the subdistrict officials, soldiers, police, schoolteachers, pupils, and representatives of the fourteen villages in the subdistrict wore uniforms, marching and lining up in military fashion. Only the wives of the village officials, representing the women's association of each village, wore traditional Javanese dress, but even there, color and style were unified, creating the impression of uniforms. The *camat*, wearing the military-style official dress signifying his rank and surrounded by soldiers in field uniform, made a dignified appearance before those assembled, accepting their salute. After the national flag was raised ceremoniously, gazed at and saluted by all, he mounted a platform and delivered a passionate speech exhorting loyalty to the state. The overall effect was reinforced by the uniforms and the standardized postures and body movements of the crowd, further emphasizing the center upon which the ritual was focused.

According to villagers' recollections, so many people participated in the ceremony in front of the subdistrict office during the Sukarno period that the village was almost emptied, and political fervor was the dominant note of the gathering. The villagers assembled in groups within each village according to party affiliation—the Partai Nasional Indonesia (PNI; the Indonesian Nationalist Party), the Partai Komunis Indonesia (PKI; the Indonesian Communist Party), the various Muslim parties, and so on—and marched to the subdistrict office. The vigorous, evocative speeches, the demonstrative, militant parades, and the tension and minor clashes between members of different parties further heightened the crowd's excitement and enthusiasm. When a radio address by Sukarno, a legendary hero and an unparalleled public speaker, was broadcast over loudspeakers, the people, intoxicated by his rhetoric, were drawn together by this potent symbol of personal greatness, overcoming their differences. Rather than being a state ritual, the ceremony was the ritual of a communal society engaged in fighting. The memory of the declaration of independence proclaimed by Sukarno and Mohammad Hatta on August 17, 1945, and the subsequent four and a half years of guerrilla warfare against the Dutch provided a mythic prototype for the ritual. The new society's communal model was probably the various spontaneously generated militias in which the villagers themselves had fought. By reenacting the drama of the establishment of the Republic, the Independence Day celebration fused past and present, transforming the past into the eternal present shared by the entire community. In the communal ecstasy they experienced in the here and now, the people discovered the state to be on their own side.

In Anderson's words, the Sukarno period was characterized by "the penetration of the state by society,"[14] whereas the Suharto period "is best understood as the resurrection of the state and its triumph vis-à-vis society and nation."[15] The 1975 ceremony still retained the outward form of mobilization of the masses. The direct appeal of the leaders to those assembled and the dependence on mass mobilization were the expressive form of the centrality at the birth of the Republic. However, the participants were all directly linked to the state organization and were mobilized in accordance with a predetermined program. If the previous ceremony had represented the drama of an emerging, unstructured society, the 1975 ceremony represented the hierarchical structure of the completed state apparatus. It was an opportunity for those involved in state administration symbolized by their uniforms to assert themselves.

That evening a rock band from town was invited to perform on the field where the ceremony had taken place, and the number of subdistrict residents attending was much greater than during the day. The *camat* appeared once again on stage, this time in casual attire, and greeted the crowd in a joking manner, making everyone laugh. For several days thereafter, amateur groups performed plays, dances, and gamelan music in most villages.

To summarize, the 1975 Independence Day celebration comprised three well-balanced parts: the long period of communal labor under the boiling sun to build a new society, the dignified ceremony that was the peak of the ritual, and the relaxed evenings of entertainment for the people. But with the decline in the enthusiastic mass participation in politics that had been common before 1965, loss of interest in state rituals was inevitable. Formerly, the local political party organization had been the main channel for political mobilization of the people. At the beginning of the Suharto period, however, the PKI, which had been influential in rural areas, was completely dissolved, after which the other parties were prohibited from establishing

---

[14]Anderson, "Old State, New Society," pp. 482–83.

[15]Ibid., p. 487.

branches at the subdistrict or village level. The resultant political vacuum was filled by the web of the state organizations, epitomized by the Ministry of the Interior, the army, and the police. The village-official class, which formerly had organized the people's political activities, opted for its position as the lowest rung on the ladder of state officialdom. Though remnants of mass politics could still be found in the *camat's* stirring speech in front of the subdistrict office, overall the ceremony was now a gathering designed for the members of the lowest unit in the state apparatus. The change in the ritual context of the Independence Day celebration from the ritual of a fighting communal society to the ritual of a triumphant state is seen more clearly in subsequent years.

V. The Ritual of Communal Labor

Although the Independence Day celebrations of 1978 and 1980 differed from that of 1975 in scale, their form remained much the same. The greatest differences from the 1975 celebration were the discontinuation of the ceremony held in front of the subdistrict office, the diminished role of the evening entertainment, and the expanded role of communal labor, changes that destroyed the balance of the celebration's three components.

The ceremony that had been held at the subdistrict office in 1975, within the sphere of village life, was conducted only at the regency office in 1978. The village officials and leaders of the youth group and civil defense corps still participated; but once they had left for the regency office early in the morning on motorcycles decorated with miniature national flags, the village returned to peace and quiet, and nothing noteworthy occurred for the rest of the day. The elderly headman of Darman had retired in 1975 after serving for almost thirty years and had been replaced by a younger man who was a college graduate. The new headman was always at the subdistrict or regency office and had the reputation among the villagers of seldom being available when they needed to discuss something with him.

The former headman had been a Muslim rear-guard leader in the guerrilla warfare during the war of independence and was the leader of village society when it was relatively independent from state administration. Under the New Order, however, village headmen came to function more as officials at the lowest echelon of the state apparatus. This tendency is clearly seen in Independence Day celebrations, in which the village officials are mobilized by the higher levels of the state apparatus. Instead of involving the people directly in the state ritual, unifying them by means of common symbols, the celebration aims to gather together all the members of the state apparatus at the regency level.

The entertainment had also lost its vigor. A village amateur troupe continued to perform *lagendriyan*, a form of drama created in the nineteenth century at the court of Mangkunegara,[16] though on a smaller scale than before. Such performances had ceased to be regarded as official village events, however, and the troupe was in financial straits because it no longer received village funds or private donations from the headman and other influential villagers.

According to villagers' recollections, dramatic performances had been extremely popular during the Sukarno period, when ordinary people participated in politics. The village officials had taken the initiative in organizing troupes to perform *wayang*

---

[16]For information on this drama form, see Theodore Pigeaud, *Javaanse Volksvertoningen* (Batavia: Volkslectuur, 1938), p. 79.

orang and other forms of traditional theater, an endeavor solidly supported by the village as a whole. But with the spread of depoliticization and the development of a consumer culture under the New Order, people's interests and activities had diversified. Consequently, the performing arts had become the private activities of a small number of enthusiasts and thus had lost their broad social base.

The immediate reason they lost popularity and their official connection with the Independence Day celebration, as well as their status as activities supported by the entire village society, had to do with the personal tastes of the village headman and the *camat*. In general, the spontaneous nature of the Independence Day celebration declined under the Suharto regime, while the initiative of the state increased.[17] Even so, the performing arts might have retained a greater role had they received the personal protection of the local leaders and the active support of the villagers. But the new headman preferred to play tennis at the subdistrict-office courts with subdistrict officials and other village headmen; he had no interest in traditional dance and drama. Nonetheless, the amateur actors, as well as the village youths who played in rock bands, viewed his lack of support as stemming less from personal taste than from indifference. "He just doesn't dare do it [*tidak berani*]," they said. This was a comment not on his personal character but on his reluctance to dip into his own pocket and supply funds for various village activities. The villagers knew that such contributions represented a personal sacrifice, but that was what they expected of a headman. In anthropological terms, the headman was expected to be the center of the ritual redistribution of wealth. His role as the lowest member of the state apparatus had taken precedence over his role as the center of village society.

Although the Independence Day celebration in Darman gradually lost its festive characteristics, it never became totally severed from the masses. Reflecting the change in national priorities from political mobilization to construction and development, the focus of ritual mobilization shifted from creation of a spectacle to communal labor to set the stage for the celebration. Instead of ceremonies and performances, communal labor to decorate the village, which could appear to be trivial and routine, became central to the celebration. If ceremonial activities themselves are considered to be the focal point of the ritual, the simple work of preparation at first seems trivial and routine. As illustrated by the following discussion, however, communal labor itself is ritual in character. Such work cannot be reduced to a means serving some other end but is an end in itself, expressing something by its very formalism. Labor and ritual, which are usually regarded as polar opposites in modern productivity theory, are unified in ritual labor.

VI. ROOFTOP WRITINGS

Communal labor in connection with Independence Day was carried out every year during the six-year period of my study, changing only in terms of increasing scale. The first major project the villagers undertook was the writing of large white letters and numbers on each roof. On the day designated by their neighborhood association, the villagers climbed onto their roofs and wrote these letters and numbers with lime. The actual work was done by the male members of each family or by plasterers and

[17]For a discussion of the same trend observed in the Independence Day celebration in Yogyakarta, see Barbara Hatley, "Indonesian Ritual, Javanese Drama—Celebrating *Tujuhbelasan*," *Indonesia* 34 (1982).

painters employed for the purpose. The *camat* decided what would be written, so that the same letters could be seen on the roof of every house in the subdistrict.

One of the most common formulas was HUT RI KE-30 (in 1975), an abbreviation of the Indonesian words meaning "Thirtieth Anniversary of the Republic of Indonesia." The number was increased by one digit with each passing year. Other examples included PELITA II, meaning "Second Five-Year Development Plan," and LSD, meaning "Village Social Council," a consultative body of village leaders the formation of which was being encouraged by the government at the time. Another frequent example was the numbers 17-8-1945 – 17-8-1975, indicating the passage of time since the declaration of independence. I saw such formulas on the rooftops wherever I traveled in the provinces of Central and East Java, the combined population of which exceeds fifty million. The effect of the repetition was overwhelming. Most formulas, being written by the occupants of the houses, were crude and far from decorative, but since they were always clearly written in large characters stretching across the entire roof, they were highly visible from every direction.

The villagers also displayed national flags at their gates or doorways. But the writings on the roofs created a very different impression from the display of the national flag, which is a feature common to the state celebrations of many nations. The national flag directly symbolizes the state or nation. The relationship between the symbol and that which is symbolized is simple and clear. The symbolic content of the rooftop formulas is much more complex. The strong impression created by these formulas will be better understood if we analyze their many attributes separately. First, written characters are significant in themselves. Their large size is also important, as is the fact that they are written on the roof. Furthermore, the letters used form abbreviations not used in daily life. Finally, we should note that the formulas include numbers that represent the progress of time.

The use of writing was very limited in rural Java during the periods of the kingdoms and of Dutch colonization, when most villagers were illiterate. In the main, writing served a talismanic rather than a mundane function: the written word, being beyond ordinary comprehension, was endowed with esoteric power. After independence, public education and a modern administrative system were gradually implemented, and writing was slowly incorporated into daily life. Even in the latter half of the 1970s, however, the combined percentage of those who could not read at all and those who could recognize individual letters but could not read a sentence was high, and in many cases the written word remained on a plane divorced from daily life. Most people came into contact with writing primarily when they had to obtain government forms from the village or subdistrict office. Writing was still used for charms, as well. Knowledge of the mystical and astrological relationships between words and numbers on the one hand and individual fortune and the order of the universe on the other was considered very important in daily life. Writings executed by magicians, fortunetellers, and teachers of folk mysticism for their disciples and clients provided another important occasion of contact with the written word.

The farm villages of Java, unlike those of industrial countries, are not inundated with writings. Consequently, the act of climbing onto one's roof to write characters and the subsequent constant visual exposure to those characters has great significance. To claim that the villagers regard letters and numbers as magical symbols with mystical power would be an exaggeration. Nevertheless, that the villagers write political formulas on their own roofs and live beneath those formulas every day indicates that they accept the external authority and hierarchy from which the formulas emanate.

The large size of the characters also exerts an impact on viewers. The creation and display of huge symbols is common to political ritual. Their large size makes viewers feel disproportionately small, reducing them to minuscule parts of the structured world.

The combination of writing and roofs is also outside the order of daily life. Letters and numbers are usually written on paper. Moreover, all writings—whether government forms, widely circulated handbooks of divination and magic, or Arabic talismans obtained from magical healers—are carefully stored in a wooden box in an inner room, out of sight. Roofs, by contrast, are the most visible part of the village scene, the part most exposed to the view of outsiders. Thus, what the villagers conceal most assiduously in their private lives is exposed by the most eye-catching method when linked with state ritual. While people usually hide the source of power for themselves, the exposed writings on rooftops signify their recognition of external power and their conformity to the order it represents.

The compelling power of these rooftop writings is reinforced by the fact that the formulas used are rarely spoken. For example, HUT RI represents the initials of *hari ulang tahun* (a term used to indicate birthdays and anniversaries) and *Republik Indonesia*. There is another expression that also means "Independence Day" which is *hari kemerdekaan*. Such terms are, however, never used by the villagers in conversation. Because they are abbreviations, they sound foreign to daily life. Moreover, the words from which the abbreviations are derived are new additions to the Indonesian language that are not commonly used. In conversation, Independence Day is referred to as *pitulasan*, a Javanese noun meaning "things relating to the number seventeen." The formulas written on the roofs, lacking the connotations and nuances of everyday language, are written and seen but never spoken.

The official terminology that has been spreading rapidly since independence includes many neologisms. Numerous words have been borrowed from classical Malay or local languages and given new meanings; others are Sanskrit, classical Javanese, Dutch, or English loanwords. The use of abbreviations and acronyms is also extremely common. Neologisms, abbreviations, and acronyms are especially noticeable in the terminology of state politics and administration. They are not merely Indonesian terms foreign to the Javanese but form an independent vocabulary system that could fittingly be termed "state language." Its terminology, frequently seen and heard but divorced from the context of conversation and thus evoking no associations or connotations, is often used in plays on words by popular playwrights and comedians in Java.

Unlike the meaningless formulas of children's word games, however, this state language has meaning and power in that the ability to manipulate it connects one to the authority and power of the state. The process occurring at the state level in Indonesian is similar to that occurring in modern Japanese, especially written Japanese, in which the systematic use of loanwords from English, French, and other foreign languages greatly augments the power of those privy to specialized knowledge by excluding those who lack access to the inner circle's special vocabulary.

In short, the majority of rooftop writings consist of formulas whose meaning cannot be inferred from everyday language. Their very strangeness and lack of meaning in the context of daily life serve to demonstrate the power of the external state system.

In the Javanese kingdoms of former times, atop commemorative structures that symbolized the state, the years of their completion were often inscribed. This resembles the present custom of writing on rooftops. But to have every dwelling so adorned could only be necessary or feasible in a new state striving to become a nation-state. It is very common for a young state, or one that needs to emphasize unity under the state, to write its political slogans in large letters wherever people might see them. The rooftop formulas, however, are not slogans used to mobilize the masses or punctuate rousing speeches. They are strangely static and decorative, like the calligraphy scrolls of Chinese poems and classical passages displayed in Japanese homes. During the war of independence, the archaic word *merdeka* (independence, freedom) was resurrected. Both spoken and written, it inspired the people. The state language used today does not have such a direct power over people's thoughts and feelings, but it does have great power as an external code symbolizing the transcendent system of the state. As seen above, its power depends on its strangeness, its separation from the context of daily life.

VII. State Time and Village Time

The final point that should be discussed in connection with rooftop writings is the inclusion of numbers that represent the passage of time. In the example HUT RI KE-30, the number grows each year. In the case of PELITA II, the period is longer, but the number increases every five years. The formula 17-8-1945 – 17-8-1975 expresses the distance the passage of time has created according to the Western calendar.

The order of time indicated by these examples, created and propagated by the state, is essentially different from that by which the villagers regulate their daily lives. The term *hari ulang tahun*, day of commemoration, literally means "the day that is repeated each year" and, as already mentioned, is also used to indicate birthdays and corporate anniversaries. To the residents of Darman, and to most Indonesians, it is still a relatively unfamiliar phrase.

Excluding those who held positions in government or business under the Dutch colonial administration, as well as those who are well educated and Westernized, the majority of adult Javanese do not know when they were born or how old they are in terms of the Western calendar. The closest approximation to a Western-style birthday is *weton*. This is based on the traditional Javanese calendar, which combines five market days and seven days of the week. The *weton* of an individual is expressed as "*pon* Friday" or "*wage* Tuesday," for example, a combination that is repeated every thirty-five days. Everyone knows his or her own *weton* but never considers its position on the linear time scale. The traditional calendar indicates where one's birthday falls within a time cycle that is without beginning or end. It is a system of classifying people into 35 groups according to their birthdays, but it is not a quantifiable system.

The point is not just that the state and villagers use different calendars. The official calendar of Indonesia is the Western calendar. Under the present international system it is almost imperative that Indonesia, as a member of that system, use the Western calendar. Moreover, the simple linear, quantifiable characteristics of the Western calendar make uniform domestic administration possible. However, in addition to its technical convenience, this calendar has an ideological character. The nationalism that legitimates the state of Indonesia is based on the ideology of progress. Present conditions are measured on a linear time scale, as evidenced by such expressions as "We must make up for three hundred years of backwardness under colonial rule" and "We have made this much progress in only thirty years since independence." Because of the fact that the concept of progress is based on relative comparison, it is essential to have a single time scale that imposes a uniform order, and the Western calendar fulfills this need.

The British social historian E. P. Thompson, in his essay "Time, Work-Discipline, and Industrial Capitalism," describes the popularization of standardized, mechanized time measured by the clock in British society during the Industrial Revolution.[18] Before that, the passage of time was marked in a much more flexible and diversified manner. The rhythm and tempo of time changed freely according to circumstance and mood. If there were times when people worked night and day, there were also times when they remained idle for several days and simply enjoyed life. Uniform time measured by the clock made the structure of time external to people.

Modern society is based on a uniform time scale that depends on an external standard. A similar process of change is occurring in Indonesia. However, wage labor measured by the clock, and the coercive, mechanized tempo that governs such labor, applies at present to only a limited proportion of the population. Most people in Darman regulate their work in the paddies, in the marketplace, or on the construction site according to the position of the sun, the degree of heat, traditional work quotas, and physical fatigue. The sight of middle and high school students rushing off to school is often the villagers' sole exposure to an absolute time standard.

Society itself has not spontaneously developed a uniform, standardized time scale, but the state is using repeated rituals to instill in the masses the Western concept of the progress of time, that is, linear, quantifiable time. Independence Day, when dates and other numbers are written on rooftops, is a prime example of this strategy. Other state commemorative days have also been established: Armed Forces Day, Oath of Youth Day, Rise of the Nation Day, Miracle of the Panca Sila Day, and so on. The numbers indicating the anniversaries of these days are reinforced by signs, television news, and other media. Though it is impossible to measure the exact degree to which this type of repetition contributes to the formation of national identity, the effect of the repetition of seemingly trivial ritualistic customs on the relatively simple lives of rural villagers cannot be ignored.

VIII. RITUAL CONSTRUCTION AND COMPETITION

In addition to writing on their roofs, flying the national flag, and cleaning and repainting their houses, the villagers participate in new communal-labor projects each year. As already mentioned, maintenance work on roads, bridges, and other infrastructure was undertaken in 1975. But such labor did not involve creating something clearly new and appropriate to a state ritual; it appeared to be simply part of the daily routine. To fulfill the ritual's objective of symbolizing the progress of linear time, the Independence Day program had to contain some obviously new element each year.

Today's Independence Day ritual, unlike that of Sukarno's time, has no mythic prototype to reenact. Consequently, many difficulties arise in selecting a new project each year. When the 1978 celebration was approaching, several members of the youth group in Darman proposed replacing the decorative bamboo gates that were set up

---

[18]E. P. Thompson, "Time, Work-Discipline, and Industrial Capitalism," *Past and Present* 38 (1967).

each year at village and hamlet entrances with permanent structures of concrete blocks. The resultant gates, constructed at nine sites in the village, were crude miniatures of the decorative gates (*gapura*) erected at the entrances to Javanese palaces and mausolea. Though clumsy and inartistic, they were new, and the people were satisfied with the outcome. When the work was done and Independence Day was over, however, the villagers faced a problem: what communal-labor program could they plan for the next Independence Day?

In 1980 the village leaders and youth group devised a still more ambitious project. Until then the roads of each hamlet had been lined with bamboo fences. The plan was to replace these with cement-block walls, erecting a small gate at the entrance to each residence. This was a major construction project requiring far more funds, materials, and labor than any previous undertaking. Money was raised even by selling the glasses, dishes, lamps, and other utensils communally owned by neighborhood groups for use in the feasts accompanying family rituals. The young men took turns working all-night shifts during the final week in order to complete the work by Independence Day—an unprecedented occurrence in Darman. Every hamlet was lined with a long concrete wall, and the walls, gates, and house façades were painted in two tones of green. The same formula as that on the roofs, HUT RI KE-35, was inscribed on the gate of each house.

The look of the village was transformed. The variegated bamboo gates and fences of the past were supplanted by standardized structures whose artificial appearance demonstrated the village's unity as part of the state. The communal solidarity that had previously been expressed by people's emotions and ideology, and by the clothes they wore and the way they stood and moved during ceremonies and performances, was now expressed by a static physical structure.

The village leaders who promoted this ritual construction praised the change in the village's appearance made by the long cement-block walls and gates as a sign of *maju,* or progress. As is common in developing countries promoting modernization, the way of thinking that sees *maju,* "progress," and *kuno,* "backwardness," as polar opposites has deeply penetrated Indonesian society, reaching to the lowest stratum of villagers, who lack both education and status. To use the example of a house, walls woven of bamboo laths and a thatched roof are *kuno,* while brick walls and a tile roof are *maju.* The villagers of Darman often expressed pride in having most of their houses made of brick, a sign of progress. Given this concept of progress, people found it fairly easy to accept cement-block walls as superior to bamboo fences.

One major reason the plan was feasible was that the construction work was ritualistic and decorative in character, offering no obvious practical benefit. The irrigation facilities, roads, and bridges in Darman and surrounding villages were well maintained, and improvements were not urgently needed. Nevertheless, farmers who owned paddies often suggested plans for improving and extending peripheral irrigation canals, but the plans always fell apart owing to conflicts over how to allot funds and who would benefit in what way. But it seldom even occurs to people to oppose ritual construction work intended solely to demonstrate the concept of progress, hard though it is to define just what that means in technical-rational terms; it is easier to endorse the abstract concept of progress as a "good thing." No one can say precisely what is more progressive about a concrete wall than a bamboo fence. Personally, I found the concrete walls rather grotesque. However, when the plan was implemented and the village was given a new look, the people accepted the outcome because they could relate it to the general notion of progress.

Ritual construction is closely tied to ritual competition. One reason the villagers were so enthusiastically involved in the project was the intervillage competition organized by the government. This competition was part of a nationwide event. A competition was organized between the villages of each subdistrict. The winner in each subdistrict then participated in the regency competition, and those winners advanced to the provincial competition. Finally, the top province and the top village in the nation were selected in Jakarta. Darman was placed second in the 1980 Central Java competition, the year the village walls and gates were rebuilt. The desire to strive for first place in the next provincial competition spread through the village, encouraging the people to work harder.

There are two important points to note about this competition. First, the state has changed the nature of the everyday communal relationship among neighbors. The villagers' sense of belonging is focused on the hamlet (*dukuh*), the smallest component of the village (*kelurahan*) as an administrative unit. Identification with one's hamlet, a community that ordinarily is not particularly exclusive or cohesive, is reinforced by communal labor and by uniform walls and gates, and is then transformed into identification with the village, which is linked to the state through the administrative hierarchy.

Second, work discipline has been closely tied to linear time. Communal labor for the Independence Day celebration consists of projects that mobilize a large number of people. The day of completion is fixed, and thus the work is strictly governed by the linear progress of time. Though communal labor for public works is not new to the villagers, tying work to a set deadline is uncommon. The ritual labor for Independence Day must be completed several weeks before August 17 because subdistrict, regency, and provincial officials visit the village on set dates to select the winner of the competition. In effect, the time discipline of a modern factory has been imposed on the village.

The all-night shift work in 1980, which was the spontaneous response of the villagers themselves, was an unprecedented experience for them. The main impetus behind the planning, and especially the implementation, of this work schedule was the competition. Just as with sports events, people become very involved in the outcome of competitions that clearly rank the entrants' efforts. The competition also has the indirect result of insinuating into the life of the village work discipline measured by the standard of linear time, like futuristic technology on display at an exhibition.

Darman is situated in a lowland area surrounded by mountains and endowed with an abundant water supply. The work of paddy cultivation is not bound by a uniform schedule. Thanks to high temperatures, plentiful sunshine, and an abundant water supply the year round, the fields can be planted at any time. Women who contract to plant rice for a certain amount of money per field will occasionally work all night when demand is high. In general, however, work is not regulated by an absolute, external time discipline but is regulated by the rhythm of the human body as it adjusts to the alternation of day and night, the amount of sunshine, and changes in the weather. In Javanese villages, whose society has not yet been transformed by the internalization of modern time through economic and technological imperatives, organized labor for state rituals and time discipline at schools serve to familiarize the villagers with linear time. Thus communal labor for the Independence Day celebration has not merely changed Darman's appearance; it has also added new concepts of time and work discipline to the principles that govern village social relations.

IX. Conclusion

In the foregoing I have discussed the ways in which the people of one farm village in Central Java celebrated Independence Day. The state of Indonesia, having emerged from its troubled infancy and established an independent institutional framework, strove to formulate a nation-state from above through government initiatives. In the process, the relationship of the villagers to the Independence Day ritual changed greatly.

If the usual features of modern state ritual are mass mobilization, festive parades, and lavish spectacles, the case study presented in this paper constitutes a very modest, slow-paced example. Festivals that liberate people from the routine of daily life are one type of ritual. The Independence Day celebration in the time of Sukarno, when society was still relatively free of state restrictions, was of this type. Under Suharto however, the celebration appears to have become a means of binding people to the New Order that the state is striving to establish. Of course, restriction and coercion are inherent characteristics of rituals; but when true ritual power is exercised, the participants have no sense of being coerced.

The Independence Day celebration of the Sukarno period, remnants of which survived in 1975, severed people from their daily routine, and the parades and rallies transformed them into militant political entities. The year 1945 did not belong to the past but was an integral part of the present. The Independence Day celebration was more the ritual of a fighting communal society than a state ritual.

The present Independence Day celebration, by contrast, is a state ritual aimed at transforming society as a whole into a national entity bound to the state. The year 1945 is firmly in the past. To confirm the ever-widening distance between the present and that past, the current year of the anniversary of independence is emphasized and new events are planned each year. The rooftop writings and the annual village face lift symbolize the common passage of time and the people's common distance from the past. The state ritual demonstrates to the people who are mobilized both the ideology of progress, which denies the past in the effort to move forward continuously, and the perspective of linear time, which underlies this ideology.

It is a common assumption that the realm of routine work and production and the realm of festivities are polar opposites and that ritual belongs to the latter. As long as we view ritual in this perspective, the present state of Indonesia appears to be diminishing the role of ritual and promoting material progress through the application of routine systems. The central event of the Independence Day celebration in Jakarta in 1985, the fortieth anniversary of independence, was the Exhibition of Indonesian Production (Pameran Produksi Indonesia) in Merdeka Square, in the center of the city.[19] The change in the focus of Darman's celebration from ceremony and entertainment to village-improvement labor projects can be viewed as reflecting the main objectives of the present Indonesian state: developing the economic base and increasing production. At least, these are the reasons the state gives for sponsoring the ritual. In reality, however, the Independence Day celebration represents the ritualization of production and work themselves. Mass mobilization for state ritual has been achieved by assimilating village communal labor into a ritual form that is an end in itself and transforming this labor into ritual competition.

[19]For information on this exhibition, see "Sebuah Laparan Perjuangan 40 Tahun," *Tempo* (August 10, 1985), pp. 12–13.

Anderson's argument, presented toward the beginning of this paper, emphasizes the differences between state and society and the rift between the two. He maintains that the link between the distinct entities of state and nation tends to be viewed too easily as simple and self-evident. If we accept his view, we must ask what the relationship between the two is, what Anderson's tiny hyphen represents. The systemic channels linking state and society include tax collection, the police, the courts, and the recruitment and promotion of officials. This paper attempts to point out that ritual also plays an important role. Ritual is not on the same plane as other systems. Each system has its own degree of ritual character. Given the need for a state to control its society, the more important the occasion, the more the state tends to turn to ritualization. State ritual is not limited to colorful pageants in the capital or grandiose commemorative structures. As discussed above, it can also be found in the time order and work discipline of daily life. In the broadest terms, it is the application of an external, universal model to the structure of space and time in everyday life.

When considering Southeast Asian countries' state- and nation-building efforts, there is much to be gained from regarding state ritual in this broader context, since the state's central problems are reflected in its constantly changing rituals.

———————

This paper was originally published under the title "Mura to kokka gyōji" [The village and state ritual] in Hara Yōnosuke, ed., *Tōnan Ajia kara no chiteki bōken* [Intellectual adventures in Southeast Asia] (Tokyo: Libroport, 1986), pp. 31–68.

4

JAVANOLOGY AND THE AGE OF RANGGAWARSITA: AN INTRODUCTION TO NINETEENTH-CENTURY JAVANESE CULTURE

Kenji Tsuchiya

INTRODUCTION

On May 25, 1899, Raden Adjeng Kartini (1879–1904), the daughter of a Javanese aristocrat in the port city of Jepara on the Java Sea, wrote the first of a series of letters to a Dutch woman, E. H. Zeehandelaar. These letters, of which this first was written in her father's home, the official residence of the Jepara *kabupaten*, just after Kartini had turned twenty, were later collected and published in 1911 by J. A. Abendanon, chief of the Department of Education and Religion of the Indies government from 1900 to 1905, under the title *Door Duisternis tot Licht* [Through darkness to light].[1] Kartini's first letter began with the words "Ik heb zóó verlangd kennis te maken met een 'modern meisje'" (I have been so anxious to make the acquaintance of a "modern girl").[2] In the Japanese translation of this collection, *modern meisje* is rendered aptly as *atarashii jidai no otome* (a girl of the new age).[3] The Dutch word *modern* demarcates the new age of the twentieth century from the colonial society of the nineteenth.

The twentieth century saw the beginning of the Pax Neerlandica, with the Dutch colonial government's establishment in both name and form of the Netherlands East Indies (Nederlandsch Oost-Indië), entailing the institution of a centralized colonial administrative system and the maintenance of "tranquillity and order" (*rust en orde;* in Javanese, *tata tentrem*) throughout the colony. This century was envisaged as an age in which "de *Ethische* koers in de koloniale politiek" (the ethical course in colonial policy), an enlightened colonial policy aimed at the "growth and development" (*bloei en ontwikkeling*) of the indigenous society, would be magnanimously implemented.[4]

---

[1]R. A. Kartini, *Door Duisternis tot Licht*, 5th ed. (Amsterdam: Nabrink, 1976; 1st ed. 1911).

[2]Ibid., p. 1.

[3]R. A. Kartini, *Ankoku o koete—Wakaki ran'in josei no shokanshū* [Beyond darkness: Letters of a young woman of the Netherlands East Indies], trans. Kiyona Ushie (Tokyo: Nisshin Shoin, 1940), p. 15.

[4]To the Netherlands itself, the advent of the new age was symbolized by the coronation of Queen Wilhelmina on September 6, 1898, in Amsterdam's Nieuwe Kerk. "De *Ethische* koers in de koloniale politiek" is taken from the title of a 1901 pamphlet by P. Brooshooft, editor of the newspaper *Locomotief*. See H. J. de Graaf, *Geschiedenis van Indonesië* (The Hague and Bandung: van Hoeve, 1949), pp. 454, 460.

Dutch society saw in the fact that a bright, enterprising young woman like Kartini expressed herself in the Dutch language the advent of a new age in indigenous society.[5]

The twentieth century was a new age for Indonesia, as well. It saw the birth of a nationalism that envisaged the colonial territory of the Netherlands East Indies as the future community of Indonesia and the development of a multifaceted movement (*pergerakan*) to build this community. It was at this time that the Dutch word *modern* was naturalized as *modérn* and became popular with nationalist leaders and young people to express the concept of a better tomorrow. Ever since, *modérn* has had a positive connotation in Indonesia. Kartini heralded the *modérn* age in Indonesia, and she is included in the hagiography of her people as a pioneer in the struggle for the *modérn* and as the first *pahlawan* (hero) of the age of nationalism.[6]

That the Netherlands and Indonesia, each for its own reasons, publicly revere Kartini, and that Kartini herself used the Dutch word *modern* at the beginning of the collection of letters that represents her "voyage of self-discovery,"[7] indicates clearly that the years around 1900 marked the birth of an age, both in the history of Dutch colonialism and in the history of Indonesian nationalism. This fact is also reflected in academic research on modern Indonesian history, particularly the history of nationalism, much of which focuses on developments beginning around the turn of the century. In what amounts to an academic tradition, discussion of nationalism begins with Kartini and the Budi Utomo, founded in Batavia (Jakarta) in 1908. In this sense, the Dutch colonial government, the Indonesian nationalists, and the academic world share the same understanding of the Netherlands East Indies and the *modérn*.

This is only natural. The emergence of nationalism as *Indonesian* nationalism presupposed the union of the whole of Indonesia (theoretically, all the colonial territory from Sabang to Merauke—*van Sabang tot Merauke*) under a centralized system converging on Batavia (particularly in terms of administration and education); and that system was established only in this century.

But when one considers the language that the nationalists of the beginning of the century used to express themselves—Kartini is an excellent example—or to make their political appeals, one immediately recognizes the overwhelming superiority of the Dutch language. By "superiority" I mean that Dutch was used more frequently than any other language to express certain phenomena, ideas, and feelings. The world was objectified through Dutch.

There are three aspects to this phenomenon. First, that most of the early nationalists recorded their ideas and political messages in Dutch was a reflection of the fact

---

[5]That Kartini was seen as heralding a new age is clearly expressed in the title Abendanon gave to the collection of her letters (the darkness/light dichotomy and the evolutionary process suggested by the phrase "through darkness to light"). The publication of these letters inspired the inauguration of a number of social projects in the Netherlands bearing Kartini's name, such as the Kartini Fund, established in 1912. On these projects, see Sitisoemandari Soeroto, *Kartini Sebuah Biografi* (Jakarta: Gunung Agung, 1977), especially chap. 12.

[6]There are numerous Indonesian translations of Kartini's letters and many critical biographies of her in Indonesian. To list only a few: R. A. Kartini, *Habis Gelap Terbitlah Terang*, trans. Armijn Pane (Jakarta: Balai Pustaka, 1938); Pramoedya Ananta Toer, *Panggil Aku Kartini Sadja* (Bukittinggi and Jakarta: Nusantara, 1962); Soeroto, *Kartini Sebuah Biografi*.

[7]"Voyage of self-discovery" is the phrase of John Smail, in David J. Steinberg, ed., *In Search of Southeast Asia* (Oxford: Oxford University Press, 1971), p. 281. See also Akira Nagazumi, *Indoneshia minzoku ishiki no keisei* [The formation of Indonesian national consciousness] (Tokyo: University of Tokyo Press, 1980).

that they were born into the social class that read, spoke, and wrote Dutch. With the development of the *pergerakan*, their audience expanded, and the Indonesian language eventually took the place of Dutch as the nationalists' common language—the *sumpah pemuda*, or "youth pledge," of 1928 is a symbolic expression of this—and use of Dutch eventually declined, disappearing at least from the written (*tulisan*) world of printed matter. But in some cases it remained the most effective means of self-expression, as seen in the letters written by Sutan Sjahrir while in exile in the late 1930s.[8]

Second, the phenomena, ideas, and feelings that characterize the new age are all expressed in Dutch loanwords, such as *modérn*. The early nationalists and their *pergerakan* frequently used words like *partij* (party), *organisatie* (organization), *voorzitter* (chairman), and *vergadering* (meeting)[9] both in writings in Indonesian and in the spoken language (*lisan*), such as speeches and discussions, whether in Indonesian or in local languages. All these terms express something having to do with the new age, the new spatial dimension. Some of these Dutch loanwords were later replaced by Indonesian equivalents, but most passed intact into Indonesian, and many became key words. The cultural debate (*polemik kebudayaan*) of the mid-1930s centered on such Dutch key words.[10]

Third, special terms used in Indonesian writings were often explained in Dutch or followed by Dutch equivalents in parentheses. One can find many examples of this in the writings of nationalists. The following passages appear in articles in Taman Siswa organs in the 1920s and 1930s:[11]

barang yang nyata (realiteit)[12]

Systeem pengajaran itu bersifat pengajaran igama, ilmu dan pengatahuan dunia (zedelijk dan sociaal).[13]

Menurut adatrecht kita, maka perempuan kita itu berhak jadi kuli (burger), oleh karenanya ia mempunyai hak memilih (stemrecht) juga.[14]

---

[8]Sjahrazad, *Indonesische Overpeinzingen* (Amsterdam and Jakarta: Djambatan, 1945).

[9]On *vergadering*, see Takashi Shiraishi, "Shoki Isuramu dōmei (1912–17)—Indoneshia zenki minzoku undō" [The early Sarekat Islam (1912–17): The first stage of the Indonesian national movement], *Ajia keizai*, vol. 22, nos. 7, 8 (July and August 1981).

[10]Achdiat K. Mihardja, Polemik Kebudajaan (Jakarta: Perpustakaan Perguruan Kementerian P. P. dan K., 1954). For more on the cultural debate, see Haruki Yamamoto, "'Indoneshia' no bunkaronteki imi—1930 nendai no bunka ronsō o tōshite" [The cultural meaning of Indonesia as seen in the cultural debate of the 1930s], *Nampō bunka*, no. 8 (1981).

[11]On the Taman Siswa, see Kenji Tsuchiya, *Indoneshia minzokushugi kenkyū—Taman Shisuwa no seiritsu to tenkai* [A study of Indonesian nationalism: The establishment and development of the Taman Siswa] (Tokyo: Sōbunsha, 1982). (An English translation of this work is now available: *Democracy and Leadership: The Rise of the Taman Siswa Movement in Indonesia*, trans. Peter Hawkes [Honolulu: University of Hawaii Press, 1987].)

[12]Ki Hadjar Dewantara, "Faidahnja Systeem Pondok," *Wasita*, November 1928, p. 43.

[13]Ki Hadjar Dewantara, "Systeem Pondok dan Asrama itulah Systeem Nasional," *Wasita*, November 1928, p. 40. The passage reads: "The educational system has the quality of religious, scientific, and secular (ethical and social) education."

[14]Raden Supomo, "Deradjat Perempuan Indonesia Didalam Adatrecht," *Wasita*, December 1928, p. 93. The passage reads: "According to our customary law, our women have the rights of *kuli* [citizens] and hence have the right to choose [the right to vote]." The term for customary law, *adatrecht*, is a compound of the Indonesian *adat*, "custom," and the Dutch *recht*, "law."

Ada salah suatu sebab, saya katakan, dalam arti kebatinan (psychologisch) karena banyak dari bangsa kita dengan disengaja atau tidak (bewust of onbewust)...[15]

untuk Ketitisan Sang Hyang Wenang, untuk dapat membawa wahyu, untuk mempunyai inzicht, untuk mempunyai doorzicht dalam masyarakat...[16]

In the first four examples certain Indonesian terms are repeated or defined in Dutch in parentheses, while in the fifth the Javanese words *Ketitisan Sang Hyang Wenang* and *wahyu* are used along with the Dutch terms *inzicht* and *doorzicht*.

We have mentioned three aspects of the superiority of the Dutch language in the eyes of the early nationalists; but in terms of the world of Javanese—the linguistic space in which Javanese is the mother tongue—this superiority was simply the result of Dutch having infiltrated Javanese. For Kartini, the world of Javanese was objectified through Dutch, and many Javanese nationalists who came after her defined various phenomena and ideas in Dutch. In fact, Dutch definitions often extended to the territory of their own culture, that is, to the "meaning structure" of their world.

The development of nationalism and the *pergerakan* led to the gradual decline in the superiority of Dutch and its replacement by Indonesian as the new language of a new people. It was the academic world above all that enabled Dutch to maintain its potential for superiority. Writing anything about Javanese history or cultural history (*wayang, serat,* literature and so on) meant first perusing all the literature in Dutch (the same holds true even today).[17] The enormous volume of work on Java in Dutch created the tradition of *Javanologie,* and any Indonesian who wished to participate in this tradition had to read extensively in historical materials under Dutch Javanologists, study at the University of Leiden, and submit a thesis—in Dutch—on the findings of one's research on Javanese culture. R. M. Ng. Poerbatjaraka (1884–1957), whose work will be discussed later, is a good example.[18]

One could say, then, that the *modérn* age of the twentieth century emerged as the result of a period during which Dutch infiltrated the Javanese language. Thus, twentieth-century Java must be considered in the context of the preceding period. This necessitates addressing a number of problems independently. My paper is an attempt to outline the problems and suggest solutions, focusing on two points. First, I will elucidate the process by which Dutch infiltrated the world of Javanese. Naturally, in this process the concrete expansion in Java of the world of Dutch—the expansion of

---

[15]Gadjah Mada, "Didiklah kamu sendiri," *Pusara,* December 1931, p. 43. The passage reads: "There is a reason, I should say, in a spiritual (psychological) sense why many of our nation, intentionally or not (consciously or unconsciously) . . ."

[16]Ibid., June 1932, p. 50. The passage reads: "to [bring about] the reincarnation of Sang Hjang Wenang, to be able to bring divine light, to have perceptiveness, to have insight into society . . ."

[17]To give just one example, over half the references cited in *Tjeritera Dewa Rutji,* a tale that expresses the psychology of the Javanese extremely well, are in Dutch—the result of the Javanology discussed in the present paper. See A. Seno Sastroamidjojo, *Tjeritera Dewa Rutji, Dengan Arti Filsafatnja* (Jakarta: Penerbit Kinta, 1961).

[18]Poerbatjaraka studied Malay and Dutch from childhood and studied the Javanese classics with Hendrik Kern. He was employed by the Batavia Museum in 1910 and later went to Leiden, where he studied Javanese classics as an assistant to J. A. G. Hazeu. He received his doctorate in 1926 at the age of forty-two with a dissertation titled "Agastya in den Archipel." See Benedict Anderson, "Politik Bahasa dan Kebudayaan Jawa," *Prisma,* November 1982.

the bureaucracy and of plantations—was important. Here, however, I will concentrate on Javanology, discussing the process by which it was established in Java. Second, I will examine the cultural activity that occurred at the *kraton* (Javanese courts) after Dutch contact. Since the *pujangga* (court poets) at the *kraton* were the bearers of Java's linguistic tradition, I will concentrate on the encounter between the *pujangga* and Dutch Javanologists, focusing on the fate of Ranggawarsita (1802–1873), a great *pujangga* who served the *kraton* in Surakarta.

The period dealt with extends from the second half of the eighteenth century to the end of the nineteenth century, and particularly the period from the mid-nineteenth century onward, in the principalities (*vorstenlanden*) of Surakarta and Yogyakarta in Central Java. By outlining the cultural history of the so-called Java core region (*kejawen*) in terms of a modern-traditional (Javanology-*pujangga*) polarity, I will examine the linguistic world of Javanese.

I. The Establishment and Development of Javanology

Dutch research on Java goes back to the time of the VOC (Vereenigde Oostindische Compagnie; Dutch East India Company), 1602–1799, but only became institutionalized in the first half of the nineteenth century. The voluminous works on Java published by Thomas Stamford Raffles and John Crawfurd, which grew out of the brief period of British rule (1811–1816), stimulated further research, which advanced rapidly when Java came under the direct rule of the Dutch government in 1816, with Godert A. G. P. van der Capellen as governor general.

Below I will examine Dutch research on Java from three angles: its institutionalization, research on the Javanese language, and research on Javanese literature.

The Institutionalization of Javanese Studies

(a) The training of "Java experts" and the Institute
for the Javanese Language in Surakarta

After the VOC established a base at Batavia at the beginning of the seventeenth century, it concluded various treaties, mainly trade agreements, with the kingdom of Mataram in Central Java. By 1705 Batavia had concluded 111 trade agreements with Mataram.[19] The language of communication between the two parties was Javanese, and throughout the eighteenth century the VOC used interpreters and translators, most of whom were Eurasians.[20]

The first systematic measures to train Dutch "Java experts" were taken during van der Capellen's term as governor general (1816–1826). With a view to smoothing relations with "native chiefs" (*inlandsche hoofden*), in 1819 the governor general inaugurated a policy of training young colonial administrators in indigenous languages for a set period at Batavia, Surabaya, Yogyakarta, Makassar (Ujung Pandang), Ambon, and Malacca.[21] These young administrators were called *élèves* (pupils).[22] This marked the beginning of systematic study of Malay and Javanese within the colonial

---

[19]On the number of agreements, see Selo Soemardjan, *Social Change in Jogjakarta* (Ithaca, NY: Cornell University Press, 1962), p. 10.

[20]E. M. Uhlenbeck, *A Critical Survey of Studies on the Languages of Java and Madura* (The Hague: Nijhoff, 1964), p. 43.

[21]*Encyclopaedie van Nederlandsch-Indië*, vol. 3 (The Hague and Leiden: Nijhoff and Brill, 1919), 167.

[22]Uhlenbeck, *A Critical Survey*, p. 44.

administrative system. The program was administered by the Department of Interior Administration (Binnenlandsch Bestuur) of the Indies government, which meant that officials in the posts of assistant resident, secretary, and inspector (*opziener*) would begin functioning as Java experts of Javanese language and society. From among these *élèves* emerged the eminent Javanologists A. D. Cornets de Groot, Jr., and P. P. Roorda van Eysingga (1796–1856).

In 1830, when Johannes van den Bosch became governor general (a post in which he served until 1833) and the Culture System (Cultuurstelsel) was inaugurated, the Dutch government went over the heads of the Mataram court officials, expanding at a stroke the opportunities for contact with local chiefs. It thus became more important than ever to train Dutch people who could function in Javanese and in Javanese society.

In 1832 an institution whose sole purpose was the training of Java experts was set up in Surakarta. This was the Institute for the Javanese Language in Surakarta (Het Instituut voor de Javaansche Taal te Soerakarta). Behind its establishment was J. F. C. Gericke (1800–1857), a German linguist who had studied Javanese since 1827, when sent to the East Indies by the Netherlands Bible Society (Nederlandsche Bijbelgenootschap). The decision to establish the institute was made on February 27, 1832, and it opened on October 29 of that year with Gericke as director.[23]

Van den Bosch's successor as governor general, J. C. Baud (who served until 1836), not only was interested in training Java experts but also had close relations with the Netherlands Bible Society, and therefore actively supported Gericke and his institute.[24] According to an 1833 report, the institute, housed in a large mansion in Surakarta, had nine students, who received a stipend for three years from the government and spent six hours a days studying, mostly Javanese and some general knowledge of Javanese people and society. The students also attended a *wayang* performance once a week and occasionally took field trips to historical sites like Borobudur and the temple complexes at Prambanan and Dien.[25]

The institute played a major role in the development of Javanology in two ways. First, it helped people who started out as *élèves* become Javanologists. Among those connected with the institute who made great contributions to Javanese studies were, in addition to Gericke himself, C. F. Winter and J. A. Wilkens, both Eurasians.[26]

Winter (1799–1859), who was born in Yogyakarta and died in Surakarta, spent his entire life in Java. His father worked as a translator in Surakarta from 1806 onward, and Winter himself was familiar with the world of Javanese from childhood. In 1818 he became an assistant translator (*adjunct-translateur*), in accordance with his father's wishes, and was promoted to translator in 1825.[27] He became a researcher at the institute when it opened in 1832, and in 1835 he began teaching Javanese, along

---

[23]*Encyclopaedie*, vol. 1 (1917), p. 783; H. Kraemer, "Het Instituut voor de Javaansche Taal te Soerakarta," *Djawa*, vol. 12, no. 6 (1932), p. 272.

[24]Kraemer, "Het Instituut," p. 270.

[25]Ibid., p. 273.

[26]On Winter and Wilkens being Eurasian, see P. van der Veur, "Introduction to a Socio-Political Study of the Eurasians of Indonesia" (PhD. dissertation, Cornell University, 1955), pp. 49, 83. Van der Veur estimates that there were 1,750 Eurasians in Java in 1815, 14,000 in 1854, 44,000 in 1860, 95,000 in 1905, and 240,000 in 1930. See ibid., pp. 24–25.

[27]Biographical data from *Encyclopaedie*, vol. 4 (1921), pp. 786–87.

with Gericke.[28] Gericke returned to the Netherlands in 1837, but Winter continued teaching at the institute until it closed early in 1843. During this time, Winter's knowledge of Java attracted favorable attention in the Netherlands, particularly his important contribution in the compilation of a Javanese-Dutch dictionary. He also published a number of treatises on Javanese literature. Winter provided the first information on the basis of which the Dutch academic world was able to pursue systematic research on Java. In fact, his contemporaries hailed him as a "nutrient source" (*voedende bron*) of Javanese studies at the Royal Academy (Koninklijke Academie) in Delft, a school for colonial administrators.[29]

Wilkens (1813–1888) made an even greater contribution to dictionary compilation. He was born in Gresik in East Java and died in Surakarta. Except for three years in the Netherlands (1848–1851), he lived in Central Java at the same time as Ranggawarsita (1802–1873). In 1833 he joined the institute, becoming an instructor in 1835 and assisting Winter in the compilation of a Javanese-Dutch dictionary. In 1848 Wilkens went to Delft with a Javanese from Surakarta, Sastratama, where he worked on the dictionary as an assistant to Taco Roorda (1801–1874) until 1851. Upon returning to Java, he collaborated with Winter again and, after Winter's death in 1859, continued work on the dictionary alone, compiling a Javanese word list of forty-three hand-written volumes. This was incorporated in its entirety in the dictionary's fourth edition, *Javanese-Dutch Dictionary* edited by Gericke and Roorda, published in 1901. Wilkens also wrote treatises on *wayang* and Javanese history.[30]

The institute's bilingual instructors such as Winter and Wilkens acted as bridges between the Javanese and the Dutch and thus contributed to the transformation of Java experts into Javanologists. As we will see, with the institutionalization of Java studies in the Netherlands itself the mission of the institute ended and it was closed.

The institute's second important role was that, by the simple fact of its location in Surakarta, it led to Surakarta's assuming a central position in Dutch research on Java. As it happened, since the latter half of the eighteenth century the royal house of Surakarta, the Kasunanan, had enjoyed a literary resurgence that Theodore Pigeaud has termed a renaissance.[31] Because Dutch research on Java concentrated on the literature of Surakarta, the Dutch were able to approach the heart of Javanese *kraton* culture. A situation was thus created in which the bearers of that culture, the *pujangga*, discussed Javanese language and culture with Javanologists and "nutrient sources" like Winter and Wilkens. The nineteenth-century Surakarta *pujangga*, one might say, inhabited two worlds, two cultures. On the one hand, they were at the cutting edge of the tradition of esoteric knowledge that flourished in court culture during the literary renaissance; on the other hand, they were in direct contact with the agents of the Dutch academic world.

(b) Courses on Java

At the same time that Java experts were being trained in the Indies, the training of colonial specialists and research on Java became institutionalized in the Netherlands itself. This process began in 1836 with lectures on Java at the officers' school in Breda. The aim was to equip officers who were to be sent to Java with a basic knowledge of

---

[28]Kraemer, "Het Instituut," p. 272.

[29]*Encyclopaedie*, 4: 786.

[30]Biographical data from *Encyclopaedie*, 4: 782–83; Uhlenbeck, *A Critical Survey*, pp. 50–51.

[31]For details, see Theodore Pigeaud, *Literature of Java*, vol. 1 (The Hague: Nijhoff, 1968).

Javanese and Malay. The first lecturer was van Eysingga. When he left for Java in 1843, J. J. de Hollander took over.[32]

The next step was the introduction of Javanese studies into Dutch educational institutions, for which Roorda, an Orientalist specializing in linguistics and philosophy, was responsible.[33] In 1834 he took up a teaching post in Amsterdam, and since de Groot's Javanese grammar was now available in the Netherlands, he turned his attention to Javanese. Roorda's assistant was J. A. Palm, who had studied Javanese for three years in Java under Gericke and Winter. In 1839 Roorda created a printing type for the Javanese script, and in 1841 he proposed the training of Dutch colonial officials in Javanese, which he maintained was urgently needed for the efficient implementation of policy in the Indies. His proposal was acted on two years later, in 1843, when the Royal Academy was established in Delft. Roorda was appointed head instructor, lecturing on the languages, geography, and ethnology of the Indies as well as teaching Javanese. Now that a training center for colonial officials existed in the Netherlands itself, the Institute for the Javanese Language in Surakarta was closed. The establishment of the Royal Academy also meant that research on Java and the Javanese language could take firm root in the Dutch academic world.

Another landmark in the process of institutionalizing research on Java was the transfer in 1864 of the Javanese studies program at the Royal Academy to the University of Leiden. (The training course for colonial officials remained in Delft until 1900.) Roorda and the other instructors moved to Leiden, as well. In the words of E. M. Uhlenbeck, "From this moment onwards the study of Javanese languages, history and ethnology became intimately connected with the old tradition of the scientific study of Oriental languages for which the university of Leiden was renowned already in the 17th century."[34] Uhlenbeck, the seventh professor of Javanology at the University of Leiden, is not being partial. The Javanese language and literature courses there under Roorda (1864–1874), Hendrik Kern (1874–1877), A. B. Vreede (1877–1908), J. C. G. Jonker (1909–1920), J. A. G. Hazeu (1920–1928), C. C. Berg (1928–1949), and Uhlenbeck (since 1949) have made Leiden the Dutch center of Javanology and, indeed, a mecca for all who wish to do research in this field, whatever their nationality.

(c) Research institutes

The mid-nineteenth century thus saw the center of Javanese research move from Delft to Leiden, which went on to produce many eminent scholars and a large body of research. The same period saw the establishment of a number of new research institutes and the improvement of existing ones, thus widening the base of Javanese research. The most important such institutes were the Royal Batavian Society of Arts and Sciences (Koninklijk Bataviaasch Genootschap van Kunsten en Wetenschappen) and the Royal Institute of Linguistics and Anthropology (Koninklijk Instituut voor de Taal-, Land- en Volkenkunde van Nederlandisch-Indië).

---

[32]Uhlenbeck, *A Critical Survey*, p. 45.

[33]For data on Taco Roorda's life and works, see Uhlenbeck, *A Critical Survey*, pp. 45–46; Hendrik Kern, "Taco Roorda," in Koninklijk Instituut voor de Taal-, Land- en Volkenkunde, ed., *Hondred Jaar Studie van Indonesië 1850–1950* (The Hague: Smits, 1976), pp. 6–14. Kern's memorial essay was written in 1928.

[34]Uhlenbeck, *A Critical Survey*, p. 59.

The Royal Batavian Society of Arts and Sciences was founded in April 1778.[35] Its purpose was to collect "all information that contributes to the development of the economic activities of the VOC," which it continued to do even under Raffles's administration. The society's activities entered a new phase under van der Capellen. Receiving government support, it undertook a wide range of activities in various arts and sciences. From the first, the society had concentrated on natural sciences, such as geology, botany, natural resources, and water utilization; to these were now added cultural and social research. Beginning in 1843, under W. R. Baron van Höevell, a vigorous effort was made to collect and classify materials on the archaeology, history, language, geography, and culture of various regions of Indonesia, and a museum was opened in the center of Batavia (the forerunner of the present National Museum) to house archaeological and ethnological materials.[36]

In addition to cataloguing materials pertaining to archaeology and ancient history, from 1799 onward the society published many monographs. Regular publication of the *Tijdschrift voor Indische Taal-, Land- en Volkenkunde uitgegeven door het Bataviaasch Genootschap van Kunsten en Wetenschappen* (TBG) began in 1853. Thus, in the mid-nineteenth century the society came to function as a research and documentation center—exploring, excavating, and collecting and organizing information in various fields of the social sciences and humanities, mainly on Java, and publishing its findings in the *TBG*.

While the Royal Batavian Society of Arts and Sciences dealt with a wide range of Indological studies, the Royal Institute of Linguistics and Anthropology restricted itself to a narrower range of studies and thus had a more sharply defined character as a research institute. It was established under the leadership of J. C. Baud in Delft in June 1851 but moved to The Hague in 1864.[37] (It is presently located in Leiden.) Founded to promote the development of "language, land, and culture" in Dutch overseas territories, the Royal Institute concentrated on collecting written materials, both published and unpublished; publishing research findings in its *Bijdragen tot de Taal-, Land- en Volkenkunde van Nederlandsch-Indië, uitgegeven door het Koninklijt Instituut voor Taal-, Land- en Volkenkunde van Nederlandsch-Indië* (BKI) and its monograph series; addressing policy issues and recommending more effective policies; and conducting scholarly exchange with other research institutes in the Netherlands, its colonies, and other countries. To serve these ends, the Royal Institute began publishing the *BKI* on a regular basis in 1852 and established a library in 1878.

The Royal Institute, along with the University of Leiden, served as a center of Javanese research and documentation. Its tradition of documentary research, dealing chiefly with history and linguistics, was transmitted through the *BKI*, which became a major medium for communicating findings in Javanology.

JAVANESE-DUTCH DICTIONARIES AND RESEARCH ON THE JAVANESE LANGUAGE

Above, I have discussed the institutionalization of Dutch research on Java in the nineteenth century. Next I will describe how Javanese studies developed in the course of that process. It is clear that the Dutch devoted considerable time and energy to research on the Javanese language, during which they built up a tradition of such research. Thus was the tradition of Javanology established in the nineteenth-century

---

[35]*Encyclopaedie*, 1: 773–74.

[36]Ibid., p. 773.

[37]*Encyclopaedie*, vol. 2 (1918), pp. 157–58.

Dutch academic world. Let us consider the various stages of the process in chronological order.

(a) From the VOC to Raffles

Javanese-Dutch dictionaries were produced from the time of the VOC's first contact with Java, limited though they were. A VOC document dated 1646 refers to a "Malay-Javanese-Dutch dictionary," a portion of which was published between 1706 and 1708 by A. Reland, a Dutch Orientalist active in the early eighteenth century. The first Javanese-Dutch dictionary, *Lexicon Javanum*, was compiled in 1706, although the editor is unknown. This dictionary, a copy of which is believed to have been sent to Reland by the Minister of Colonies at the time, Petrus van der Vorm (1644–1731), includes examples of *krama* and *ngoko* as well as the Javanese calendar and syllabary.[38] (*Krama* and *ngoko* are forms of speech uniquely Javanese that establish the relationship between speakers—typically, indicating whether the relationship is one between inferior and superior or one between equals. Evidently the use of *krama* and *ngoko* was already widespread in Java at the beginning of the eighteenth century.)[39]

In addition to these rudimentary Javanese-Dutch dictionaries, several Dutch people (N. Engelhard, J. C. M. Radermacher, H. C. Cornelius, and others) are known to have been interested in Javanese. True research, however, began only in the early nineteenth century, under British rule. The many pages devoted to descriptions of the Javanese language and literature in Raffles's two-volume *History of Java* (1817)[40] and Crawfurd's three-volume *History of the Indian Archipelago* (1820)[41] were particularly important. Crawfurd had studied Malay, and between 1811 and 1816, as Resident of Yogyakarta, he had frequent contact with high officials of the *kraton;* he was, in fact, deeply involved in the split of the Paku Alam from the royal house of Yogyakarta, the Kasultanan, in 1813.[42] Crawfurd also collected materials that the German scholar Wilhelm von Humboldt (1767–1835) used in preparing his essay on Kawi (Old Javanese), posthumously published between 1836 and 1839.[43]

(b) Bible translation

I have already mentioned that Gericke was sent to Java by the Netherlands Bible Society. The society's activities, particularly its Bible-translation projects, played an important part in promoting Dutch Javanese studies.

Bible translation was first undertaken in the time of the VOC, in response to the needs of Protestant missionaries. A Malay translation published in 1692 was used for proselytizing throughout the Indonesian archipelago, but it was only with the establishment of the Netherlands Bible Society in 1814 that translation of the Bible into

---

[38]Uhlenbeck, *A Critical Survey*, p. 43.

[39]On the establishment of research on *krama* and *ngoko*, see Anderson, "Politik Bahasa."

[40]Thomas Stamford Raffles, *The History of Java*, 2 vols. (London: Black, Parburg, and Allen, 1817; 2d ed. 1830).

[41]John Crawfurd, *History of the Indian Archipelago*, 3 vols. (Edinburgh: Archibald Constable, 1820).

[42]*Encyclopaedie*, 1: 534; Soekanto, *Sekitar Jogjakarta, 1755–1825* (Jakarta: Mahabarata, 1952).

[43]Uhlenbeck, *A Critical Survey*, pp. 43–44. On Humboldt, see Kenkichi Kameyama, *Funboruto— bunjin, seijika, gengo gakusha* [Humboldt: Man of letters, politician, linguistic scholar] (Tokyo: Chūō Kōron Sha, 1978). For Humboldt's research on Kawi, see ibid., pp. 233–49.

local languages, including Javanese, was undertaken in earnest.[44] It was considered essential to train specialists with accurate and extensive knowledge of these languages, and Gericke's dispatch to Java in 1827 was the first attempt to do this. The German missionary G. Bruckner had already prepared a Javanese translation of the Bible in 1823, which was published in 1829, but Gericke was given the task of creating a better translation.[45] He began work in 1835 and completed his translations of the New and Old Testaments into Javanese script in 1848 and 1854, respectively. The former, however, was severely criticized by Roorda, who had been an adviser to the society since 1836, and publication plans were canceled. Roorda himself undertook preparation of a new version. His translation was published in 1860, and editions revised by P. A. Jansz (1820–1904) were published in 1890 and 1893. Quite a few Javanese editions of Bible stories and hymns were also published from 1860 onward.

There are three points of interest in connection with these translation endeavors. First, the people involved were all leading specialists on Java and thus were actively engaged in the establishment of institutions for Javanese studies, Gericke's Institute for the Javanese Language in Surakarta and Roorda's Royal Academy in Delft being the prime examples. Second, these efforts, particularly the compilation of Javanese-Dutch dictionaries, were part and parcel of wide-ranging research on linguistic culture. Third, through this activity a close-knit scholarly lineage (Bruckner-Gericke-Roorda-Jansz) was formed, corresponding to the stages of its evolution (criticism-revision-criticism-revision). This third point is seen even more clearly in the field of dictionary compilation and grammar research, which I will discuss next.

(c) Compilation of Javanese-Dutch dictionaries: The scholarly lineage

Nineteenth-century Dutch research on the Javanese language proceeded along several parallel and sometimes overlapping lines: Bible translation, dictionary compilation, preparation of texts on conversational usage, and grammar research. Having discussed Bible translation, let us now review the other strands in chronological order.

The first Javanese grammar to be published since the appearance of Raffles's and Crawfurd's studies of Java was prepared by Bruckner, who lived in Semarang and Salatiga from 1814 onward. His basic Javanese grammar was completed in 1823 and published in Bengal in 1830.[46] The following year an introductory grammar and a Javanese word list by Gericke were published. Then, in the period when van der Capellen's policy of training *élèves* was in vogue, two such *élèves*, van Eysingga and de Groot, produced studies on the Javanese language. De Groot's grammar was published in 1833, and van Eysingga's Javanese dictionary and grammar was published in 1835.

Thus the first half of the 1830s saw the publication of four Javanese grammars. De Groot's, regarded as the best, was reissued in 1843 with a foreword by Gericke and annotations by Roorda. Favorably reviewed by P. J. Veth (1814–1895), author of *Java, Geographisch, Ethnologisch, Historisch,* and by Wilkens, it became the basis of subsequent research on Javanese.

Roorda began to play a central role in Javanese research in the 1840s, both his dictionary and his grammar being of signal importance. He occupied a key position

---

[44]*Encyclopaedie,* 1: 428.

[45]For details, see Uhlenbeck, *A Critical Survey,* p. 53.

[46]Ibid., p. 44.

in the channel of institutionalized information gathering (Surakarta-Delft-Leiden) that, as we have seen, developed in Javanese studies and that involved such researchers as Gericke, Winter, and Wilkens and their Javanese informants.

In 1843 Roorda produced a supplement to the Javanese word lists compiled by Bruckner, van Eysingga, and others. Four years later, in 1847, he completed the first systematic Javanese-Dutch dictionary,[47] augmenting, revising, and editing Gericke's draft manuscript. Revised editions of the Gericke-Roorda dictionary appeared in 1875, 1886, and 1901, the 1901 edition becoming the standard one. Javanese word lists compiled by Winter and Wilkens and the findings of de Groot and others formed the basis of the first edition, and further research by Winter and Wilkens was incorporated in later editions. Gericke died in 1857, Winter in 1859, and Roorda himself in 1874, but the work of revision was continued by A. C. Vreede (1840–1908), Roorda's son-in-law, and A. B. Cohen Stuart (1825–1876), who prepared the 1875 edition, and by Vreede and Kern (1833–1920), who prepared the 1886 edition. The 1901 edition was prepared by Vreede and J. G. H. Gunning. It was in the course of this dictionary-compilation project, spanning nearly half a century, that the lineage of Javanology in the Netherlands took form.

Twentieth-century efforts to compile a Javanese-Dutch dictionary to replace the 1901 one were spurred by the remarkable burgeoning of Javanese studies. Pigeaud, who lived in Surakarta and Yogyakarta from 1926 to 1946, played a key role in the compilation of a new dictionary, in addition to his many contributions to the study of Javanese culture.

Roorda was also at the center of research on Javanese grammar in the mid-nineteenth century. In 1855 he published a major work analyzing the phonetics, sentence structure, and script of the Javanese spoken and written in contemporary Surakarta, *Javaansche grammatica benevens een leesboek tot oefening in de Javaansche taal*, based on data collected mainly by Winter and Wilkens.[48] Revised editions appeared in 1874, 1882, 1893, and 1903. This project, while regarded as a milestone in research on Javanese, also touched off a vigorous academic debate. The debate was initiated in 1864 by the brilliant linguist H. N. van der Tuuk (1824–1894), who had already published important findings on the Batak language of North Sumatra. Van der Tuuk criticized Roorda's work on grammar from the viewpoint of comparative linguistics. The ensuing controversy lasted until Roorda's death ten years later. Through this critical study, van der Tuuk broke new ground in the infant study of the comparative languages of various localities, beginning in the mid-nineteenth century. His research was fruitful not only for Batak and Javanese but also for Sundanese, Balinese, and Kawi. Such scholars as J. L. A. Brandes (1857–1905), Adriani, and de Zwister Brandstetter studied under him.[49]

This nineteenth-century research on Javanese, centered on the preparation of dictionaries and grammars, laid the foundations of Dutch Javanology: it was during this period that its institutions and training procedures were refined, paving the way for the succession of eminent scholars who established its lineage.

---

[47]Ibid., p. 47.

[48]Ibid., p. 50.

[49]R. Nieuwenhuys, "Herman Neubronner van der Tuuk," in Koninklijk Instituut, ed., *Honderd Jaar Studie*, pp. 1–5.

(d) Other works on the Javanese language

Besides the above-mentioned Javanese-Dutch dictionaries and grammars, a number of specialized dictionaries, works on conversational usage, textbooks, and other works on Java were produced, particularly in the latter half of the nineteenth century.

In response to the increased opportunity to study Javanese, texts incorporating grammar, conversational usage, and character dictionaries were published by Jansz in 1862, by de Hollander in 1886, and by G. J. Grashuis in 1892.[50] Many examples of Javanese usage had already been collected by Winter and Wilkens. In addition, collections of Javanese riddles (*cankriman*), short charades consisting of two lines (*wangsalan*), and proverbs, sayings, and idiomatic expressions were published by S. Keyzer (1863), Jansz (1872), Poensen (1877), W. Hoezoo (1878, 1887), J. Kreemer (1883, 1886), and R. Atmasoepana (1897), all Dutch men. Encyclopedic works on Javanese society were also written, including L. T. Mayer's two-volume chronicle of village life (1897), van der Berg's collections of Javanese social titles (1887, 1902), and Poensen's accounts of social life (1864 onward). Studies of speech levels (Jansz in 1883, C. F. Winter's son F. L. Winter in 1892, G. J. Oudesmans in 1894, A. H. J. G. Walbeehm in 1897) and dialects (Poensen's 1870 collection of East Java dialects, C. te Mechelen's 1879 collection of peasant dialects) also appeared. The end of the nineteenth century also saw the publication of guides like *De Javaansche Geestenwereld*, edited by H. A. van Hien and published in four volumes between 1894 and 1896.[51]

This kind of research developed further in the twentieth century. The Java Institute (Java Instituut), established in Surakarta in December 1919 in accordance with Decree 75 of the governor general, and its journal, *Djawa*, published monthly from 1921 to 1941, played an important role, as did the multivolume *Encyclopaedie van Nederlandsch-Indië* (1917–1940). This encyclopedia included information on every aspect of the Netherlands East Indies collected by the Dutch since the nineteenth century.

(e) Javanese participation: The nineteenth century

So far, we have looked at the development of nineteenth-century Javanology conducted by the Dutch, particularly language research. However, we must not overlook the fact that Javanese people also participated, first as informants to Dutch researchers and later as researchers in their own right, thus bearing some of the responsibility for Dutch research on Java. In short, Javanese themselves participated in the process of defining the world of Javanese in Dutch.

The use of Javanese informants began to increase in the 1840s, when Roorda, in Delft, and Winter and Wilkens, in Surakarta, began their collaboration on a Javanese-Dutch dictionary. When Roorda's assistant Palm returned to the Netherlands in 1835, after three years of research in Java, he took with him a Javanese aristocrat, Raden Panji Poespawilaga.[52] The two assisted Roorda in designing type for Javanese script. In 1839 Roorda completed the design and had the type cast at the Johannes Enschedé foundry in Haarlem.[53] Needless to say, this development greatly facilitated the publication of Javanese documents and research findings. Since the type was based

---

[50]Uhlenbeck, *A Critical Survey*, p. 55.

[51]Ibid., p. 79.

[52]Ibid., p. 50.

[53]Ibid., p. 46.

on the script used at the Surakarta *kraton*, the Surakarta script became the standard Javanese script.[54]

As has already been noted, Sastratama was with Wilkens when the latter worked under Roorda in Delft from 1848 to 1851, helping in the preparation of the Gericke-Roorda dictionary. And when the second revised edition of the dictionary was published by Vreede and Kern, in 1886, it included new data provided not only by such Dutch scholars as Kern, J. J. Meinsma, Poensen, and P. van der Broek but also by the Javanese aristocrat Raden Mas Ismangoon Danu Winata.[55] Ismangoon was born in 1852 in Yogyakarta but went to the Netherlands at an early age. He graduated from the Hoger Burger School in Leiden in 1870, took the course for colonial administrators in Delft, and returned to his homeland in 1875 as an official in the Department of Interior Administration. Following an illness, he went to Delft once again, where he earned his living as an instructor of Javanese and married a Dutch woman. He died in Magelan in 1895. He was widely respected in Dutch society as one who had bridged the gap between Javanese and Dutch people.[56]

All three of these Javanese participated directly in the process of establishing Dutch Javanology, and the case of Ismangoon shows that bilingual Javanese intellectuals were involved in research on Java in the Netherlands in the latter half of the nineteenth century. Before the end of the century, Javanese were publishing scholarly work of the same sort as Dutch Javanologists. A collection of proverbs and idioms compiled by Makoendhasastra was published in 1886, and a collection of *wangsalan* compiled by Atmasoepana was published in Surakarta in 1897. Ki Padmasoesastra provided more data than anyone else on the everyday speech of Javanese peasants, publishing his findings in 1896, 1900, 1907, and 1911. He also edited a Javanese grammar (1897–1898) and coauthored papers with D. F. van der Pant on everyday speech in the Surakarta region that were published in the *TBG* in 1885 and 1886. As we will see, Padmasoesastra also collected, edited, and published Ranggawarsita's works. Meanwhile, R. M. Tjandra Negara published a paper on Javanese locutions, with an afterword by Kern, in the *BKI* in 1878, and published a list of loanwords in Javanese (a major subject of research since Humboldt's time) in the same journal in 1880.[57]

All these Javanese scholars but Tjandra Negara published in Javanese script. With him, however, work by Javanese scholars began to appear in scholarly journals in Dutch. And as we have seen, papers were also published under joint Dutch-Javanese authorship. This pattern became more common in the twentieth century. Javanese researchers published papers in Dutch, often with long lists of works in Dutch as references. This was true not only in the field of Javanese-language studies but also in other fields, such as Javanese history (particularly ancient history), archaeology, culture, and literary history.

What this means is that through the development of Dutch research on the Javanese language—beginning with individual Javanese words and extending to Javanese linguistic culture as a whole—both meanings and correlations were defined and explained in Dutch and, via publication, came to be shared. The colonial govern-

---

[54]Pigeaud, *Literature*, 1: 25. Beginning in 1918, Javanese works were printed in the Latin alphabet rather than Javanese script. See Uhlenbeck, *A Critical Survey*, p. 76.

[55]Uhlenbeck, *A Critical Survey*, p. 48.

[56]*Encyclopaedie*, 2: 173.

[57]The information in this paragraph is from Uhlenbeck, *A Critical Survey*.

ment's stipulation, in 1893, of the Javanese of the Surakarta region as the standard Javanese language to be taught in modern schools throughout Java[58] symbolizes the essence of Javanology: the world of Dutch determining the shape of the world of Javanese.

THE STUDY OF JAVANESE CULTURE AND LITERATURE

(a) Research by Dutch Javanologists

In the latter half of the nineteenth century the Dutch studies discussed above gave rise to scholarly research in various fields related to linguistics: Kawi, inscriptions, *serat* and *babad, wayang,* and poetry. Uhlenbeck's classification of this research shows what a wide range it covers: (1) Kawi, (2) manuscript collection, (3) inscriptions, (4) *tutur* (pre-Islamic religious philosophy and cosmology), (5) Islamic teachings, (6) the *Mahābhārata,* (7) *serat* (tales) and *babad* (chronicles), (8) *kidung* (ancient chants), (9) *kakawin* poetry, (10) *wayang,* (11) premodern literature, and (12) legal codes and systems.

In the study of Kawi, which Humboldt pioneered, the nineteenth century saw the publication of van der Tuuk's dictionary on Kawi (1879, 1881), Kern's linguistic and grammar research (1876–1877, 1898–1906), Winter and van der Tuuk's Kawi-Javanese dictionary (1880), and van der Tuuk's four-volume Kawi-Balinese-Dutch dictionary (1897, 1899, 1901, 1912). In the twentieth century, J. Gonda and P. J. Zoetmulder further advanced research in this field.

The University of Leiden and the Batavia Museum engaged actively in the collection of manuscripts, and in 1892 Vreede published a catalogue of documents in the University of Leiden archives. The collecting and cataloguing of manuscripts continued in the twentieth century.

Research on inscriptions began in the mid-nineteenth century. R. T. A. Friederich (1854–1857), Cohen Stuart (1875), van der Tuuk (1876–1877), and Brandes (1877) were among those who transcribed and translated inscriptions. In the twentieth century Kern, Poerbatjaraka (a Javanese), Pigeaud, W. F. Stutterheim, J. G. de Casparis, and L. C. Damais published numerous studies.

Research on *tutur* only began in earnest in this century, but the study of popular Muslim mysticism tinged with pre-Muslim Javanese religious speculation (research on *suluk* [Islamic mystical songs] and *primbon* [Javanese almanacs]) commenced in 1881 with Gunning's collection of *primbon,* which originated in the sixteenth century. In the twentieth century, *primbon* texts were often published in *Djawa.*

Research on the *Mahābhārata* also began in the nineteenth century. In 1849 Friederich obtained an ancient manuscript of this Hindu epic on Bali, part of which van der Tuuk published in 1871. Kern published a partial translation in 1877. In 1893 H. Juynboll published both the text and a translation. Work on the text and translation has been continued in this century by Gonda (1936), A. A. Fokker, Jr. (1938), and Zoetmulder (1950).

More research has been done on *serat* and *babad* than on any other form of literature. Indeed, these, along with *wayang* and premodern literature, make up the "great tradition" of Javanology. The *Pararaton* [Book of kings], dating back to the Majapahit period, was edited and translated by Brandes and published in 1897. N. J. Krom's revised edition, prepared with the help of Jonker, H. Kraemer, and Poerbatjaraka, was published in 1920. In 1847 Friederich published a partial translation of a Balinese

---

[58]Ibid., p. 65.

chronicle, *Usana Bali*, and a portion of the Gelgel poem *Pamañcangah*, edited by Berg, was published in 1929.

A great number of *babad* were compiled in the courts of Java from the mid-eighteenth century onward, and in the nineteenth century many of these chronicles were edited, translated, annotated, and published. Portions of the *Babad Tanah Djawi* were published in the Javanese newspaper *Bramartani* (called the *Djurumartani* for a time) between 1870 and 1875. In 1874 the entire work was edited and published by Meinsma, followed by an annotated second edition in 1877 and a third edition in 1903. All three versions were published in Javanese script. Finally, in 1941, the Royal Institute published a version in the Latin alphabet with a translation by J. L. Olthof and an index compiled by A. Teeuw.

Many other *babad* were published: *Babad Bedhahipun ing Mangir* and *Babad Dipanegara* (Semarang: Van Dorp, 1872), Babad Petjina (Van Dorp, 1874), *Babad Gijanti* (Yogyakarta: Kolff-Buning, 1874; reprinted 1908, 1923), *Babad Parambanan* (Surakarta, 1902), *Babad Mataram* (Surakarta, 1904–1905), *Babad Demak* (Singapore, 1909), and *Babad Dipanegaran* (Surakarta, 1909). J. Knebel's translation of the *Babad Pasir* appeared in 1900, and van der Broek's translation of the *Babad Kedhiri* was published in 1902. The *Babad Tjerbon*, edited by D. A. Rinkes and annotated by Brandes, was published in 1911.

Babad were also published by the colonial government's own publishing agency, the Balai Pustaka, established in 1908: *Babad Bedahipun Keraton nagari Ngjogjakarta* (1913), *Babad Mangir* (1913), *Babad Panambangan* (1918), *Babad Madja lan Babad Nglorog* (1935), *Babad Patjitan* (1935), *Babad Pathi* (1937), *Babad Arungbinangan* (1937), *Babad Gijanti* (twenty-one volumes, 1937–1939), and *Babad Tanah* Djawi (thirty-one volumes, 1939–1941).

Meanwhile, Brandes and R. A. Husein Djajadiningrat published numerous analyses of *babad* in the *TBG* and other journals, considerably raising the level of scholarship in this field. In the twentieth century a number of Javanologists, including Berg, G. W. J. Drewes, de Casparis, Pigeaud, and H. J. de Graaf, engaged in lively debate on the analysis of *babad*.[59]

Research on *kidung* only began in the twentieth century. So, for all practical purposes, did that on *kakawin*. In 1894 on Bali Brandes discovered a manuscript of the famous *kakawin* titled *Nagarakertagama*, believed to have been written by Prapanca in 1365. The text was first published in 1904. Kern published it in the Latin alphabet with a translation in 1919, and between 1960 and 1963 Pigeaud published it in five volumes, with English translation, notes, and index.

There have been numerous studies of *wayang* since the mid-nineteenth century, mainly of the texts used by the *dalang*, the *wayang* storyteller. In most cases researchers have edited and translated the *lakon*, the complete text of the story and dialogue narrated by the *dalang*, rather than the *pakem*, the summary used by the *dalang*. In 1846 Wilkens published a translation of *Pragiwa*, and Roorda's edited versions of two *lakon*, *Palasara* and *Pandu*, appeared in 1869. Poensen's translation of *Palasara* was published in 1872, while J. van der Vliet's translation of *Pandu* appeared in 1879. Te Mechelen published edited versions of six *lakon* in 1882 and 1884, and twenty-three *pakem* in 1897. Van Dorp in the late nineteenth century and the Balai Pustaka early in the twentieth century began publishing a great number of *wayang* texts, the Balai

---

[59]Ibid., p. 128.

Pustaka alone issuing 146 by 1932.[60] Also in the twentieth century, a *dalang* training institute was established in Surakarta, and in 1930 *Pakem Sastramiruda*, a manual for training *dalang*, was published.

Studies of premodern literature consisted of research on the literature of the renaissance that began in the mid-eighteenth century. As in the case of *wayang*, Van Dorp published numerous texts beginning in the late nineteenth century, while the Balai Pustaka did the same beginning early in this century. The way had been paved by some of the leading scholars of Javanese: Gericke published a translation of *Wiwihadjarwa*, with a commentary, in 1844, and Winter and Roorda published a condensed version of the *Serat Rama* in 1845 and the entire text in 1847. Van Eysingga (1849), Cohen Stuart (1860), and Friederich (1878) also edited or translated literary texts, and in 1873 a Javanese, M. Ng. Kramaprawira, published an edited version of *Dewa Rutji*.

In the last of Uhlenbeck's categories, legal codes and systems, Winter was the first to report on trials in Surakarta (1843), while Roorda and D. L. Mounier were the first to translate and comment on codes (1844). The accumulated information and research eventually bore fruit in C. van Vollenhoven's voluminous work on customary law, *Adatrechtbundels* (1918–1931).

(b) Javanese participation: *Djawa*

As we have seen, Dutch research on Java in the nineteenth century consisted primarily of research on the Javanese language, particularly in relation to compilation of a Javanese-Dutch dictionary, with Roorda, Winter, and Wilkens playing a central role. In the latter half of the nineteenth century Javanese people also became involved in the study of history and literature as well as linguistic research. Their participation is seen best in the scholarly scientific journal *Djawa*, published between 1921 and 1941. The journal's aim, set forth in the inaugural issue, was to develop "the indigenous culture of Java, Madoera, and Bali" by "in the first place promoting and disseminating knowledge of their culture,"[61] and indeed it contained a wealth of articles providing new insights and facilitating the flow of information in every field of Javanese studies.

Looking at *Djawa* from the viewpoint of Javanese participation in Javanology, the following points emerge. The first has to do with the journal's style. Except for the title, printed in Javanese script, the entire journal was in Dutch; it could just as well have been titled *Bijdragen tot Javanologie*. The readership was thus limited to those who were interested in Java (Javanology) and could read Dutch. It is clear, too, from the fact that the journal's first editorial office was in Weltevreden, a central district of Batavia (it later moved to Yogyakarta), and the fact that it was printed by G. Kolff in Weltevreden that Dutch-speaking readers in Java formed the main group of subscribers. It is safe to assume that a considerable number of Javanese (and Sundanese) were included. Here, in other words, we see Javanese obtaining the latest ideas on various aspects of their own culture from a journal published in Dutch.

This is related to a second point, the composition of the journal's editorial staff. *Djawa* was published by the Java Institute, whose members at the time of its foundation included the head of the Mangkunegara family, K. G. P. A. A. P. Prangwedono,

---

[60]C. Hooykaas, "Javaansche Uitgaven van Volkslectuur (Balé Poestaka)," *Djawa*, vol. 12, no. 2/3 (1932), pp. 93–115.

[61]"Ter Inleiding," *Djawa*, vol. 1, no. 1 (1921), p. 1.

who served as honorary chairman; Djajadiningrat, the chairman; S. Koperberg, the secretary; and a committee member in the Netherlands, P. J. Gerke. There were also fifteen commissioners, eight of whom were Dutch and seven of whom were Javanese. The Dutch commissioners included B. J. O. Schrieke, B. ter Haar, and Kiewiet de Jong, while the Javanese commissioners included Soeriodiningrat, Koesoema Oetaya, and Poerbatjaraka, as well as Umar Said Tjokroaminoto of the Sarekat Islam (Association of Islam).[62]

The composition of the editorial staff also reflected cooperation between Dutch and Javanese. When the journal began publication in 1921, it had three Dutch editors, J. Kats, Koperberg, and J. W. Teillers, and two Javanese editors, Djajadiningrat and Poerbatjaraka. Ten years later in 1931 the ratio remained the same, the Dutch being Drewes, Kats, and Koperberg, and the Javanese being Djajadiningrat and M. Soeriodiradja. The ratio changed in 1941, the final year of publication; the two Dutch editors were Koperberg and J. L. Moens, and the two Javanese editors were R. Sidarta Dibjapranata and B. P. H. Purbaja. All the Javanese scholars named played a central role in the development of Javanology, evaluating the findings of Javanese research together with their Dutch colleagues.

II. Ranggawarsita and His Times

A particularly interesting aspect of the development of Dutch Javanology is the fate of traditional Javanese intellectuals. "Traditional intellectuals" refers to the bearers of the great tradition of the Java *kraton*, the people who, under the patronage of the kings, recorded in Javanese script the tales and chronicles exalting the kings, an act that was a manifestation of their power to penetrate the mysteries of the universe and discern the destiny of this world. They were the custodians of the world of the esoteric, and their writings were preserved in the *kraton* as *pusaka*, the sacred regalia.

Those who held this function in the Java *kraton* were the court literati known as *pujangga*. The last and greatest *pujangga* of the nineteenth century was Ranggawarsita, who served the Kasunanan. The years of Ranggawarsita's life (1802–1873) correspond almost exactly to those of Taco Roorda's (1801–1874), the man who made the greatest contribution to the establishment of Dutch Javanology. Also of interest is the fact that in the mid-nineteenth century, when Winter and Wilkens, Roorda's "nutrient sources," were in Surakarta scouring Javanese literature and defining every word they found in Dutch for the bilingual dictionary they were helping him compile, Ranggawarsita was living in the same city and was at the height of his career as a *pujangga*. Thus the father of Javanology and the custodian of the world of esoteric knowledge converged on the same temporal and spatial plane.

Javanology presupposes the exoteric; publication is the natural end product of interviews and the collection, classification, and analysis of materials. The esoteric, however, is by definition mysterious, although it too involves dissemination in the opaque manner of the *lisan* (oral) tradition. The *kraton* was the center of the world of the Javanese (and of the Javanese language) because it was the repository of this *lisan* tradition. And of all the *pujangga*, Ranggawarsita has attracted the most attention among twentieth-century Javanese; he seems most relevant to them, for he touches the deepest core of their being.[63] Javanology objectified this world of the esoteric,

---

[62]"Het Java-Instituut," *Djawa*, vol. 1, no. 1 (1921), pp. 65–66.

[63]On the relationship between Ranggawarsita's message and the situation in Surakarta in the latter half of the 1970s, see Teruo Sekimoto, "Sawito jiken no bunkaronteki kōsatsu" [Cultural

made it, indeed, a key subject of research, subjecting it to scrutiny under the penetrating light of Western scholarship and thus fixing its place in the universal scheme of modern knowledge. The manifold achievements of Javanology discussed in part one illustrate this process.

One could say, then, that nineteenth-century Java, particularly Ranggawarsita's world, was one in which two paradigms coexisted, in which the paradigm of Javanology permeated and interacted with the paradigm of the world of the esoteric as Dutch permeated Javanese. To show this clearly, we must now completely shift our focus from Dutch scholars and scholarship to Javanese *pujangga* and their works. Below I will attempt to analyze the age in which Ranggawarsita lived and to describe the traditional Javanese intellectual world as it was in the nineteenth and early twentieth centuries. I will begin by surveying the literary activity of the *kraton* in the years before Ranggawarsita, after which I will discuss Ranggawarsita himself.

The Literary Renaissance

As I have already mentioned, the latter half of the eighteenth century saw the literary florescence in the Kasunanan (Yogyakarta) that Pigeaud calls a renaissance. Nor was this florescence confined to the Kasunanan: the same phenomenon could be seen in the other three royal houses of Java—the Kasultanan, the Mangkunegara, and the Paku Alam. Why did this burst of literary activity occur at that particular time?

(a) Systems and technology

One can point to two conditions that encouraged a literary florescence, both of which were clearly related to the presence of the Dutch in Java (both the VOC and the Indies government). First, with the breakup in the mid-eighteenth century of the kingdom of Mataram (in 1755 Surakarta and Yogyakarta broke away; in 1757 the Mangkunegara broke away from Surakarta; and in 1813 the Paku Alam broke away from Yogyakarta), the presence of the Dutch was a prerequisite for the maintenance of "tranquillity and order" *tata tentrem* among the royal houses. The Dutch acted as arbitrators in this civil strife, established the conditions of the division, specified the scale of each royal house (the number of inhabitants of each territory and the amount of court income), and, having the right to veto the appointment of high court officials, acted as guardians of the internal affairs of the royal families. It was the Dutch presence that enabled the royal houses to avoid the disputes with external enemies and the internal conflicts that had been endemic since the establishment of Mataram at the end of the sixteenth century.

In fact, despite the coexistence of three (later four) royal houses in Central Java from the mid-eighteenth century onward—rather, because of the stabilization of this coexistence—all enjoyed an age of peace. Competition among the royal houses now took the form not of disputes leading to invasion or political subjugation but of rivalry that spurred each royal house to try to outdo the others in establishing, in the eyes of its own vassals and subjects, the superiority of its claim to legitimacy as inheritor of the great tradition of Java. This became still more crucial at the time of the emergence of a new royal line. Anxiety over the advent of a new century in 1774 (the year 1700 in the Javanese calendar), an occurrence that in Javanese tradition coincided with the rise and fall of kingdoms, spurred the royal houses to embark on

considerations of the Sawito affair], in Chūsei Suzuki, ed., Sennen ōkokuteki minshū undō no kenkyū [Studies on millenarian movements] (Tokyo: University of Tokyo Press, 1982).

great new undertakings. All these factors stimulated the mystical act of recording events, in other words, the creation of *serat* and *babad*. A new kingdom and a new age were to be created through language.[64]

The second condition has to do with the technology of recording the written word in general, not just *serat* and *babad*: new developments in paper making, book making and book binding, printing, and print media that resulted from contact with the Dutch.

Before paper, pen, and ink were available in Java, writings were inscribed on stone, copper sheets, or palm fronds called *lontar* or, in Javanese, *kropak*. Of these, *lontar* was the medium used most widely and over the longest period of time. (*Lontar* were produced in East Java and Madura until the beginning of the twentieth century.) In addition *dluwang*, a kind of cloth made from tree bark, had been in use since the arrival of Islam.

This situation changed when Chinese and Arabian paper began to be imported with the commencement of the VOC's trading activities in the seventeenth century. Paper manufactured in the Netherlands was first imported to Java around that time, as well as writing instruments, and became the favorite of all the royal courts. Pigeaud notes that imported paper was a major factor in the literary renaissance of the eighteenth and nineteenth centuries.[65] The supply of paper increased tremendously when the Dutch began actually manufacturing paper in Java around the turn of the twentieth century. All these changes dramatically increased the opportunities for writing and thus the production of written works, which no longer had to be incised.

The increased paper supply was accompanied by the introduction of book-making and book-binding techniques. Arabian book-making and book-binding methods using sheepskin were known in the eighteenth century, but in the nineteenth century Western methods were introduced and came into wide use in Java. The creation of type for the Javanese script in 1839 enabled the mass production of Javanese literature. The appearance, in the late nineteenth and early twentieth centuries, of publishers that published widely in Javanese, such as Van Dorp in Semarang, Tan Khoen Swie in Kediri, Kolff-Buning in Yogyakarta, and the Balai Pustaka in Batavia, enlarged the market for Javanese books. Publishing received a further boost with the 1918 Spelling Ordinance (Spellingstelsels), finalized in 1926, which stipulated the use of the Latin alphabet instead of Javanese script.[66]

The existence of paper, type, and a market also enabled the regular publication of newspapers and magazines in the mid-nineteenth century. The newspaper *Bramartani*, which carried stories from *serat* and *babad* as well as reports of "strange happenings" in Java, began publication in Surakarta in 1855. It ceased publication after a year but resumed ten years later, in 1865. The editor at that time was Jones Portier, and Ranggawarsita was an editorial adviser. The paper's name was changed to

---

[64]M. C. Ricklefs, *Jogjakarta under Sultan Mangkubumi, 1749–1792: A History of the Division of Java* (London: Oxford University Press, 1974); Kenji Tsuchiya, "Jokujakaruta—chūbu Jawa ni okeru 'miyako' no seiritsu to tenkai" [Yogyakarta: The establishment and development of a capital in Central Java], *Tōnan Ajia kenkyū*, vol. 21, no. 1 (June 1983).

[65]Pigeaud, *Literature*, 1: 35–37.

[66]Uhlenbeck, *A Cultural Survey*, p. 76.

Djurumartani for a time, but was changed back to *Bramartini* in the reign of Sultan Paku Buwana IX (r. 1861–1893).[67]

(b) Literary activity

The above-mentioned technological changes both made it easier for the *pujangga* of the *kraton* to write and increased their opportunities for doing so. Meanwhile, the incentive for writing existed in full measure in all the courts of Java, generating the mid-eighteenth-century literary renaissance. Let us now examine that literary activity itself, focusing on the Kasultanan (Yogyakarta) and the Kasunanan (Surakarta).

According to Ricklefs, the Kasultanan had a stronger tendency than the Kasunanan to use *serat* and *babad* to demonstrate its authenticity, making the creation of *serat* and *babad* an important part of the process of establishing the kingdom. The Serat Surja Radja is said to have been compiled in 1774 (1700, or the beginning of the eighteenth century, in the Javanese calendar) by the prince Kandjeng Gusti, who was later to become Hamengkubawana II (r. 1792–1810, 1811–1812, 1826–1818). This long story, in the guise of fiction, begins with the Javanese king Surja Djaja Amisesa and relates the division of the kingdom and its reunification. Ricklefs believes that it actually prophesies that the Kasultanan will become the court of a united Java. There is also a *babad* compiled by the *pujangga* Raden Tumenggung Djajengrat in 1777 (1703 in the Javanese calendar). This lengthy *babad* (over 1,400 pages), which has no title and is referred to simply as the *Babad Kraton*, suggests, through a narrative that begins with Adam's creation of the world and ends with the establishment of Kartasura in 1680 (a supplementary volume extends the story to the destruction of Kartasura in 1742), that the Kasultanan is the rightful successor of the Kartasura *kraton*, in other words, the kingdom of Mataram.[68]

Literary activity also flourished in the Kasunanan: the *pudjangga* compiled new *babad*, rewrote old tales, and composed new tales and poems. The most distinguished work around the turn of the nineteenth century was that of the *pujangga* Raden Ngabehi Jasadipura (1729–1802).[69] He composed the *Babad Gijanti* at the beginning of the nineteenth century and rewrote in contemporary Javanese the epic poems *Brata Yuda*, *Serat Rama*, *Minta Raga*, *Nawa Rutji*, *Dewa Rutji*, and *Ménak Amir Hamza*. His son Jasadipura II received the title Sastra Nagara (National Man of Letters) for his contributions to Surakarta's literature. In addition to continuing his father's rewriting of the classics, he wrote the *Babad Pakĕpung*. It was also in Surakarta that the *Babad Tanah Djawi* was composed, during the reign of Paku Buwana IV (r. 1788–1820). By rewriting Kawi classics in the language of the day, a process known as *jarwa* (modernization of Kawi), the Jasadipura father and son created the nineteenth-century genre of "paeans to the glorious past." Incorporated into *wayang* as subject matter for the *dalang*'s *lakon*, their works deeply penetrated Javanese society.[70]

But the *pujangga* were not the only ones responsible for the Surakarta renaissance. The monarchs Paku Buwana III (r. 1749–1788), Paku Buwana IV, and Paku Buwana V (r. 1820–1823) also wrote. Paku Buwana IV left such works as the *Serat*

---

[67]Andjar Any, *Raden Ngabehi Ranggawarsita, Apa yang Terjadi* (Semarang: Aneka, 1980), pp. 46–47.

[68]Ricklefs, *Jogjakarta*, introduction, chap. 7.

[69]On Surakarta literary activity centering on Jasadipura and his son, see Pigeaud, *Literature*, 1: 235–43.

[70]Ibid., p. 239.

Wulangreh and the *Sekar Kinanti*,[71] and Paku Buwana V, known as Pangeran Adipati Anom before his accession to the throne, commissioned the *Serat Tjentini*, sometimes referred to as the "encyclopedia of Java."[72]

RANGGAWARSITA

Ranggawarsita, true heir to the *pujangga* tradition of the courts of Java, wrote many works. Yet with him the tradition of *pujangga* ends. In terms of Java's cultural history, the nineteenth century can be described on the one hand as the age in which the lineage and tradition of Javanology were established and on the other as the age when the lineage and tradition of the *pujangga* ceased to exist. The establishment of Javanology and the cessation of the tradition of the *pujangga* are, in fact, intrinsically related.

By discussing this point in the light of Ranggawarsita's life and his encounter with Javanology, I will examine the fate of Java's traditional intellectuals in the age when Javanology was being established. I will begin with a sketch of Ranggawarsita's life based on two biographical works by Andjar Any (published in 1979 and 1980 respectively).[73] I use these sources partly because they are the only critical biographies of Ranggawarsita that exist and partly because these works, published more than a century after Ranggawarsita's death, illustrate beautifully the manner in which the legacy of Ranggawarsita has been transmitted by the Javanese from the time of his death to the present and how he is perceived by the Javanese. Then, after reviewing Ranggawarsita's works, I will consider his fate, and that of the *pujangga* in general, in the age that saw the first flowering of Javanology.

(a) Ranggawarsita's life

Following is the life of Ranggawarsita as retold by Andjar Any.[74]

Raden Ngabehi Ranggawarsita was born into the Jasadipura family in the Baluwarti district of Surakarta on March 15, 1802; his childhood name was Bagus Burham. Jasadipura, who died the year Burham was born, was his great-grandfather; Jasadipura's son Jasadipura II (Sastra Negara) was his grandfather. Burham lived in Surakarta until he was twelve years old, when he was sent to the *pesantren* (Muslim boarding school) of Tegalsari Gusti, located southeast of Ponorogo, with his servant/guardian Ki Tanudjaja, to study the traditional Javanese *ngèlmu* (learning). At the time, this *pesantren*, directed by Kyai Imam Besari (Kasan Besari), was the most noted in Java.[75]

Ponorogo, located 120 kilometers southeast of Surakarta at the southeastern foot of sacred Mount Lawu in Central Java, has appeared in Javanese historical docu-

---

[71] Ibid., pp. 108–9, 237.

[72] R. M. Ng. Poerbatjaraka, *Kapustakan Djawi* (Jakarta: Penerbitan Djambatan, 1952), pp. 150–51. Although the Mangkunegara and the Paku Alam were smaller than the Kasultanan and the Kasunanan, they also had *serat* and *babad* of their own histories.

[73] Andjar Any, *Rahasia Ramalan, Jayabaya, Ranggawarsita dan Sabdapalon* (Semarang: Aneka, 1979); Andjar Any, *Ranggawarsita*.

[74] The notion of the retold (*diceriterakan kembali*) life of Ranggawarsita is based on a conversation between the author and Andjar Any on January 27, 1983, in Surakarta.

[75] Tegalsari Gusti still exists. Most of the buildings are now modernized, but the building in which Ranggawarsita studied and his room have been preserved just as they were. The building is used as a dormitory for *santri* (religious students). The floor consists of bamboo slats; Ranggawarsita's room, the last on the right, is only 1.5 meters by 2.5 meters.

ments since ancient times. It was known as a place where many eminent men had undergone ascetic training in their youth or to which they had repaired to withdraw from the world temporarily. At the beginning of the nineteenth century boys from all over Central Java, particularly the sons of high officials, were sent to the Tegalsari *pesantren* to study *ngèlmu*. For Burham, the eight years from the time he went there at the age of twelve (1814) to the time he was taken on by the Surakarta *kraton* as a low-ranking scribe (*mantri carik kadipaten anom*) at the age of twenty (1822) were literally a *samadi*, an ascetic journey.

Known as a mischief-maker from an early age, Burham showed no interest in study when he entered the Tegalsari *pesantren*, nor did his behavior improve. Kyai Besari tried to bring Burham to his senses by forbidding the other pupils to associate with him, but to no avail. Finally he expelled Burham. Attended by Tanudjaja, the youth began a life of wandering. The pair went first to nearby Desa Moro, where Tanudjaja knew someone, and from there to Madiun and on to Kediri, in East Java. Meanwhile, a youth named Kromoleyo, whom Kyai Besari had sent after them, was told of their whereabouts in a dream and, finding them, conveyed Kyai Besari's message to come back to the *pesantren* and start afresh. Kyai Besari, in fact, having studied together with Burham's grandfather, was particularly concerned about the boy's future.

Burham returned to the *pesantren*, but he was no better behaved than before. At that time Ponorogo was suffering from a drought, and the *pesantren* was short of food. Kyai Besari divided the boarders into groups of five or six and told them to go to the homes of local aristocrats and wealthy people and beg in the style of mendicant priests. Burham, however, persuaded his group and went off to enjoy fishing in the rivers and playing in the hills. He was severely reprimanded both by Kyai Besari, who had learned of his escapades, and by Tanudjaja.

"All was still, and so was Bagus Burham. Suddenly, as if he had received divine light, Bagus Burham began to speak."[76] This experience, Andjar Any writes, marked Burham's "conversion" and the beginning of his transformation into the great poet Ranggawarsita, who could "discern even the voices of birds and beasts."[77] After that, Burham engaged in austerities (*tapa*) every night by the river to the west of the *pesantren*. He continued these practices for forty days, eating nothing but one banana a day. On the final night Jasadipura appeared to him in a dream. When Burham followed his great-grandfather's command to pull his ear, Jasadipura entered the youth through the ear.

Meanwhile, Tanudjaja, who was attending his master and was also in a half-dream, half-waking state, felt light descend from heaven and enter a pot he was holding. When the two removed the lid, they found a big fish inside. Burham ate everything but the head and tail, which Tanudjaja ate, and from this time on a light signifying divine revelation (*wahyu*) shone on Burham's head.

After that Burham made phenomenal progress in his studies. He was able to chant the Koran without a single mistake, and his words penetrated to the very souls of his listeners. Kyai Besari bestowed on him the name Mas Ilham, a name that soon became known throughout Ponorogo, its bearer frequently being called on to deliver sermons (*kotbah*) to the villagers.

---

[76]Andjar Any, *Ranggawarsita*, p. 27.

[77]Ibid., p. 28.

Upon finishing his studies, in 1817 Burham returned to Surakarta, accompanied by Kyai Besari, and was warmly welcomed by his family after his three-year absence. He celebrated his circumcision that year. He found favor with Panembahan Buminata, younger brother of Paku Buwana IV, who conferred on him the traditional learning of the royal family. Paku Buwana IV saw great promise in Burham and in October 1819 made him an assistant scribe (*abdi dalem carik kadipaten anom*) at the *kraton*. In 1820 Paku Buwana IV died and was succeeded by his son Sugandi, who became Paku Buwana V. But the new king did not like Buminata and therefore, despite the latter's repeated recommendations, kept Burham in a low post. Meanwhile, in November 1821 Burham married Raden Adjeng Gombak. Her father was Kandjeng Adipati Tjakraningrat, the *bupati* of Kediri and Buminata's adopted son. Burham was nineteen years old.

After this Burham and Tanudjaja traveled once again. Seeking a more advanced teacher, Burham visited Kyai Tunggul Wulung in the village of Ngadiluwih, in East Java. After staying there seven days, at Kyai Wulung's suggestion he visited Adjar Wirakantha, who lived south of Banyuwangi, on the eastern tip of Java. Like Kyai Wulung, Wirakantha realized immediately that Burham possessed unusual powers. Wirakantha then told Burham of Ki Adjar Sidalaku, who lived in Tabanan, on Bali, and had some ancient *lontar* in his possession. Burham went to Bali and spent ten days with Sidalaku, who bestowed on him the power of prescience and gave him a number of *lontar*. Burham then went back to Java, stopping in Kediri to see his wife and father-in-law before returning to Surakarta. Upon his return to Surakarta, in 1822, Burham was given the name Mas Ngabehi Sarataka and, as already mentioned, was employed as a low-ranking scribe in the *kraton*. His long pilgrimage was over.

The political situation in Java was extremely unstable at that time. In 1823 Paku Buwana V abdicated, and his son Supardan ascended the throne as Paku Buwana VI (r. 1823–1830). But the Java War (1825–1830), led by the disaffected prince Diponegoro, led to a rise in anti-Dutch sentiment in Central Java. Both Paku Buwana VI and Burham were ostensibly on the side opposed to Diponegoro, but they were said to be secretly in sympathy with the rebels. This led to the arrest of Burham's father and his execution in Batavia. Then Paku Buwana VI himself was arrested and exiled to Ambon, where he died in 1849. A rumor spread that Paku Buwana's arrest was the result of Burham's father having divulged the secret relationship among Paku Buwana VI, Diponegoro, and Sentot, the commander of Diponegoro's forces, and this was later to lead to rumors of antipathy between Paku Buwana VI's family and Ranggawarsita's family (particularly the rumor that Ranggawarsita was killed on the orders of Paku Buwana IX, who was a son of Paku Buwana VI).

After Paku Buwana VI's exile R. M. Malikies Solikin, a son of Paku Buwana IV, ascended the Surakarta throne in 1830 to become Paku Buwana VII (r. 1830–1858). It was during his reign that Burham reached the height of his career as a *pujangga*. He had attained the position of chief scribe (*panewu sadasa kadipaten anom*) in 1826, during Paku Buwana VI's reign, and was awarded the name Raden Ngabehi Ranggawarsita III in 1830. (Though his father had been known as Ranggawarsita II, unqualified references to Ranggawarsita are understood to indicate Ranggawarsita III). In 1844 Jasadipura II, *pujangga* to the Kasunanan, died. Responsibility for the family fell on Ranggawarsita, and the following year, on the advice of his patron, Buminata, he followed in his grandfather's footsteps and took up the post of *pujangga* in Surakarta. The inauguration ceremony took place on September 14, 1845. With this the *pujangga* Ranggawarsita was born.

Ranggawarsita spent the rest of his life as a *pujangga*. Both his wife, Gombak, and his patron, Buminata, died in 1848, and his mother died in 1852. The year his mother died Ranggawarsita remarried, his wife being the daughter of R. M. P. Djajengmardjono. Meanwhile, after the death of Paku Buwana VII in 1858, R. M. Kusen, another son of Paku Buwana IV, became Paku Buwana VIII (r. 1858–1861). When he died, Paku Buwana VI's son ascended the throne to become Paku Buwana IX. Ranggawarsita died during his reign, having served six monarchs.

The rapid turnover in rulers indicates what a turbulent age the Kasunanan passed through in the nineteenth century. During this period Ranggawarsita was educated in traditional Javanese learning and became a *pujangga*, writing numerous tales, adapting classics, and composing poetry. Many people visited him at home, among them such aristocrats as B. R. M. Harja Gondakusuma (who was later to become Mangkunegara IV), Pandji Dipakusuma, and Pandji Ismubrata. Foreign visitors included Winter, whose relationship with Ranggawarsita will be discussed in some detail later.

Besides his role as a master of classical Javanese literature, Ranggawarsita performed such services for the king and high officials as interpreting dreams, foretelling the future, and even curing illnesses. These abilities show that he possessed the qualifications traditionally associated with a *pujangga*. The word *pujangga* derives from *bujangga*, whose first meaning is "snake," its second, "one who accompanies the king." *Pujangga* eventually came to mean "person of knowledge" (*cendekiawan*), "spiritual teacher" (*rokhaniawan*). A *pujangga* was considered to fulfill eight qualifications: excellence in literary endeavors, fluency in Kawi, skill in language manipulation (plays on words), eloquence, mastery of the spoken and written word, familiarity with the world (everything from the *halus*, or refined, to the *kasar*, or coarse), understanding of human emotions and thought, and finally, possession of a superior memory.[78] This understanding of what constituted a *pujangga* presupposed the belief that proficiency in literature and language was equivalent to proficiency in the Javanese esoteric world; therefore the ability to interpret dreams, foretell the future, and exhibit magical powers was only what one would expect of a *pujangga*.

The final years of Ranggawarsita's life, when he was out of favor with Paku Buwana IX, were far from happy. His famous poem *Serat Kala Tida* [The age of madness],[79] a requiem for the age in which he lived, was written after 1861, during the period of friction with Paku Buwana IX. Ranggawarsita died on December 24, 1873, eight days after writing the poem *Serat Sabda Djati* [True words], in which he is said to have prophesied the day of his death.[80]

---

[78]Ibid., p. 103.

[79]This poem, the most popular of Ranggawarsita's works in later generations, has been studied by numerous scholars in Indonesia and elsewhere. It is because of this poem that the phrase *zaman edan* (age of madness) is so often associated with Ranggawarsita. Studies of the poem include Benedict Anderson, "The Time of Darkness and the Time of Light," in Anthony Reid and David Marr, eds., *Perceptions of the Past in Southeast Asia* (Singapore: Heinemann Educational Books [Asia], 1979); Anderson, "Politik Bahasa"; Kamadjaja, *Zaman Edan* (Jakarta: U. P. Indonesia, 1964); Kamadjaja, *Zaman Edan, Pembahasan Serat Kalatidha Ranggawarsita* (Yogyakarta: Proyek Javanologi, 1983); Takashi Shiraishi, "'Jinminshugi' o megutte—Chiputo Mangunkusumo vs Sutattomo Suriyokusumo" [*Pandita* versus *Satria*: The dispute between Soetatmo Soeriokoesoemo and Tjipto Mangoenkoesoemo], *Tōnan Ajia kenkyū*, vol. 17, no. 4 (1980); Sekimoto, "Sawito jiken."

[80]Whether Ranggawarsita died a natural death or was murdered was debated in the pages of the Jakarta newspaper *Sinar Harapan* in 1979 and 1980. The debate grew out of the poet's

From this summary of Andjar Any's accounts of the life of Ranggawarsita, we can see how this *pujangga* came to occupy the place he did in the world of the Javanese (the world of the Javanese language). Through his use of *sandiasma*[81] he demonstrated his mastery of the Javanese language. He showed himself to be a prophet as well, foretelling, in a play on words known as sengkalan, the 1945 "advent of the golden age" (that is, Indonesian independence).[82] And by adapting the prophetic writings of Djajabaja and thus reviving them in his own age, he came to be seen as part of the millenarian tradition of Javanese mysticism.[83]

Most important, through the many supernatural qualities associated with him, particularly his ability to discern "the voices of birds and beasts"—which came to be interpreted as meaning that he was a "poet of the people [*rakyat*]," one who listened to the voice of the people—he became an integral part of the tradition of the Javanese, particularly the world of *lisan* rather than *tulisan*. Ranggawarsita's works, especially his poetry, have lived on not so much through being printed and sold by publishers as through being quoted by nationalists in their speeches and recited at village gath-

---

having supposedly prophesied the date of his death in *Serat Sabda Djati*. For details, see Andjar Any, *Ranggawarsita*, pp. 71–99. Around the same time, a seminar on Ranggawarsita was held at the University of Indonesia. These activities indicate the heightened interest in Ranggawarsita in the Indonesian academic world in the latter half of the 1970s.

[81] *Sandiasma* is the technique of slipping a name or title into the words of a poem. Ranggawarsita was the originator of this technique and often wove his name into the lines of his poems. In the following example, from the poem *Wedhayatmaka*, the final syllable of the first or second word of each line together spell "Radyan Ngabehi Ronggawarsita." See Andjar Any, *Ranggawarsita*, pp. 106–7. The syllables in question are italicized.

> Tanpanta*ra* ngesthi tyas hartati;
> Lir wini*dyan*, saraseng parasdya,
> Ringa ri*nga* pangriptane,
> Tan dar*be* labdeng kawruh,
> Mung ngruru*hi* wenganing budi,
> Kang mi*rong* ngaruhara,
> Ja*ga* angkaragung,
> Minta lu*war* ring duhkita,
> Awya kong*si* kewran lukiteng kinteki,
> Kang ka*ta* ginupita.

[82] It is in *Djaka Ladang* that Ranggawarsita prophesies independence in 1945. The pertinent lines are as follows:

> Sangkalane maksih nunggal jamanipun;
> Neng sajroning madya akir;
> Wiku Sapta ngesthi Ratu;
> Adil parimarmeng dasih;
> Ing kono kersaning Manon:

The four words of line 3 also indicate the numbers 7, 7, 8, and 1, respectively (a *sengkalan* play on words). These lines can be paraphrased as follows: "We are now halfway there; finally, in 1877, all people will be visited with justice. It is the will of God." The year 1877 in the Javanese calendar corresponds to 1945, the year of the Indonesian declaration of independence. See Andjar Any, *Rahasia Ramalan*, pp. 21–24; Sekimoto, "Sawito jiken."

[83] Andjar Any, *Rahasia Ramalan*, p. 114.

erings; thus they have been transmitted orally from generation to generation.[84] In this world of oral tradition Ranggawarsita more than any other *pujangga* has continued to be revered a master of the world of the esoteric.

This point is related to what I wrote above about Andjar Any's retelling of Ranggawarsita's life. His accounts provide an almost complete list of the biographical items that, through the ages, have gone into the making of the traditional Javanese hero (or, in Ranggawarsita's case, the great *pujangga*). We have the unruly youth, the sudden conversion occasioned by recollection of the times of an illustrious ancestor, the faithful servant, the period of wandering, the practice of austerities, the bestowal of *wahyu* as the climax of a half-dream, half-waking state, the second ascetic journey, the mastery of ancient esoteric knowledge, the acquisition of mysterious powers (one day suddenly reciting the Koran "in a voice of unearthly beauty," discerning "the voices of birds and beasts," demonstrating a superhuman memory, and so on; and especially, demonstrating prophetic powers, such as interpreting dreams and foretelling the future).[85] It is precisely because the story of Ranggawarsita's life can be framed in this traditional set of terms that he has lived on in the minds of the Javanese as a *pujangga* without parallel, a hero of "glorious Java's golden age," a figure ranking with the saints of the *wayang*. The concrete fact that he lived in nineteenth-century Surakarta and was a contemporary of Roorda, the great Dutch authority on Java, becomes irrelevant, and he is added to the ranks of the saints as a timeless "great *pujangga*."[86] Thus has he been given a place as a true master of the esoteric in the oral tradition of the Javanese.

---

[84]Detailed discussion of Ranggawarsita's reemergence in the nationalist period lies outside the scope of this paper, but one major episode is worth mentioning here: the rumor that spread at the time of the arrest, in 1929, of Sukarno and other leaders of the PNI (Partai Nasional Indonesia; Indonesian Nationalist Party) that they were planning a 1930 uprising. This rumor spread in the *pergerakan* after Ranggwarsita's *Djaka Ladang* was published in the newspaper *Darma Kanda*. The *sengkalan* in the lines reading

> Para sudagar ingargya,
> Jroning jaman keneng sarik;
> Marmane sak-isining rat;
> Sangsarane saya mencit;
> NIR SAT ESTHINING URIP
> Iku ta sengkalanipun
> Pantoging nandhang sudra

(All things are experiencing sadness; the age of sadness will end in the year of *nir sat ersthining urip*) yields the year 1860 in the Javanese calendar, or 1930 in the Western calendar. See Andjar Any, *Rahasia Ramalan*, p. 7. For a striking portrayal of how Ranggawarsita's works provided spiritual nourishment to the Javanese involved in the nationalist movement, see Pramoedya Ananta Toer, *Bukan Pasar Malam* (Jakarta: Balai Pustaka, 1959), chaps. 13, 16.

[85]Benedict Anderson, "The Idea of Power in Javanese Culture," in Claire Holt, et al., eds., *Culture and Politics in Indonesia* (Ithaca, NY: Cornell University Press, 1972).

[86]Ranggawarsita's grave, in the village of Palar in Kraten Regency, Central Java, is sacred to the Javanese. On November 11, 1953, a bust of Ranggawarsita was unveiled in central Surakarta in a ceremony attended by President Sukarno and Minister of Education Mohammad Yamin. In their speeches, both Sukarno and Yamin emphasized Ranggawarsita's role as a "poet of the people." See Kamadjaja, *Zaman Edan* (1964), pp. 11–32. On November 10, 1955, Ranggwarsita's grave was rebuilt as a shrine by the government, and he and his family were laid to rest in a marble mausoleum.

(b) Ranggawarsita's works

Ranggawarsita produced an enormous opus. In Pigeaud's view, his greatest work is the *Pustaka Radja*, a compilation and adaptation of ancient Javanese tales and legends. In this work Ranggawarsita arranges events in Javanese history according to a calendar of his own devising. The introduction, *Paramajoga*, and part of the body of the work were published in Surakarta and Yogyakarta between 1884 and 1892. Some of Ranggawarsita's imitators, such as Sumahatmaka of the Mangkunegara, copied his style, issuing the unpublished wayang tales in a volume titled *Pustaka Radja Madya*. Pigeaud classifies *Serat Kala Tida* as didactic poetry, and says that works in the same style were later published by others.[87]

At the end of his 1980 biography of Ranggawarsita, Andjar Any lists fifty-six works by the *pujangga*.[88] One of them is a Kawi-Javanese dictionary (Dutch version) coedited with Winter, with whom, as we will see, Ranggawarsita had a very close relationship. Also listed are three works that Ranggawarsita adapted, Jasadipura's versions of the *Brata Yuda*, *Djajabaya*, and *Paniti Sastra*. I will not go into further detail; suffice it to say that Ranggawarsita produced an impressive number of works as a *pujangga*.

How did scholars of Javanese literature, both Ranggawarsita's contemporaries and those who came later, evaluate his works? Poerbatjaraka's scathing criticism more or less sums up their judgment. In *Kapustakan Djawi*, a history of Javanese literature, Poerbatjaraka focuses his critique of Ranggawarsita on four works: *Paramajoga*, *Serat Djitapsara*, *Pustaka Radja*, and *Serat Tjemporet*. Yet according to Andjar Any, Poerbatjaraka holds Ranggawarsita in much less esteem than his predecessors Jasadipura and Jasadipura II, writing caustically that "Ranggawarsita quoted his grandfather's works and won popularity by getting them published in a newspaper [the *Bramartani*]."[89] Poerbatjaraka himself adds that because Ranggawarsita lacked a thorough knowledge of Kawi, frequently he used it inappropriately and the meaning is obscure.[90] And "as for the *serat Pustaka Radja*, the greater part of it is just R. Ng. Ranggawarsita's nonsense."[91]

I believe that Poerbatjaraka's evaluation expresses the judgment of Ranggawarsita and his age that grew out of the development of Javanology in Java itself. Let us, then, examine the way in which Ranggawarsita was involved—was compelled to become involved—with this Javanology.

(c) Ranggawarsita and Javanology

As we have already seen, it was in the mid-nineteenth century, when Ranggawarsita was active as a *pujangga* at the Surakarta *kraton*, that the Institute for the Javanese Language in Surakarta was established. This was also the period in which Winter and Wilkens were carrying out research on Javanese literature in Surakarta and compiling a Javanese-Dutch dictionary, the period in which the Dutch were beginning to work actively to establish Javanology as a field of study. This means that, as

---

[87]Pigeaud, *Literature*, pp. 110, 170–71.

[88]Andjar Any, *Ranggawarsita*, pp. 114–16.

[89]Ibid., p. 76. It is not clear what text by Poerbatjaraka Andjar Any is quoting.

[90]Poerbatjaraka, *Kapustakan Djawi*, p. 154.

[91]"Tjekakipun serat Pustaka-radja, punika sabagean ageng sangat, namung isi omong-kosongipun R. Ng. Ranggawarsita." Ibid., p. 157.

Pigeaud suggests, the Dutch (and the Dutch language) began infiltrating the *kraton* in Surakarta, thus influencing Javanese literature.[92]

Ranggawarsita had direct contact with Dutch scholars in this period, and his relationship with Winter linked him to the mainstream of Javanology. According to Andjar Any, Winter frequently visited Ranggawarsita to consult him on the Javanese language and literature.[93] Ranggawarsita's rich store of knowledge and phenomenal memory made him an indispensable informant. Thus from the start Javanology was in direct contact with the pinnacle of traditional Javanese learning (*ilmu kejawen*). Ranggawarsita's collaboration with Winter in the editing of the Kawi-Javanese dictionary is a good example of the way Javanology operated at the time. Pigeaud writes that Dutch scholars in nineteenth-century Surakarta, such as Gericke, Winter, and Wilkens, had contact with the court *pujangga* in order to learn Javanese.[94] And of course *pujangga* meant, first and foremost, Ranggawarsita. According to Uhlenbeck, the second volume of the Javanese conversation book *Javaansch Zamenspraken*, edited by Winter and published in Amsterdam in 1858, contained *wangsalan* and *pracekan* (parables and precepts) with commentaries by Ranggawarsita, an indication of what an invaluable source of information he was.[95]

A number of episodes convey a more concrete idea of the relationship between Ranggawarsita and Winter. One has to do with the circumstances in which Gondakusuma (1811–1881) became Ranggawarsita's disciple. Gondakusuma, known as the author of the didactic poem *Wédatama* and other works, was close to Ranggawarsita; Pigeaud describes them as friends.[96] Ranggawarsita, Winter, and Gondakusuma all belonged to the same generation: Winter was three years older than Ranggawarsita, who was nine years older than Gondakusuma.

The story has it that Gondakusuma had heard of Ranggawarsita's reputation and wanted to study with him but had not had an opportunity to meet him. Winter, learning of this, arranged a meeting. He sent a messenger to Ranggawarsita's house to say that he wanted to bring Gondakusuma to see the *pujangga*. He also arranged to have food delivered to Ranggawarsita's house so that he would be sure to have something on hand to serve his guests. Although Ranggawarsita had a good income, he was very extravagant and often had to go out to a nearby *warong* (foodstall) to get something to serve his guests because there was nothing in the house. Being a close friend (*sahabat dekatnya*), Winter knew this. On their first meeting Ranggawarsita greeted Gondakusuma with deference and prophesied that he would become the master (*pangeran*) of the Mangkunegara. Indeed, in 1849 Gondakusuma became Mangkunegara IV, and a close relationship was forged between Ranggawarsita and the Mangkunegara.[97]

This anecdote makes it clear that Winter was on friendly terms with both men and also that he could skillfully cut through the intricate rules normally involved in arranging a meeting between a *pujangga* of the Kasunanan and a future ruler of the

[92]Pigeaud, *Literature*, pp. 109–10.

[93]Andjar Any, *Ranggawarsita*, p. 106.

[94]Pigeaud, *Literature*, p. 109.

[95]Uhlenbeck, *A Cultural Survey*, p. 56.

[96]Theodore Pigeaud, "Uit de Pers: In Memoriam R. Ng. Ranggawarsita," *Djawa*, vol. 12, no. 2/3 (1932), pp. 137–38.

[97]Andjar Any, *Ranggawarsita*, pp. 49–50.

Mangkunegara. Not only did Winter have access to the royal families of Central Java, he was at home in their culture.

Another episode has to do with the *"persdelict* affair," touched off when a comment critical of the colonial government appeared in the *Bramartani*, the newspaper on which Ranggawarsita served as an editorial adviser. When the resident of Surakarta, Hendric Mac Gillavry, learned of this, he called in the editor, Jones Portier, and demanded an explanation. Portier told him that all the articles in Javanese were edited by Ranggawarsita, and that Ranggawarsita either had written or had intentionally included the article in question. It later became clear that the article had been written by someone else, Ki Purwowidjaja, and that Ranggawarsita had had nothing to do with its publication, but the incident led to his resignation. Winter is said to have compensated Ranggawarsita for the trouble caused him, while Gillavry presented him with a memento in recognition of his services.[98] It is not clear whether this was C. F. Winter, who died in 1859, or his son (or even Wilkens), but it is clear that the colonial government was suspicious of Ranggawarsita and that Winter had the role of conveying its views to the *pujangga*.

Winter's role in transmitting the government's wishes is even more obvious in an episode that seems to have taken place before 1835. One day Winter went to Ranggawarsita to convey the government's wish that he go to the Netherlands to teach Javanese. Ranggawarsita was poor at the time, and Winter found him in the yard behind his house planting a banana tree. Winter took in the situation at once, gave him the 150 *rupiah* he had with him, and conveyed the government's request that he go to the Netherlands to teach Javanese at a salary of 1,000 *rupiah* a month. Ranggawarsita turned down the offer on the grounds that he was already employed at the *kraton* and suggested that Poespawilaga (evidently his brother) go in his stead. As it turned out, Poespawilaga did go. (As we saw in the first part of this paper, he went with Palm to Delft, assisted Roorda, and contributed to the creation of type for Javanese script.) Andjar Any writes that Ranggawarsita's refusal of this request made the government even more wary of him.[99] But as this episode also shows, Ranggawarsita was offered the opportunity, through Winter, of participating directly in the mainstream of Javanology, which was linked to Roorda.

All three episodes portray contacts between Ranggawarsita and Dutch Javanologists in which the *pujangga* proudly maintained his honor. Actually, however, *pujangga* in the mid-nineteenth century were in a very difficult position.

I would like to examine this point with the help of Anthony Day's excellent dissertation on nineteenth-century Javanese literature.[100] Day points out that while Javanology in mid-nineteenth-century Java focused on ancient history and literature, the *kraton*'s own interest in ancient times, and consequently in Kawi, which had flourished in the time of Jasadipura (from the latter half of the eighteenth through the early nineteenth century), had waned considerably. As an illustration, Day quotes a passage from the reminiscences of a Javanese published in *Javaansch Zamenspraken* edited by Winter. The translation is Day's.

---

[98]Ibid., pp. 64–65.

[99]Ibid., pp. 65–67.

[100]Anthony Day, "Meanings of Change in the Poetry of Nineteenth-Century Java" (PhD dissertation, Cornell University, 1981).

It can be said that no one knows *kawi*, except those who are descendants of *pujangga*; ability (*kasagedan*) in kawi only descends to their own children and grandchildren. Among Javanese who are not descendants of *pujangga*, only a very few are willing to study *kawi*, because it can not be used for speaking. It is only used for texts meant for reading. The second reason, of course, is that kawi has no use (*faedah*) for earning a living. It is different with you Dutchmen who devote yourselves to expanding your skill (*pagunan*), knowledge (*kawruh*) and ability (*kasagedan*), because these lead to profit, fame and honor.[101]

The speaker's main point is that "Javanese who are not descendants of *pujangga*" are not interested in Kawi. But of greater interest is what the last sentence reveals, namely, that while Dutch Javanologists study Kawi because it brings them "profit, fame and honor," the study of Kawi brings the Javanese no monetary benefit whatsoever. This was as true of the *pujangga* as of any other Javanese.

What was happening was that Javanologists were taking the place of the *kraton* as patrons of the *pujangga*. It goes without saying that this brought about a basic change in the significance of the *pujangga*. Once masters of esoteric knowledge, they were now becoming Javanology informants. A dialogue in *Javaansch Zamenspraken* depicts the relationship between Javanologists and *pujangga* in concrete terms. The conversation, translated by Day, takes place between Tuwan Anu (Mr. X) and Raden Ngabehi Kawireja, apparently a *pujangga*.

Tuwan Anu:
    How many pages of my copy of the Old Javanese *Bratayuda* have you been able to gloss?
Raden Ngabehi Kawireja:
    I've done four pages already, which I've brought for you to inspect. Here they are. Is this what you wanted me to do?
Tuwan Anu:
    Yes, in fact. Here on top, I take it, is the prose gloss which explains the Old Javanese; below is the complete text (lit. "sounds") of the original?
Kawireja:
    Yes.[102]

Here we see the informant, Kawireja, preparing explanations of fragments of a Kawi text under orders from his patron, Tuwan Anu. The results of this joint research become the property of the research institute for which Tuwan Anu is acting, are published in the Dutch academic world, and become part of the legacy of Dutch Javanology. Ancient writings, carefully preserved in the *kraton* as sources of esoteric knowledge, are thus, through the mediation of Javanese informants, added, one by one, to the inventory of Javanology. The "museumization" of the *kraton*[103] may have brought "profit, fame and honor" to the Dutch Javanologist, but to the *pujangga*-informant it brought nothing but a bare living, if that. In fact, eventually Dutch Java-

---

[101]Ibid., p. 188.

[102]Ibid., p. 38.

[103]As Javanese intellectuals like to say, "The *kraton* has become a museum" (*Kraton menjadi musium*).

nologists began passing judgment on their Javanese informants' knowledge of Javanese literature and Kawi.

In short, this was a period when *pujangga* were being hired as informants, a period that ended with the *pujangga's* knowledge itself being scrutinized in the light of the scholarly tradition of Javanology. And Ranggawarsita lived in the midst of this harsh age. (The Kawireja in the above dialogue could have been Ranggawarsita himself.)

As early as 1860, while Ranggawarsita was still alive, Cohen Stuart pointed out that Ranggawarsita's knowledge and understanding of Kawi were incorrect.[104] At the end of the nineteenth century the Royal Batavian Society of Arts and Sciences established that his *Pustaka Radja* was not based on "original" Kawi accounts.[105] Assessment of Ranggawarsita from the viewpoint of Javanology continued into the twentieth century, producing Poerbatjaraka's caustic criticism. Finally, Javanology ceased to concern itself much with Ranggawarsita. (He was taken up again as a subject of research in Indonesian studies only in the latter half of the 1970s, a century after his death.)[106]

Thus it was that in the mid-nineteenth century Javanology, which was in a privileged position in every respect—research institutes, organization, funding, and market—turned the traditional intellectuals of the *kraton*, the *pujangga*, into mere informants. And as the gap between the world of the "righteous Javanese king and his court" depicted in ideal terms by the *pujangga* and that of the real king and his court grew ever wider, the tradition of the *pujangga* became the object of Javanologists' research on literature and ancient history and was thus subsumed into the world of contemporary Western thought. The *kraton* indeed became a museum, and the tradition of the *pujangga* died out.

CONCLUSION

In this paper I have first looked at the establishment and development of Javanology in both the Netherlands and the Netherlands East Indies in the nineteenth century; I have then presented an overview of the life of Ranggawarsita, a *pujangga* who lived at that time, and of his world. As its title indicates, my paper is no more than a preliminary study; all the points discussed herein call for further research. Nevertheless, the following conclusions can be drawn from my overview.

First, examination of the establishment and development of Javanology fails to reveal any indicator of a decisive division between the nineteenth and twentieth centuries. The tradition of Javanology was established in the mid-nineteenth century in the heart of the Dutch academic world (the University of Leiden being the classic example), and that tradition continued to develop even more vigorously in the twentieth century.[107] Unlike the case of Kartini, the *modérn* age of Javanology touched the Central Java *kraton* long before the twentieth century began.

---

[104]Day, "Meanings of Change," p. 187.

[105]Ibid.

[106]See notes 79 and 80.

[107]In 1976 the Royal Institute published a history of Indonesian studies to commemorate its one hundred twenty-fifth anniversary: *Honderd Jaar Studie van Indonesië, 1850–1950*. Nowhere in this volume, which pays tribute to the contributions to Javanology of van der Tuuk, Roorda, and others, do we find any periodization that distinguishes the nineteenth from the twentieth century.

Second, traditional Javanese learning (*ilmu kejawen*) and the tradition of the world of written Javanese (*jagad tulisan*) was totally and directly absorbed into the field of Javanology. The world of written Javanese, as the object of Javanology, thus transcended the limits of time and space to become part of the Dutch academic world, there to be analyzed, defined, and given form. Through this process Java's ancient history (restoration and reconstruction of inscriptions and ruins) and classical literature, which the Javanese themselves had already forgotten, were restored and put on display.

Third, the nature of the *pujangga* changed in the process. Javanese intellectuals in Ranggawarsita's time were hired as Javanology informants and in some cases, such as that of Poespawilaga, were even physically taken over by their Javanologist patrons and shipped off to the Netherlands. Such intellectuals lived a double life, as masters of esoteric knowledge on the one hand and as convenient informants on the other, the former function growing ever weaker as the latter grew stronger. The natural culmination of this process was that the Javanese themselves gradually began to participate in Javanology, publishing in the pages of journals like *Djawa*. Eminent Javanese scholars like Poerbatjaraka eventually emerged. And if they found the *Pustaka Radja* to be "nonsense," this too was the result of the development of Javanology. As one Indonesian wrote in the early 1930s, "In the pages of [the newspaper] *Aksi* a pure Indonesian scholar recently described the history [*babad*] portrayed by Ranggawarsita as 'flatus' [*entoet beroet*]. According to him, the only true history books are those written by scholars [*doctor-doctor*] devoted to learning."[108] In the light of Javanology, it was inevitable that Ranggawarsita should be judged harshly.

Fourth, as Andjar Any shows, Ranggawarsita and his world nevertheless continued to live on in the world of the Javanese language. We are speaking here not of the world of accurately kept written records, *jagad tulisan*, but of the world of spoken language, *jagad lisan*. This is the world that succeeded best in avoiding infiltration by the Dutch language and by Javanology. The main reasons for this are the Dutch style of indirect rule and the fact that the main interest of Javanology lay in the world of the written word and in ancient Java. In the world of the people (*rakyat*), Ranggawarsita was still a master of esoteric knowledge. Here he continued to be known first and foremost as a great prophet. After independence, the government of the Republic bestowed on him the title Pujangga Rakyat, "Poet of the People." The *pergerakan*, the movement for an independent Republic of Indonesia, regarded Ranggawarsita as a poet beloved of the people, a prophet who, within the *kraton* that the colonial power was rendering powerless, foretold the destruction of that colonial power and the coming of the golden age (*zaman mas*). The prophet lives on in the word *parandene* (nevertheless) in the *Serat Kala Tida*, transcending time and space.

Fifth, Ranggawarsita's double existence—as the Ranggawarsita of Javanology and the Ranggawarsita of the world of spoken Javanese—reflects the linguistic duality that became increasingly evident in Java from the mid-nineteenth century onward. This was, first, a process of written Javanese being infiltrated by written Dutch. Eventually, the act of a Javanese "writing" meant, ipso facto, writing in Dutch. Javanese participating in the tradition of Javanology, as well as the early-twentieth-century intellectuals and nationalists of whom Kartini was a forerunner, were the carriers of this method of linguistic expression. This gave rise to a dual-language situa-

---

[108]Gadjah Mada, "Didiklah kamu sendiri," *Pusara*, February 1932, p. 82. See also Tsuchiya, *Indoneshia minzokushugi kenkyū*, chap. 7, sec. 2 (*Democracy and Leadership*, chap. 5, sec. 3).

tion involving Javanese, the mother tongue, and Dutch. The addition of Malay as the Indonesian national language further complicated Java's linguistic situation. More generally, the division between Ranggawarsita's world of spoken Javanese and the Dutch world of Javanology that passed judgment on him indicates the split between the *lisan* tradition and the *tulisan* tradition in Java.

The phenomena outlined in the above five points define the cultural parameters of the rise and development of nationalism in twentieth-century Java. But since the purpose of this paper is to provide an overview of the tulisan world of nineteenth-century Java, discussion of the internal continuity between that world and Indonesian nationalism or of the cultural prescriptions that the dismantling and reconstitution of nineteenth-century Javanese culture exerted on nationalism belongs to another paper.

This paper was originally published under the title "19 seiki Jawa bunkaron josetsu: Jawagaku to Rongowarushito no jidai" [Introduction to nineteenth-century Javanese culture: Javanology and the age of Ranggawarsita] in *Tōnan Ajia no seiji to bunka* [Culture and politics in Southeast Asia], edited by Kenji Tsuchiya and Takashi Shiraishi (Tokyo: University of Tokyo Press, 1984), pp. 71–172.

The spelling of Indonesian and Javanese words in the English version of this paper follows the new orthography (*ejaan baru*), which has been in use since 1970. However, the spelling of personal names and titles and of the titles of written works follows that used in the sources in which they appear, which is basically the old orthography (*ejaan lama*), which was in use until 1970.

Finally, I would like to thank the following colleagues, who in different ways helped me in the writing of the paper: Benedict Anderson, James Siegel, Amrih Widodo, Sidney Jones, Roger Downey, Takashi Shiraishi, Saya Shiraishi, and Noriaki Oshikawa. Naturally, none of these friendly critics should be held in any way accountable for the text's deficiencies, which are wholly my responsibility.

5

POPULAR CATHOLICISM IN THE NINETEENTH-CENTURY PHILIPPINES: THE CASE OF THE COFRADÍA DE SAN JOSÉ

Setsuho Ikehata

INTRODUCTION: EVANGELIZATION AND BROTHERHOOD

Roman Catholic missionary efforts in the Philippines began when the islands came under Spanish control in the latter part of the sixteenth century. In the approximately 330 years of colonial rule under the Spanish union of church and state, Catholicism became the dominant religion of the Philippines. There was a considerable spread, however, in the time at which Catholicism was introduced to and established in different regions. In the lowlands of Luzon, where Catholicism penetrated most deeply, missionary work began in the 1570s, and the faith was fairly well established by 1630–1640. Jesuit priests began systematic proselytization in the lowland areas of the Visayas around 1600, though substantial conversion of the inhabitants apparently began in the 1650s. On the other hand, full-scale evangelization in the mountainous areas of northern Luzon did not begin until the eighteenth century. The people were converted, at least nominally, by the end of the century, but subsequent shortages of clergy, together with the Philippine Revolution, led to the neglect or discontinuation of pastoral care, and in the end Catholicism failed to take firm root. Almost no missionary efforts reached the mountainous areas of the Visayas throughout the period of Spanish rule. On Mindanao, Jesuit missionaries began working in the northern coastal region in the seventeenth century. After the expulsion of the Society of Jesus in 1768, however, the region was largely neglected by the Church.[1]

Catholicism not only reached various parts of the Philippines at different times but also incorporated elements of animism, that is, belief in spirits called *anito*, and other elements of indigenous culture. Philippine Catholicism thus developed unique traits. In terms of doctrine, liturgy, organization, and religious paraphernalia, it differed significantly not only from the orthodox Catholicism prescribed by the Vatican but also from the Catholicism of evangelist Spain and of the Spanish colonies in Latin America (particularly Mexico), from which it had been transmitted to the Philippines.

According to John N. Schumacher, SJ, a distinctively Philippine Catholicism emerged in the initial stages of the evangelization process, and its individuality continued to develop throughout the subsequent historical process. The "Philippiniza-

---

[1]John N. Schumacher, SJ, "Syncretism in Philippine Catholicism: Its Historical Causes," *Philippine Studies* 32 (1984): 261–69.

tion" of Catholicism was particularly pronounced in the years from 1770 to 1830. Early in this period, Spain implemented the principle of monarchical authority over the Church, advocated by Charles III (r. 1759–1788), in the Philippines as well. Under that policy the Jesuits were expelled from the Philippines,[2] the friar orders were subjected to royal and episcopal control, and indigenous priests were hurriedly trained and ordained. As a result, the cure of souls in many parishes (*paroquia*) passed from the Spanish regular clergy to hastily trained indigenous secular (*clero*) priests. Some parishes in remote areas were left without priests.

Spain was caught up in a succession of wars involving its European neighbors, through the French Revolution and the Napoleonic Wars and into the 1830s. Within Spain there was continuing conflict between liberals and the religious orders. The effect on the Philippines was a reduction in the number of Spanish regular priests and a decline in the power of the religious orders. Meanwhile, indigenous secular priests were being trained and ordained so rapidly that they lacked an adequate grasp of Catholic doctrine and liturgy. In Schumacher's view, these circumstances facilitated the blending of Catholicism with indigenous beliefs.[3]

What actually was this Philippine Catholicism, the Catholicism that had been formed through this historical process and was believed in and practiced by the Philippine people? Few studies have dealt with this question. For the period of Spanish rule, I know of only one work that comes squarely to grips with the subject, *Religious Life of the Laity in Eighteenth Century Philippines: As Reflected in the Decrees of the Council of Manila of 1771 and the Synod of Calasiao of 1773* by M. Caridad Barrion, OSB.[4] Her analysis, however, is based on decrees of the Council of Manila of 1771[5] and written resolutions of the Synod of Calasiao of 1773,[6] as the book's subtitle indicates. Thus, her description is limited to the religious life of the laity as observed by Spanish priests; developments beyond their purview are ignored. Documents written by the people involved would be the ideal sources for presenting a true image of popular Philippine Catholicism, particularly the details of beliefs and practices, but in the Philippines, with its long history of colonial rule, there is little prospect of locating such records. The paucity of such sources inevitably limits the scope of Barrion's work.

Collection of data on popular Catholicism in the colonial Philippines is difficult as a rule. The subject of this paper, the Cofradía de San José, is an exception. The Cofradía was organized in the 1830s in the southern Tagalog region of Luzon. Persecution by the Spanish authorities drove the members to mount a futile uprising, and

---

[2]As a result, the post of parish priest was left vacant in 130 *pueblos* (towns) in the Visayas and on the north coast of Mindanao.

[3]Schumacher, "Syncretism," pp. 257–61.

[4]M. Caridad Barrion, OSB, *Religious Life of the Laity in Eighteenth Century Philippines: As Reflected in the Decrees of the Council of Manila of 1771 and the Synod of Calasiao of 1773* (Manila: University of Santo Tomas Press, 1961). See also John N. Schumacher, SJ, *Readings in Philippine Church History* (Quezon City: Ateneo de Manila University Press, 1979); John Leddy Phelan, *The Hispanization of the Philippines: Spanish Aims and Filipino Responses, 1565–1700* (Madison: University of Wisconsin Press, 1959), pp. 31–89.

[5]The Council of Manila was convened by the archbishop of Manila, Basilio Sancho de Santa Justa y Rufina, from May to November 1771.

[6]The Synod of Calasiao was convened by the bishop of Nueva Segovia to enforce the decrees of the Council of Manila. It was held in Calasiao, Pangasinan Province, during the week of Pentecost in 1773. Eleven friars from the Nueva Segovia diocese attended.

the Cofradía was destroyed after less than ten years of life. Its unfortunate fate, however, led to the seizure of records of the Cofradía's activities by the authorities. These are preserved in the Philippine National Archives in Manila as the Apolinario de la Cruz Papers, hereafter referred to as the AC Papers.[7] (Since these documents are also important sources for the historical study of Tagalog, twenty-two of the AC Papers that were most important in writing this paper are included in Appendix II.) At the time that I wrote my first paper on the Cofradía de San José,[8] I could not fully decipher these Tagalog documents, which I had received on microfilm. Fieldwork conducted in 1982 and 1983, however, gave me an opportunity to study the originals and decipher most of them. That research brought to light much new information about the Cofradía and enabled me to take a different approach in this paper, in which I will attempt to describe the activities of the Cofradía as a means of clarifying the nature of popular Catholicism in the Philippines in the first half of the nineteenth century.[9]

The term *cofradía* originally referred to an association of lay Catholics, with piety and charity as its main objectives. Basically, the members' aims were to deepen their faith and practice Catholic brotherhood. The five religious orders engaged in early missionary work in the Philippines[10] promoted the establishment of *cofradías* as organizations to deepen Catholic converts' sense of identity and solidarity as Catholics.[11] In that sense, *cofradías* were the organizational basis for the steady development, in terms of both doctrine and organization, of Philippine Catholicism.

Cofradías organized during the period of Spanish rule can be classified into three types. Some were organized and spread by religious orders. Examples of this type include the Congregation of the Most Holy Virgin of the Annunciation (Congregación de la Santísima Virgen, also known as La Anunciata), organized in 1600 by the Jesuits of the Seminary of Saint Joseph (better known as San Jose Seminary [Seminario de San José]) in Manila; the Confraternity of the most Holy name of Jesus (Cofradía de Santísimo Nombre de Jesús), organized by the Augustinians early in the seventeenth century; and the Venerable Third Order of Saint Francis (Venerable Orden Tercera de San Francisco), organized by the Franciscans in 1729.

A second type of *cofradía* was organized by cathedrals or parish churches. Examples include the Confraternity of the Most Holy Sacrament (Cofradía de Santísimo Sacramento), organized by Manila Cathedral early in the seventeenth century,

---

[7]These papers include letters by members of the Cofradía, listed in Appendix I; a memorandum by Octabio Ygnacio San Jorge; a 610-quatrain poem relating the history of the Cofradía; a membership list; receipts; affidavits by members recorded by Spanish officials; reports by Spanish authorities, including Father Manuel Sancho, the Lukban parish priest; and other documents.

[8]Setsuho Ikehata, "San-Hose shintodan no hanran: 19 seiki Firipin ni okeru komunitasu undō" [The uprising of the Cofradía de San José: A *communitas* movement in the nineteenth-century Philippines], in *Chūsei Suzuki*, ed., *Sennen ōkoku teki minshū undō no kenkyū: Chūgoku, Tonan Ajia ni okeru* [Studies of popular millennial movements in China and Southeast Asia] (Tokyo: Tokyo Daigaku Shuppankai, 1982), pp. 441–90.

[9]I would like to express my gratitude to the Japan Foundation for sponsoring my fieldwork under its Scholars Abroad Program. As a result of that research, in the present paper I have amended some of the information in my 1982 paper on the Cofradía de San José (see note 8).

[10]The five religious orders engaged in missionary work in the Philippines were the Augustinians, Discalced Augustinians, Dominicans, Franciscans, and Jesuits.

[11]Phelan, *The Hispanization of the Philippines*, p. 74.

and the Venerable Congregation of Saint Peter, Principal of the Apostles (Venerable Congregación de San Pedro, Principe de los Apostoles), organized by the same cathedral in 1698.

A third category of *cofradías* included those formed on the initiative of laymen, subsequently receiving spiritual guidance from churches or religious orders.[12] The best-known example is the Brotherhood of Mercy (Hermandad de la Misericordia). This *cofradía*, organized in 1594 by Spanish laymen in Manila, was modeled on a *cofradía* of the same name established at the end of the fifteenth century in Lisbon. Consequently, the Manila government and archdiocesan authorities supported the Hermandad de la Misericordia, which engaged in a vigorous program of economic and charitable activities.[13]

In the Philippines, many parishes, the basic units in the organization of the Church, were equivalent territorially to *pueblos* (towns) in the government's administrative organization.[14] A parish usually included more than one branch of these *cofradías* as well as a *cofradía* organized in that parish. The approval of both the governor general, as the representative of the king of Spain, and the diocese was required to organize a *cofradía*. According to Barrion, however, only a very few of the large number of *cofradías* that existed in the latter half of the eighteenth century had received official approval.[15] Unauthorized *cofradía* activities probably became widespread because Church discipline had relaxed considerably by that time.

The Cofradía de San José, the subject of this paper, was an unauthorized *cofradía* organized by lay believers. However, there is an obstacle to regarding it as just another unauthorized *cofradía*: it was deliberately founded as a secret society. Why did the Cofradía de San José conceal its existence from the authorities from the time of its formation? That is the question with which I would like to begin exploring the Cofradía's activities over the approximately ten years of its existence.

I. The Secret Early Years of the Cofradía de San José

Although several papers on the Cofradía de San José have been published, the only full-scale study based on surviving Cofradía manuscripts is that by Reynaldo Clemeña Ileto.[16] Even Ileto, however, treats only the history of the Cofradía after 1840, when it made its activities public; the history of its early period has remained unknown.

This obscurity was intentional, as a letter dated August 3, 1840, demonstrates. This letter was sent by the head of the Cofradía, Apolinario de la Cruz (referred to

---

[12]René B. Javellana, SJ, of Ateneo de Manila University suggested this threefold classification, but I gathered and organized the data.

[13]For *cofradías* in Manila in the first half of the seventeenth century, see Emma Helen Blair and James Alexander Robertson, eds., *The Philippine Islands, 1493–1898*, 55 vols. (Cleveland: Clark, 1909), 20: 240–42. For *cofradías* throughout the Philippines in the latter half of the eighteenth century, see Barrion, *Religious Life of the Laity*, pp. 81–87. For *cofradías* throughout the Philippines in the first half of the nineteenth century, see Manuel Buzeta and Filipe Bravo, *Diccionario Geográfico, Estadístico, Histórico de las Islas Filipinas*, 2 vols. (Madrid: Imprenta de D. José C. de la Peña, 1850), 1: 166–68. Note that the information in the last two sources is incomplete.

[14]Some parishes in thinly populated districts included two or three *pueblos*.

[15]Barrion, *Religious Life of the Laity*, p. 82.

[16]Reynaldo Clemeña Ileto, *Pasyon and Revolution: Popular Movements in the Philippines, 1840–1910* (Quezon City: Ateneo de Manila University Press, 1979), pp. 37–91.

hereafter as Apolinario) to his aide and the second highest-ranking leader of the Cofradía, Octabio Ygnacio San Jorge (Octabio). It reads in part: ". . . and the letters that you keep there from 1832 to 1839 should be disposed of together with all our other documents." (. . . at saca ang m̃ga sulat mong nangaririyan at yniyngatan na may mañga fecha ñg tauong 1832 años hangan 1839 a.ˢ ay iiong pag aalisin na sa casama ñg ating m̃ga papeles.)[17] The letter is dated shortly after the Spanish authorities began investigating the Cofradía; 1832 is the year in which it was founded. Apolinario's letter indicates that at that point he, as the head of the Cofradía, feared that knowledge of its activities in the period from its establishment through 1839 might be revealed to nonmembers, and particularly to the Spanish authorities. Thus he ordered Octabio to destroy letters and other records of its history (Cofradía members, using the Spanish term, called these documents *apunte*). In fact, there are only two Cofradía de San José documents dating from before 1840 in the AC Papers.[18] This evidence that the Cofradía deliberately concealed its history makes that history even more intriguing.

Fortunately, a valuable historical document that does reveal the Cofradía's secret history has been preserved in the Philippine National Archives. It is a poem of 610 quatrains entitled *History of the Confraternity, which Brother Apolinario de la Cruz founded in the town of Lucban, written and put into verse by me to better excite the hearts and souls of all the brothers in the mentioned confraternity deducated to our father Saint Joseph* (*Historia de la Cofradía que fundó el Hermano Apolinario de la Cruz en el pueblo de Lucban, trabajada y puesta en verso por mí para poder mejor estimular los corazones y ánimos de todos sus hermanos a la insinuada Cofradía, dedicado a nuestro padre San José*), referred to as the Poem hereafter. This work is, I believe, a verse rendering of events that Apolinario narrated to some Cofradía members around June 1841.[19] However, the version of the Poem preserved in the Philippine National Archives is not the Tagalog original but a copy of the translation into Spanish made by the Spanish authorities.

The Poem is Apolinario's appeal to Cofradía members to maintain unwavering faith despite the authorities' persecution of the organization. The Poem describes the Cofradía's history of hardship and suffering and affirms the group's orthodoxy. The Poem, of course, presents the history of the Cofradía from Apolinario's point of view, and we must check it against secondary sources to extract the facts from it. Nonetheless, in attempting to understand Apolinario's inner world, we must accept his worldview as it is, however hard it may be to understand from our perspective. (The same is true in studying Apolinario's letters.) The Poem is not a sophisticated verse; Apolinario, as the narrator (or author), was inconsistent in his choice of voice, for instance, switching between the first and the third person. But let us let him speak.

The Poem compares the organization that was the starting point for the Cofradía to a *talang* (or *mabolo*) tree, describing the group's origin as follows:

> In the year eighteen hundred
> thirty-two, counted
> by the date
> current in the whole world

---

[17] Appendix II-E-5.

[18] Appendix II-A, II-E-1.

[19] This estimate is based on the time of the last events described in the Poem.

Through an admirable divine Prodigy,
incomprehensible to me,
at the entrance to the territory
where the town of Lucban is located

A marvelous tree grew,
beautiful to the sight from top to bottom;
but without any leaf or flower,
and as they say, with only short branches

It was cared for by someone from Abang,
a careful youth who tried to guard secretly,
the tree that I have mentioned,
Listen attentively to me.

En el año de mil ochocientos
treinta y dos, contados
por la fecha
que siga en todo el mundo,

Por un admirable Prodigio divino,
incompresible para mí,
en la entrada del territorio
donde está el pueblo de Lucban

Nació un árbol maravilloso,
hermoso a la vista desde arriba hasta abajo;
pero sin ninguna hoja ni flor,
y según dicen con cortas ramas.

Estaba al cuidado de uno de Abang,
jovan cuidadoso que procuró guardar secreto,
el árbol que Ilevo dicho,
escuchadme con atención. [8–11][20]

This section of the Poem tells us that the Cofradía de San José originated as an association established in Lukban, Tayabas Province (now Quezon Province), in 1832. Apolinario de la Cruz, a young man of the village of Abang, led the association, and people gradually began to gather around the *talang* tree. At Christmas that year, people began calling Apolinario the father of the association. They planned a *festejo* to be held a year after the association was founded. The *festejo* included a novena (*novenario*) dedicated to Saint Francis. After the *festejo* they made an offering to the church, attended mass, and then founded a *pobre Cofradía*.[21]

---

[20]The bracketed figures are the quatrain numbers I have assigned.

[21]Poem, quatrains 42–43.

The Poem thus supports a date of 1833 for the formal establishment of the Cofradía.[22] Every *cofradía* had a patron saint to intercede for its members, who had an interest in the temporal benefits to be received from the patron saint. Since the ceremony establishing the Cofradía was held after a novena dedicated to Saint Francis, its initial patron saint was presumably Saint Francis, not Saint Joseph.[23] The evidence that the Cofradía de San José changed its patron saint is also a sign of its origin as a grass-roots, indigenous organization rather than one established under the auspices of a church or religious order. It is thought that the founders of the Cofradía initially chose Saint Francis as their patron saint because the southern Tagalog region, in which Tayabas was located, had been under the jurisdiction of the Franciscans since the sixteenth century and thus the local people held Saint Francis in great veneration.

In February 1834, probably during Lent, Apolinario suggested that members of the Cofradía make a journey to a distant mountain. As the following section of the Poem indicates, the trip was a devotional pilgrimage.

Like an Army this Assembly marched,
equipped with everything necessary
and prepared to suffer every burden,
to battle an enchanted land.

Without rest by day or night, this Army
marched to combat the said land,
their arms and shields being
the extraordinarily big Rosaries worn around their necks.

They carried a candle as guide, and a flag
that was the public banner of all their victories
and their swords were their knees poised for adoration,
by which they sensed evil deeds.

Semejante a un Ejército marchó esta Junta,
provista de todo lo necesario
y dispuesta a padecer los trabajos que sufrió,
para ir a pelear a una tierra encantada.

Sin descansar este Ejército ni de día ni de noche,
marchaban a combatir la expresada tierra,
siendo sus armas y broqueles
los Rosarios que llevaban al cuello de extraordinaria grandeza.

Llevaban una candela por guía, y una bandera
que era estandarte público de todas sus victorias

---

[22]The Poem mentions only the year 1832, when the Cofradía was founded. The other years reflect my inferences.

[23]That the guardian saint of the Cofradía was initially Saint Francis is also suggested by the document in Appendix II-A.

y sus espadas eran sus rodillas preparadas para la adoración,
por cuyo medio conocían a las obras malas. [71–73]

The pilgrims' destination, the enchanted mountain, appears from geographical indications to have been Mount Banahaw. Thus, it is presumed that the Cofradía pilgrimage was an early version of the Mount Banahaw pilgrimage, still widely practiced in Lent. After the pilgrimage the Cofradía organized its *principales* into a board,[24] which immediately resolved that "every member should read the *pasión* left us by God" (no hay nadie que no esté leyendo / la pasión que Dios Padre nos dejó a nosotros).[25] Thus the Cofradía de San José stressed the recitation of the *pasyon* even during its early years.

The following year, 1835, the Cofradía celebrated Lent with great devotion. Immediately after Octaves, however, an event occurred that rocked the young organization. Apolinario decided to part from the members and work as a lay brother (*donado*) in the San Juan de Dios Convent Hospital in Manila. As the name indicates, a famous convent was attached to this hospital, which the Franciscan Order administered for the Spanish. Apolinario decided to serve as a *donado* there to "awaken the members from their lethargy."[26] Apparently his goal was to cultivate his ability to demonstrate forceful leadership as the spiritual leader of the Cofradía.

The ideal way to become an outstanding religious leader was not to work as a *donado* in a convent hospital but to become a friar, but religious orders were closed to indigenous people until Spanish rule came to an end.[27] The Poem states again and again that upon donning the black habit (*hábito negro*) of a *donado* in the convent hospital, Apolinario abandoned worldly pleasures and vanities to devote himself to the salvation of his soul. Apolinario accumulated considerable knowledge of Catholic doctrine and liturgy in his roughly six years of service at San Juan de Dios, which ended with his expulsion in March 1841.

Apolinario's participation in the ceremony in honor of Saint Joseph (*una función en honor de San José*) held on the nineteenth of each month at the convent hospital exerted an especially great influence on the later activities of the Cofradía. A high Spanish official, Sinibaldo de Mas y Sans, who was hospitalized at San Juan de Dios in 1841, mentions in his account of the Philippines that the friars of the convent hospital sent out a *donado* the day before the ceremony to collect alms for it. Mas y Sans states that the ceremony for Saint Joseph gave Apolinario the idea of organizing the Cofradía de San José in Lukban.[28] We know that the Cofradía de San José was founded before Apolinario went to the convent hospital. It is reasonable to assume, however, that his participation in the ceremony for Saint Joseph underlay the change

---

[24]Poem, quatrain 77.

[25]Ibid., quatrain 78.

[26]Ibid., quatrain 138.

[27]The prevailing view among Philippine historians has been that the Cofradía de San José was established and rose in revolt because Apolinario was denied entrance to a religious order owing to racial discrimination. See, for example, Teodoro A. Agoncillo and Milagros Guerrero, *History of the Filipino People* (Quezon City: Garcia, 1970), p. 123; Renato Constantino, *The Philippines: A Past Revisited* (Quezon City: Tala Publishing Services, 1975), pp. 135–36. But that view is erroneous, as this paper makes clear.

[28]Sinibaldo de Mas y Sans, *Informe sobre el Estado de las Islas Filipinas en 1842*, 2 vols. (Madrid: n.p., 1843), vol. 1; "Historia de la Dominación Española en las Islas Filipinas, desde Su Descubrimiento, hasta Nuestros Días: Parte Segunda," p. 81.

of the Cofradía's patron saint from Saint Francis to Saint Joseph and the inauguration of new activities, such as collecting alms and gathering new members.

After Apolinario left for Manila, the Cofradía members in Lukban were attacked by uneasiness, a sense that they had lost their spiritual mainstay. The board of *principales* therefore selected a successor to Apolinario in May 1836. As a symbol of his status, the *principales* conferred the title of *voto de confianza* on him.[29] The Poem refers to him only as a person from Ygan (a village located on the outskirts of Lukban), but another document supports the conclusion that he was Octabio Ygnacio San Jorge. In this document, written jointly by Apolinario and Octabio on February 6, 1837, Apolinario stated that he had entrusted Octabio temporarily with the leadership of the Cofradía and requested the elders to follow Octabio with respect.[30]

Thus, Octabio became the acting leader of the Cofradía early in 1837, while Apolinario, in Manila, sent the group instructions by letter. However, the two-tier leadership structure thus established was marred by occasional disturbances in the two men's relationship. A letter from Apolinario to Octabio dated November 9, 1838, reveals a serious rift between them. Octabio, ignoring Apolinario's advice, had held an open meeting in Lukban and had been cautioned by the authorities. That put Apolinario in an awkward position at the San Juan de Dios Convent Hospital. The two leaders were at odds over a woman, Catalina de San José, who was helping Apolinario in Manila. Apart from indicating that the Cofradía's activities were secret at the time, what is interesting about this incident is that Apolinario's mother, called head mother (*punong ina*) among the members, settled the quarrel. She presented three conditions to the two men: to decide not to expand the Cofradía further, to hold no further meetings, and to have Apolinario and Octabio part ways. The *punong ina* must have had great authority within the Cofradía, because Apolinario told Octabio in the letter, brooking no opposition, "keep still, listen, and understand the reasons for the orders coming from our head Mother" (*manayiñga cayo at enyong dengen at talastacen ninyo ang mañga cadahelanan ñg caotosang nanggaleng sa ating punong Yna*).

The following year in 1839, Apolinario returned home for the first time in four years, perhaps to mend his relationship with Octabio. The Cofradía members were delighted to have their spiritual father among them again, but Apolinario seems to have been deeply disappointed in the Cofradía's activities. He returned to Manila, worried about how to develop the Cofradía, and prayed constantly to God and the Virgin Mary.[31] Then one night the Virgin spoke to him:

> The thoughts that tormented his pensive heart
> turned to joy in the depth of the night,

---

[29] Poem, quatrains 222–25.

[30] This document, reproduced in Appendix II-A, states that Octabio was entrusted with leadership of the Cofradía in 1837, but the Poem has him selected as Apolinario's successor in May 1836. The discrepancy can be accounted for by assuming that he was selected in May 1836 and that his position was confirmed in the 1837 document.

[31] The Cofradía was devoted to the Blessed Virgin of the Rosary as well as Saint Joseph. In his affidavit, Apolinario gave the full name of the Cofradía as La Cofradía titulada del Señor San José y Voto del Santísimo Rosario and said that its only aim was to celebrate Saint Joseph and the Blessed Virgin of the Rosary. See Apolinario de la Cruz, "Declaración de Apolinario de la Cruz," *La Política de España en Filipinas* 2, no. 32 (1892): 113.

when he heard the voice of the merciful Mother
who understood and promised to make the confraternity flourish.

Las ideas que atormentaban su pensativo corazón
se trocaron en gozo en lo profundo de una noche
oyó la voz de la Madre misericordia
que compadecida, prometió hacer florecer la Cofradía. [263]

Mary seems to have given Apolinario specific instruction on ways to develop the Cofradía, as discussed below. In great delight, he immediately related Mary's words to Octabio, who announced them to all the members and obtained their agreement. This event stimulated the Cofradía to begin an ambitious expansion movement.

A detailed description of the activities undertaken to expand the Cofradía is found in quatrains 279–337 of the Poem, which describe the expansion movement using the verbs *marchar* and *caminar*. Apolinario's most trusted *principales* were involved in trying to enlarge the group. They usually went out in pairs; at first pairs visited houses in Lukban, and then extended their visits to more distant *pueblos*. The Poem describes the people as laying out carpets to welcome these proselytizers as if to welcome their guests. When they reached a *pueblo*, their first step was to find the *patron* and present him with a candle from Apolinario, in what appears to have been a symbolic statement of the arrival of the light of the Cofradía. When the pairs of *principales* had collected a certain number of new members and completed their duties, they returned to Octabio and drew up documents that they then took to Apolinario in Manila.

The southern Tagalog region in the nineteenth century

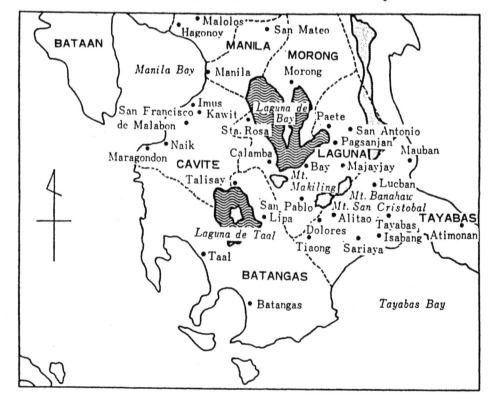

The visit to Manila included participation in a ritual. Upon arrival, the *principales* were ordered to confess and purify their souls. Then at dawn they were to eat the fruit of that eucharistic tree (*gustaron la fruta de aquel árbol eucaristico*).[32] Next Apolinario garbed each of them in a *camisa* (shirt). The *camisa* was the emblem of the title of our Mother, *el titulo de nuestra Madre*, bestowed upon those who had performed virtuous deeds. Its formal title was Servitude of the Blessed Virgin, *Esclavitud ñg mahal na Virgen*. When Apolinario heard the Virgin Mary speak to him in the stillness of the night, she promised that she would grant that title to those who performed virtuous deeds. *El titulo de nuestra Madre* spurred members to embark on proselytizing journeys and was thus a useful tool in promoting the expansion of the Cofradía. As the Virgin Mary had promised Apolinario, the Cofradía was flourishing by February 1840.

Well, having already arrived the month of February,
his greatest marvelous pleasure was
what happened to this Cofradía that we are following,
well, it sprouted very beautiful flowers.

This being extremely prodigious,
showing signs of considerable expansion even to very distant lands,
according to our eldest brother,
although it is not evident now, is like a cluster of flowers that is crushed in
    prison.

Habiendo ya, pues, llegado el mes de febrero,
fue también su sumo grado maravilloso
lo que sucedí a esta Cofradía que seguimos,
pues echó hermosisimas flores.

Siendo esto sumamente prodigioso,
dando muestras de estenderse bastante y hasta a tierras muy lejanas,
y según dice nuestro hermano mayor,
aunque ahora no está manifiesto, es un Ramillete de flores que está oprimido en una
    cárcel. [391–92]

The Cofradía spread in the three southern Tagalog provinces of Tayabas, Laguna, and Batangas. Specifically, it had members in the *pueblos* of Lukban, Tayabas, Pagbilao, Sariaya, and Tiaon in Tayabas Province, in the *pueblos* of Majayjay, Nagcarlan, Lilio, Magdalena, and San Pablo in Laguna Province, and in the *pueblo* of Lipa in Batangas Province. The membership grew to between forty-five hundred and five thousand.[33]

On April 1, 1840, the Cofradía presented a petition to the Lukban church, stating that Apolinario and his fellows wished a mass to be said for their *cofradía* on the nineteenth of each month[34] and requesting formal licence of the Cofradía. The name of the group was mentioned nowhere in the petition, which simply referred to Our

[32]Poem, quatrain 300.
[33]Cruz, "Declaración," *La Política* 2, no. 32 (1892): 114.
[34]Appendix II-B.

Confraternity, *Nuestra Cofradía*. It seems that a formal name, which appears in later sources, had already been agreed upon for the group: La Cofradía de Señor San José y Voto del Santísimo Rosario.[35] Apolinario and Octabio, however, continued to refer to it as the Cofradía de San José in their letters, omitting "y Voto del Santísimo Rosario." In their petition, Apolinario and his fellows stated that they realized that their petition for formal licence concerned a matter that fell under the jurisdiction of the diocese of Nueva Cáceres, but that since Nueva Cáceres was so far away they hoped that the parish priest would grant licence.[36] Clearly they were well aware of the formal requirements for establishing a *cofradía*. We must conclude that since the founders of the Cofradía had been carrying out activities in secret even though they knew that official permission was necessary, this concealment was deliberate.

The Lukban church refused to sanction the Cofradía but did agree to have a mass celebrated on the nineteenth of each month, for which it requested an offering.[37] Consequently, the Cofradía, still lacking formal licence, embarked upon more-public activities with the Thanksgiving Mass (*Misa de Gracia*) on the nineteenth of each month. That a parish church took part in the activities of a *cofradía* that lacked official recognition may appear strange, but as Barrion points out, this was not particularly unusual under Spanish rule.[38] The Cofradía de San José was singular, however, in that it kept its existence secret from the parish church until 1840.

II. ACTIVITIES OF THE MEMBERS

Below we will explore what membership in the Cofradía de San José entailed. All members were required to fulfill three duties: to recite the *Pater Noster*, *Ave Maria*, and *Gloria Patri* seven times a day; to pay monthly dues to the Cofradía; and to attend the *Misa de Gracia* celebrated on the nineteenth of each month.[39]

The daily duty of reciting three prayers seven times each suggests that prayer was the lifeblood of the Cofradía. That this was indeed so is made clear by an incident that occurred at the end of October 1841, after the arrest of five hundred people involved in the Cofradía uprising. Spanish officials interrogating those who had been spared execution asked, "What was your purpose?" "To pray" was the reply.[40] As the oath taken upon joining the Cofradía indicates,[41] the three prayers were an expression of the members' reverence for and obedience to Jesus, Mary, and Joseph. Almost all *cofradías* required the daily offering of certain prayers or hymns, repeated a specified number of times. The original goal of this daily course of prayer was to deepen members' piety through prayer. At the same time, the prayers were often associated with indulgences. In officially recognized *cofradías* founded by churches or religious orders, it was usual for members to receive indulgences and benefits from

[35]Cruz, "Declaración," *La Política* 2, no. 32 (1892): 113.

[36]At the time, the Philippines had one archdiocese and three dioceses. The Tayabas region was under the jurisdiction of the diocese of Nueva Caceres in the *pueblo* of Naga, Camarines Sur Province.

[37]Octabio made a memorandum of the church's reply, but his nonstandard orthography and awkward style make it difficult to decipher.

[38]Barrion, *Religious Life of the Laity*, p. 82.

[39]Cruz, "Declaración," *La Política* 2, no. 32 (1892): 114.

[40]Mas y Sans, *Informe sobre*, vol. 1; "Historia de la Dominación," p. 87.

[41]Appendix II-C.

the pope. For example, one could earn indulgences by performing perfectly the daily obligation of prayer.[42] The Cofradía de San José was not officially recognized, and therefore its members did not formally receive such benefits. It is possible, however, that the members believed that by reciting three prayers seven times a day they would be granted a set period of indulgence.

The second duty of membership, paying dues, was performed on the nineteenth of each month. For this reason the members called their dues by the Spanish word for nineteen, *dies y nueve*, or by a corruption of that term, *dizenuebe*. The *dizenuebe* was one *real* a month, or twelve *reales* a year, a considerable sum for humble people. Precise comparative data are lacking, but some comparisons can be made to suggest what a burden these contributions must have been. For instance, in the first half of the nineteenth century the annual tax on an adult was fifteen and a half *reales*,[43] and the cost of enough rice to support an adult for a year was about thirty-six *reales*.[44]

The Cofradía dues payment list, which is included in the AC Papers, shows that many members' dues were in arrears, an indication of how difficult payment must have been. Nonetheless, despite the financial burden it entailed, people freely chose to join the Cofradía. Clearly, it must have offered something very appealing. The Spanish authorities began investigating the Cofradía de San José because they found its collecting such large amounts of money suspicious. It should be understood, however, that while the dues were a considerable financial burden on the members of the Cofradía, they were not especially high in comparison with the dues of other *cofradías*. Planning to eradicate the Cofradía de San José, the authorities began to organize the Cofradía ni San Francisco Xavier in the *pueblos* of Lukban, Tayabas, and Majayjay around July 1841. This *cofradía* collected dues of two *cuartas* a week.[45] That amounted to a little less than half the Cofradía de San José dues. However, the sponsors of the Cofradía ni San Francisco Xavier, including the parish priests, collected a variety of alms, and almsgiving was all but mandatory. There were standard amounts for alms: one *peso* for an ordinary person (*maguinoo*) and four *pesos* for a wealthy person.[46] Thus, membership in this *cofradía* actually imposed a considerably greater financial burden than did membership in the Cofradía de San José.

---

[42]For example, the regulations of the Pía-Unión de San Antonio de Padua, founded in the late nineteenth century, required members to say the *Gloria Patri* three times a day. Performance of this duty enabled members to receive a partial indulgence of one hundred days for each day they recited the prayer. See *Estatuos de la Pía-Unión de S. Antonio de Padua y Rezo para Todo los Martes* (Manila: Tipo-Lit. de Chofré y Comp.ª, 1895), p. 11.

[43]The fifteen and a half *reales* total breaks down into a poll tax (*tributo*) of ten *reales*, a one *real* tithe (*diezmo predial*), a *pueblo* emergency fund tax (*caja de comunidad*) of one *real*, three *reales* to support the parish priest and church (*sanctorum*), and a special tax of half a *real* for the war against the Moros (*donativo de Zamboanga*).

[44]According to an unpublished report of a survey of the state of agriculture, commerce, and industry in Tayabas Province, prepared in 1823 by Father Bartolomé Galán, the parish priest of the *pueblo* of Tayabas, at the request of the Junta Económica de Industría de Manila, an adult in Tayabas Province consumed the equivalent of about six *kaban* of unhulled rice a year. The contemporary price of unhulled rice was normally six *reales* a *kaban*. Thus, a year's supply of rice for one adult would cost thirty-six *reales*. See Fray Bartolomé Galán, "Informe sobre la Provincia de Tayabas," MS dated April 8, 1823, Ayer Collection, Newberry Library, Chicago, Box 1350.

[45]*Cuartas* seems to be a misspelling of *cuartos*. In contemporary Philippine currency, one silver *peso* equaled eight silver *reales*, and one *real* equaled twenty copper *cuartos*.

[46]Letters by Octabio dated July 14, July 22, and July 29, 1841.

It is probable that the authorities were suspicious about the Cofradía dues not because the dues were high but because the funds being amassed were not in the hands of a church or religious order ultimately controlled by Spaniards but in the hands of indigenous lay leaders. In fact, the funds were used to make offerings for the *Misa de Gracia,* to pay the costs of the application for official recognition, to be discussed later, and to purchase the *Esclavitud ñg mahal na Virgen.* Almost no money remained in the hands of the Cofradía's treasurer, Father Ciriaco de los Santos.[47]

The third obligation of Cofradía members was attending the *Misa de Gracia,* celebrated on the nineteenth of each month from May 19, 1840, onward. In a letter dated May 12, 1840, Apolinario gave detailed instructions on how the monthly mass was to be celebrated and how much the offering was to be.[48] Members who lived in villages some distance from Lukban would gather in Lukban on the eighteenth to attend the mass on the nineteenth. The *Misa de Gracia* was "our Mass in honor of Saint Joseph" (*aten misa na ypinagmamalasakit sa Amang Sto San Josef*),[49] the Cofradía's patron saint.

Apolinario described the significance of attendance as follows: "You must announce to all our brothers of the said confraternity that whoever is free should try to attend Mass. In that way, they may see the brotherly life of souls. Those who, because of illness, cannot attend, nevertheless share the blessings." (At ang ypagpapahayag mo naman sa lahat na m̃ capatid natin sa naturang Cof.ª ay con sinong may calogalan, ay manyari baga na sumimba, at ñg canilang maq.ta ang pinagcacapatirang cabuhay.ⁿ ñg calolova at ang hindi man macasimba na may capansanan ay caramay rin ñg paq.ᵉnabang.)[50] The primary purpose of the monthly *Misa de Gracia* was to fuse the individual members' piety into a single flame. There was also a secondary significance, however. In response to a request for the mass to be repeated for those who were not able to attend on the nineteenth, Apolinario wrote that this could not be permitted because it would cost too much, adding that members need not worry, because "the indulgence is for the benefit of all the brethren" (*yayamang yaon ay para sa lahat na magcacapatid ang aplecacion ñg Yndolgª*).[51] Members were promised an indulgence (probably a partial indulgence) for attending the *Misa de Gracia.* It is not clear whether the rule that an indulgence would be granted to those attending a mass for a patron saint of a *cofradía* was a rule of the Church at the time or whether this was Apolinario's own interpretation. In either case, the Cofradía members believed Apolinario's assurance that an indulgence would be granted.

After the mass, the Cofradía members withdrew to the house of one of their number, Don Franco de los Santos, commonly called Cabezang (or Cabesang) Ysco Pamienta, since he was one of the village heads (*cabezas de barangay*) in the *pueblo* of Lukban, where a membership meeting was held.[52] The meeting began with recitation of the rosary appropriate for the day.[53] Next the members recited the *Salve Regina*

---

[47]He is discussed in part four.

[48]Appendix II-E-2.

[49]Letter by Apolinario dated May 18, 1840.

[50]Appendix II-E-2.

[51]Letter by Apolinario dated July 28, 1840.

[52]Teodorico T. Dolendo, "Los Sucesos del Mag-Puli," *Renacimiento Filipino,* Aug. 21, 1911, pp. 221–22.

[53]Those who recite the rosary daily meditate on the joyful mysteries on Monday and Thursday, the sorrowful mysteries on Tuesday and Friday, and the glorious mysteries on Wednesday, Saturday, and Sunday.

(*Aba Puo*) praising the blessed Virgin and the *Purijet* (a prayer of unknown content) three times each. In addition, they recited the *Ave Maria*, the *Gloria Patri*, and a prayer called the Greeting to the Saints of Serene Servitude (*Bati sa m̃ Stos na Capayapaang Esclavitud*) seven times each.[54] After the prayers letters from Apolinario to Octabio would be read. Apolinario's letters included instructions on the activities and practices that the Cofradía should be carrying out at the time. They also contained his teaching, within the context of Catholicism as he understood it, concerning the way the members should understand the daily reality confronting them and the way they should live.

The induction of new members and the appointment of new group heads (*cabecillas*) also took place at the monthly meetings. A new member was accompanied to his (or her) first *Misa de Gracia* by the member who had recruited him, his older brother (*hermano mayor*).[55] The new member then read the oath of membership at the meeting. The culmination of the meeting was a communal meal, which deepened the members' sense of unity.

The nineteenth of the month was also the occasion for collecting alms. In Apolinario's letters, this collection is referred to by the Spanish term *demanda* or the Tagalog word *lakad*.[56] Two by two the members designated by Apolinario would set out for distant *pueblos*, carrying the Chest of Saint Joseph (*caja ni Sto. S. Josef*). This custom was clearly modeled on the activity in which Apolinario participated on the nineteenth of each month at the San Juan de Dios Convent Hospital. The pairs assigned to collect alms each month had their Cofradía dues (*contribucíon*) for that month and the following month reduced to one-eighth (*mangacavalu*).[57] The alms they collected were apparently used to purchase the *Esclavitud*, as already mentioned.[58]

Thus far we have considered the activities of the Cofradía only in terms of the three duties of membership, but there were various other activities. Of these, the most important was journeys to expand the membership. In his letter of July 5, 1840, Apolinario named the *cabecillas* assigned the task of gaining new members and allocated to each *cabecilla* a specific number to be responsible for. He also forcefully argued the importance of gathering new members: "I have drawn up anew a list of those who are to gather new members so that our Cofradía de San José will run smoothly and each one does not lack enthusiasm in admitting new members in San José. [I say this] since you merely seem to follow, without inner resolve. If you really

---

[54]Appendix II-E-2.

[55]Cruz, "Declaración," *La Política* 2, no. 32 (1892): 114.

[56]According to Ileto, the Cofradía de San José called journeys made to expand the Cofradía's membership *lakaran*. See Ileto, *Pasyon and Revolution*, pp. 71–72. However, in Apolinario's letters, at least, I have found no use of the word *lakaran* for these journeys. The root of *lakaran* is *lakad*, a term Apolinario used in his letters in three senses: to set out to attend mass on the nineteenth of the month, to gather alms, and to go to Naga, seat of the Nueva Caceres diocese, with the application for official recognition of the Cofradía.

[57]Letter by Apolinario dated July 6, 1840.

[58]Attached to Apolinario's letter of July 6, 1840, is a list of the members assigned to collect *demanda* each month from July through December of that year. We can infer that the funds were used to purchase the *Esclavitud* from the following notation on the list: "These are the groups, listed by month of the current year, that take their turn in going around in the name of St. Joseph for the maintenance of the Santo Esclavitud." (Yto ang m̃ magcacalangcap sa bavat ysang buan ngayon taong lumalacad na naghalihalili ñg paglibut para cay San Josef na mantencion ñg Sto Esclavitud.)

wanted to follow, you would involve spirit and body, not merely superficial behavior. Do not treat this matter jokingly." (Lesta cong guinavang panibago na hinguil sa m̃ paghanap nang cani caniyang tavo para maaun din na mabuti ang ateng Cof.ª ñg Smo. Rosario, at nang huvag namang nag aalañgan ang loob nang ysa,t ysa ñg pagtangap ñg magsisipasoc at maq.ᵉq.ᵉcapatid sa cay Sto S. Jose, Atila mandin cayo ay sumosonod lamang ay m̃ vala sa loob. Con cayo sana ay ibig sumonod ay pagcaramayan ñg calolova,t catau-an hovag ang paembabau lamang at yian ay hivag ypaghalong biro lamang.)[59]

Expanding the membership was the responsibility of the *cabecillas*, but ordinary members also chose to take part in this effort.[60] Anyone who collected twelve new members was awarded the position of *cabecilla*[61] and one *voto*. The word *voto* is used in the AC Papers in almost the same sense as *titulo*. To be given a *voto* was to be given the *camisa* and the title *Esclavitud ñg mahal na Virgen*. In his letter of July 28, 1840, Apolinario told Octabio that he had bestowed the *Buto [voto] Esclavitud* on a woman named Fahosta Maria, and that Octabio was to inform all the members that she had attained the position of *cabecilla* by reading the document attesting to that fact at the next meeting.[62]

In addition to the title *Esclavitud ñg mahal na Virgen*, the Cofradía de San José used the title Servitude of Saint Joseph, *Esclavitud ñg Santo San Jose* (or *Esclavitud kay San Jose*). It is clear that Octabio, for one, had both *Esclavitud* titles.[63] The *Esclavitud ñg mahal na Virgen*, however, is mentioned more frequently in the sources,[64] and it is clear that the title was related to serving as a *cabecilla*. The *Esclavitud ñg Santo San Jose* is mentioned only twice in the documents.[65] Its functions and its status relative to that of the *Esclavitud ñg mahal na Virgen* are unknown.

---

[59]Appendix II-E-4.

[60]In his letter of July 6, 1840, Apolinario instructed Octabio concerning such members: "Tell them that people considered for membership, aside from those who have already been approached, [will be grouped according to town of origin]. Make a list. All should hear of my instructions written in a letter stating that new members [listed under] Lucban be in fact from Lucban, those listed under Mahayhay, from Mahayhay, those listed under Tayabas, from Tayabas. There will be exclusivity. A group will no longer be able to get members assigned to another group." (ypahayag mo ang m̃ hahanaping tavong panibago puera sa naqueta na, ang catapat na numero ay siyang tuca sa bavat ysa ygava mo ñg Quaderno, tuloy maringig ñg calahatan ang aquing belen sa ysang sulat tuloy sabihin mo na ang hahanapin ngayon nasabing tavo, ay ang taga Lucban, ay taga Lucban, ang Mahayhay ay Mahay, ang Tayabas ay pang tagTayabas, samacatuvid ay sarelinan, hindi na macapaghiheram.ⁿ.)

[61]In his affidavit, Apolinario explained that "Each group head (*cabecilla*: literally, little head) was responsible for the recruitment and care of twelve people, who were listed as having one *voto* (votive offering). If he recruited twenty-four members, two *votos*; if thirty-six, three *votos*; if forty-eight, four *votos*. When a group head was able to submit four *votos*, he became a founder who cared for the members of his group." (cada cavecilla tomaba á su cargo el reclutar y cuidar de doce personas y se señalaba en el padron como con un voto: si reclutaba veinte y cuatro, dos votos, si treinta y seis, tres, y si cuarenta y ocho, cuatro, en cuyo caso este cavecilla que habia cumplido los cuatro votos que se presentaban, quedaba á cargo del uno de los fundadores que cuidaba de el y de todos los individuos de su cavecillaje.) Cruz, "Declaración," *La Política* 2, no. 32 (1892): 114.

[62]Appendix II-D.

[63]Appendix II-A.

[64]The earliest mention is in Apolinario's letter of June 29, 1837 (Appendix II-A), in which he stated that fourteen members were about to receive this title.

[65]In Appendix II-A and in a letter dated July 12, 1841, from Father de los Santos to Octabio.

It is particularly interesting that the title *Esclavitud ñg mahal na Virgen* wielded such force to enlarge the Cofradía membership. It is possible that the *camisa* that was the outward sign of this title carried with it the graces and indulgences that people valued so highly at the time. That Apolinario appears to have purchased these *camisas* from some church leads one to make that supposition.[66] The alms that the Cofradía collected were used to pay for them, as already mentioned.

Apart from the daily prayers described earlier, Cofradía members frequently performed other devotional acts, such as saying the rosary and saying novenas. In the Philippines, devotion to the rosary had been encouraged by the Church since the early years of Catholic evangelization. Saying the rosary was part of the curriculum taught at all parish schools. The Dominicans and Franciscans did much to propagate this devotion; the rosary was said twice a day in their schools. Devotion to the rosary was still flourishing in the latter half of the eighteenth century[67] and, apparently, into the nineteenth century. The Cofradía had been founded to praise not only its patron saint but also the Blessed Virgin of the Rosary. The Poem repeatedly encourages saying the rosary. For instance, it suggests that saying the rosary regularly will bring tranquillity and recommends saying the rosary to purify one's spirit and prepare one's soul for salvation after death.[68]

In fact, Cofradía members did say the rosary on many occasions throughout the year. The instances recorded in the Poem can be divided into two categories. One is feast days in the liturgical calendar. Specifically, saying the rosary is mentioned in connection with the Feast of the Circumcision in January, the eighth day after Easter, Christmas, and the eve of Pentecost in May.[69] The second category is related to the Cofradía's activities. When something good happened, that is, something for which the members owed thanks to the Blessed Virgin, they performed this devotion in praise of the Virgin. Examples include the reorganization of the Cofradía in March 1834, Apolinario's return home after four years in 1839, the announcement to the entire membership of the policy of expanding the Cofradía, and the safe return of Apolinario's mother, who had gone to visit him in Manila.[70]

Examples of the second type are found in Apolinario's letters to Octabio, as well. For instance, when a member received the title *Esclavitud ñg mahal na Virgen* from Octabio, the recipient was to say the rosary, while meditating on the three sets of mysteries, at Octabio's house or at the nearby Hermitage of Our Lady of the Porter's Lodge, *Hermita ñg Nuestra Señora de la Portería*. On that occasion, Apolinario wrote, the first set, the joyful mysteries, were dedicated to those who had committed mortal sins. The second, the sorrowful mysteries, were dedicated to those near death and

---

[66]In his letter of June 29, 1841, Apolinario wrote to Octabio: "Please write in your report that I am waiting for the name of the priest who signed your *Esclavitud ñg Sm̃o Rosario ñg m.ᐟ na Virg.ⁿ* and the date of your reception." (At isulat mo rin sa Despacho at ynaantay co, cun sinong Pañglan ñg Paring nacafirma sa Yiong esclavitud ñg Sm̃o Rosario ñg m.ᐟ n Vir.ⁿ at cun anong fecha ñg tangapin mo.) And in a July 12, 1841, letter signed by Father de los Santos, Apolinario wrote: "I have received two *Esclavitud ñg m.ᐟ na Virg.ⁿ* and one [*Esclavitud*] kay S. Jose for our dead brothers." (Tinangap cu ang dalavang Esclavitud ñg m.ᐟ na Virg.ⁿ at ysa cay S. Jose p.ª sa namatai nateng m̃. capatid.) Apolinario was receiving *camisas* signed by a priest from some source.

[67]Barrion, *Religious Life of the Laity*, pp. 70–71.

[68]Poem, quatrains 57, 218.

[69]Ibid., quatrains 64, 142, 354, 416.

[70]Ibid., quatrains 81, 247, 268, 378.

those who were pregnant. The third, the glorious mysteries, were dedicated to the members of the Cofradía, living and dead.[71] The rosary was also said at the death of a Cofradía member, a custom we will discuss in conjunction with that of the novena.

Broadly speaking, there were two cases in which novenas were said. One, as with the rosary, was in conjunction with certain feast days. For instance, the Poem mentions a novena in connection with the Feast of the Finding of the Holy Cross (*Santacruzan*).[72] Again, the Poem relates that on the first anniversary of the founding of the Cofradía the members held a festejo and dedicated a novena to Saint Francis.[73] It is conjectured that they did this before the fourth of October, which is the annual celebration day for the saint.

The second category of novenas included those said when the Cofradía encountered difficulties and sought through this devotion of nine separate days of prayers to receive the grace of God through the intercession of the saints. For instance, in a letter dated June 1, 1840, shortly after the authorities began investigating the Cofradía, Apolinario ordered the members to say novenas of the rosary and to pray to Saint Joseph, their *mahal na patron*, "that I also be saved from danger at this present moment and be spared from all temptation; not only I but all of us here, and all of you out there, that is, all of us members of the confraternity" (*acoy yligtas din sa m̃ pañganib ñgayon Panajong yto, at ylayo sa lahat ñg tocso at hindi lamang aco di cami nañgaririni at cayo namang naririan samacatuvid ay tayong lahat nasang Cof.ª*).[74]

As official pressure on the Cofradía intensified, novenas were said more frequently, not only to seek the grace of God but also to prevent members' quitting the Cofradía and to strengthen their solidarity. When orders proscribing the Cofradía de San José were issued in Lukban, Tayabas, and Majayjay in July 1841, the *cabecillas* in Tayabas, which had no organization (*capisanan*), ordered a novena for the purpose of reinforcing the solidarity of the Cofradía.[75] When the Cofradía rebelled, in October 1841, and its members gathered in the village of Isabang, Apolinario indicated that he wished to say a novena in the Tayabas parish church, and the Cofradía negotiated with the *pueblo* officials over this. In the camp in Alitao, where the members gathered to make their last stand, they said a novena in their makeshift church right up to the day of the final battle.

A novena was also said when a Cofradía member died. On such an occasion it was customary for other members living in the same *pueblo* to gather and say a novena of the rosary. Before the prayers for each day of the novena, the participants meditated upon the mysteries of the rosary appropriate for the day. After the novena was completed, a mass was celebrated in the parish church.[76]

---

[71]Appendix II-E-5.

[72]Poem, quatrains 85–86. The Feast of the Finding of the Holy Cross is celebrated in May to commemorate the fourth-century discovery in Jerusalem by Helena, mother of the emperor Constantine, of the cross on which Jesus was crucified.

[73]Poem, quatrain 42.

[74]In this letter Apolinario ordered three consecutive novenas, the first by the people of Lukban, the second by the people of Majayjay, and the third by the people of Tayabas. After the completion of each novena a mass was to be celebrated in the *pueblo*. Because Apolinario ordered that a portrait of Saint Joseph be used in the novenas, we know that they were directed at Saint Joseph.

[75]Letter by Octabio dated July 29, 1841.

[76]A letter by Apolinario dated May 18, 1841, directs that a novena of the rosary be said following the death of two members (Santᵒ. de la Cruz and Fileciano San Juan). According to the

A novena is a series of prayers for God's grace through the intercession of the saints. The traditional Philippine belief in *anito* may have made the devotion of the novena easy to comprehend by analogy.[77] At any rate, it was widespread in the Philippines.

To summarize, the days of the members of the Cofradía de San José were filled with prayer. One must agree with the statement by members quoted at the beginning of this section: the purpose of the Cofradía was prayer.

III. A COFRADIA FOR THE POOR

In October 1841, the members of the Cofradía de San José gathered in the village of Isabang to rise in revolt. Father Manuel Sancho, the parish priest in Lukban, described the situation as follows in his report on the Cofradía, based on interviews in Lukban and on confiscated documents: "[The news of Apolinario's arrival in Isabang] was transmitted with unbelievable speed. Numbers of young and old, male and female, people of every position in society, drawn by the prestige of the founder [of the Cofradía], transformed that isolated village into a lively, if crude, camp in a matter of hours."[78]

According to Father Sancho, the Cofradía members who gathered in Isabang were an extremely diverse group. They did not appear to have been drawn from a particular social class or to have other obvious characteristics in common. The founders of the Cofradía, however, thought of themselves as developing an organization specifically of the poor. The Poem states that the pairs of members setting out on proselytizing journeys were to dress as the poor (*pobres*) and walk humbly, as the saints did, to attract people from every class.[79]

The Poem also describes a dream in which Octabio, chosen to succeed Apolinario in 1836, became aware of his mission to save the souls of the poor. One night, the Poem relates, Octabio dreamed he was drawn into the midst of a church choir. The fragrance of incense wafted through the air. For a moment he was dazed, but then he began looking around him with great interest and speaking with people. He took no notice of the powerful (*los poderosos*) around him but exchanged words with the mendicant poor (*los pobres mendigantes*). Those who were poor (*aquellos pobres*) knelt before him, weeping for joy. Octabio, having gazed upon the poverty of these unfortunate people, vowed to lead them to repent their sins.[80]

A corollary of the Cofradía's policy of saving the souls of the poor was expressed in the organization's single restriction on membership: *mestizos* could not be admitted.[81] This prohibition is mentioned in three of Apolinario's letters, those of May 12, May 26, and July 5, 1840. The relevant portion of the May 12 letter is: "and

---

record of alms for that occasion, the novena began on June 6, 1841, and lasted seven days instead of nine days. A *limos* of two *quartos* was made by each member attending.

[77]It was believed that the spirits known as *anito* would intercede with the gods so that people's wishes might be granted.

[78]Manuel Sancho, "Relación Espresiva de los Principales Acontecimientos de la Titulada Cofradía del Señor San José: Formada por el M. R. P. Fr. Manuel Sancho, Cura del Pueblo de Lucban," *La Política de España en Filipinas* 1, no. 23 (1891): 290.

[79]Poem, quatrain 312.

[80]Ibid., quatrains 236–40.

[81]A child born to a Philippine woman and a foreign man was called a *mestizo* if male, a *mestiza* if female. Unless otherwise specified, the term *mestizos* refers to men and women collectively.

concerning the admission of new members, as long as there are those who want to come in, the door is open, except of course for the *mestiza* because this is for the poor ['poor-blooded']." (at sampon ñg m̃ pagtangap hangang may napasoc ay bucas ang pinto hovag lamang ang m̃ tauong mistisa sapagca at ytoy sa Dogu ñg Pobre.) All three letters actually forbade admitting *mestizas;* but since Apolinario was almost completely unversed in Spanish, it would be risky to assume that his prohibition applied only to women of mixed blood. Father Sancho noted in his report on the Cofradía that the group excluded *mestizos;* that is, they used the masculine *mestizos* to refer to both men and women.[82]

There is another ambiguity in the Cofradía's use of the word *mestizos.* Under Spanish rule, there were two categories of *mestizos:* those who were part Spanish and those who were part Chinese. In the nineteenth century, the number of Chinese *mestizos* grew extremely rapidly, and in many cases the word *mestizos* without a modifier came to mean Chinese *mestizos.* However, it appears likely that the Cofradía de San José excluded *mestizos* of both Spanish and Chinese origin.[83]

Why was this? According to the letter quoted above, it was because "[the Cofradía] is for poor people." By extension, since the Cofradía was for poor people, it was not for wealthy *mestizos.* The question remains, however, whether mestizos as a class actually were better off than indigenous people in the province of Tayabas at the time. Since no sources on economic conditions there in the 1830s and 1840s have been found, let us review the economy of Tayabas as described in a report written in 1823 by a Spanish priest, Father Bartolomé Galán.[84]

Tayabas is extremely hilly and the soil is poor, but its agricultural production at the time was adequate. The major industry was upland dry rice cultivation; the *pueblos* of Lukban, Tayabas, Sariaya, Tiaon, and Atimonan sold their surplus rice to other *pueblos* in the province that were not suitable for rice cultivation and also to San Pablo and Majayjay (where there was already a weekly market on Mondays) in Laguna Province. In addition to rice, the people grew wheat, beans, and vegetables. Small amounts of the wheat and beans were shipped to Manila. In addition, cattle breeding was widespread in Tayabas, Pagbilao, Sariaya, and Tiaon. The report makes no mention of large landowners, but states: "Here the residents (*cuidadanos*) own all the land. They plant what they like from among the crops that will grow in this [region's] soil and sell them when and how they like." Thus, land ownership had not yet developed the pattern of large haciendas owned by religious orders or private individuals that was seen in the provinces around Manila. It appears that smallholders farming their own land were dominant in Tayabas Province.

Other industries also flourished. There were two areas of commerce: trading in surplus agricultural products between neighboring *pueblos* and buying produce locally to supply Manila, the capital. The people of the *pueblos* of Lukban and Tayabas were most active in both, but people from Gumaca, a *pueblo* to which the Cofradía did not spread, also supplied the capital.

The people of Lukban sold the surplus rice raised in their own *pueblo* at the weekly market in Majayjay and also went to the rice-producing area of Sariaya,

---

[82]Sancho, "Relación Espresiva," *La Política* 1, no. 21 (1891): 250.

[83]Since the *mestizos* were most closely related racially to the indigenous inhabitants of the Philippines, it is reasonable to assume that the Cofradía also excluded both Chinese and Spaniards; in other words, that membership was restricted to indigenes.

[84]The following information is based on Galán, "Informe sobre."

bought rice there, and resold it at the Majayjay market. They also went as far as the *pueblo* of Manbulao in Camarines Norte Province to exchange the rice produced in their own *pueblo* for that area's gold. The people of Lukban made hats, sleeping mats, clothing chests, and other objects of *buli* or *pandan* fibers.[85] These products of family workshops were taken to the commercial town of Santa Cruz, on Laguna de Bay, and from there by boat to Manila. Santa Cruz was an entrepôt for goods bound for Manila. The people of Lukban, together with people from Mauban, also went as far as the island of Polillo in Nueva Ecija Province, where they bought sea slugs, shells, beeswax, and other products of the island for transport to Santa Cruz.

The people of the *pueblo* of Tayabas, which was rich in agricultural products, took their rice to the weekly market in Majayjay, sent coconuts to Sariaya, Pagbilao, and Santa Cruz, and sold *panocha*, or *pacascas* (a kind of sugar cake), to Mauban, Atimonan, Gumaca, and other *pueblos*. In exchange for these goods, they bought rice in Sariaya, just as the people of Lukban did, taking it to the Majayjay market, and purchased fish in Pagbilao. They shipped large bags and mats woven of *buli*, as well as wheat, which were produced in Tayabas, to Manila via Santa Cruz.

In Gumaca, which had little arable land, people compensated by vigorous development of fishing and trade. They went to the nearby island of Alabat to gather sea slugs and tortoiseshell and purchased beeswax from the mountain people there in exchange for rough clothing. They also sailed south to Ragay Bay and occasionally to the island of Bulias to fish for sea slugs. The sea slugs, tortoiseshell, and beeswax were all shipped to Manila. They also took mats, vinegar, clothing, and other goods purchased in neighboring *pueblos* to Naga in Camarines Sur Province, where they exchanged them for gold and *abaca*. The *abaca* was traded in Atimonan and Mauban for high-quality cloth woven of *abaca* in those two *pueblos*. This cloth was then sent to Manila. A summary of products shipped from Tayabas Province to Manila would thus include wheat, beans, sea slugs, tortoiseshell, beeswax, and products of cottage industries, such as mats, bags, and *abaca* cloth.

The Chinese spearheaded the commercial activity in Tayabas Province, surmounting the twin barriers of the pitiless tropical climate and transportation problems to engage in trade with distant *pueblos* and islands. The town of Lukban, in the center of Tayabas Province, had the liveliest commerce and was therefore the richest *pueblo*, but it owed its wealth to the Chinese who lived there, the report tells us.[86] The Chinese mentioned, however, can be inferred to be Chinese *mestizos* in most cases. Limitations on Chinese residence began to lessen at the end of the eighteenth century, and by 1830 the restrictions on Chinese immigration to the Philippines had been considerably relaxed. Nonetheless, Chinese penetration into rural areas progressed little until the second half of the nineteenth century. Chinese *mestizos*, however, moved into rural areas and made dramatic economic and social advancement between 1750 and 1850.[87]

Another reason to believe that the Chinese mentioned in the report were Chinese *mestizos* is found in Mas y Sans' acute analysis of the Cofradía movement, written immediately after the October 1841 uprising: "Was the movement the result of a con-

---

[85]*Buli* are the fronds of a type of coconut palm. *Pandan* are the leaves of a plant belonging to the pandanus family.

[86]See "Lucban Comercío," in Galán, "Informe sobre."

[87]Edgar Wickberg, *The Chinese in Philippine Life, 1850–1898* (New Haven: Yale University Press, 1965), pp. 24–31.

spiracy? . . . Apolinario was a young man, just twenty, utterly stupid and without prestige, when he began this enterprise. If conspirators had planned an insurrection, surely they would not have used such an unimportant person. But there is no doubt that they did have at least some spirit of rebellion. The Cofradía did not admit Chinese *mestizos* [*mestizos sangleyes*]. But the Chinese *mestizos* were even more pious and wealthier than the Filipinos [Spaniards born in the Philippines]. Many such people lived in the *pueblo* of Lukban, but none participated in the Cofradía. On the contrary: when the rebels gathered in Igsaban [Isabang], the Chinese *mestizos* were extremely afraid that the rebels would come, assassinating them and looting. Moreover, it is obvious that it would give this kind of organization the greatest support to include Spaniards in its membership; nonetheless, the Cofradía de San José did not seek out Spaniards for membership or want them as members."[88] Mas y Sans tells us that there were many Chinese *mestizos* in Lukban; that although they were prosperous and pious, relationships between them and the people of the Cofradía were hostile or strained; and that the Chinese *mestizos* even feared being murdered and having their goods plundered when the Cofradía uprising occurred.

Chinese *mestizos* became increasingly active in the commercial life of the Tayabas region in the first half of the nineteenth century. A reading of Galán and Mas y Sans makes it clear that the economic gap between the Chinese *mestizos* and the indigenous peasant population was beginning to widen. Thus we can infer that when the Cofradía aimed at organizing poor people, what was meant by poor people was, basically, indigenous people who saw themselves as poor in relation to the growing wealth of the Chinese *mestizo* merchants. In short, the basic motivation behind the foundation of the Cofradía de San José was a growing sense of relative deprivation among indigenous people in a society in transition from a subsistence to a commercial economy.

There were, of course, disparities of wealth among members of the indigenous population, as well. Under Spanish rule, Philippine society had a two-class social structure: an upper class of *principalía*, who were addressed with the title Don or Doña, and a lower class of common people, whom the *principalía* oppressed in many ways.[89] The membership list of the Cofradía shows that members with the title Don or Doña accounted for only six of the twenty-three male *cabecillas* and four of the sixteen female *cabecillas*. Thus it appears that the Cofradía's members were drawn mainly from the relatively poor stratum of indigenous society.

Why did the Cofradía exclude Spanish *mestizos*? The AC Papers include a memorandum that Octabio wrote for Apolinario's use. (Since Octabio added to it whenever an incident occurred, without indicating the date, it is impossible to date the document precisely.) After the authorities investigated the Cofradía in October 1840, Octabio was summoned to the Tayabas parish church and investigated by the *vicar forane* for Tayabas Province. According to Octabio's memorandum, the *vicar forane*, after threatening the Cofradía's members with excommunication and denial of burial in consecrated ground, suddenly changed the subject and said: ". . . this Spaniard from Manila whom you dearly love was probably dirt poor in his own native land

---

[88]Mas y Sans, *Informe sobre,* vol. 1; "Historia de la Dominación," p. 88.

[89]For more on the two-class social structure, see Setsuho Ikehata, "Firipin kakumei no rīdāshippu ni kansuru kenkyū (1896 nen 8 gatsu–1898 nen 4 gatsu)" [A study of leadership in the Philippine Revolution, August 1896–April 1898], *Tōyō bunka kenkyūjo kiyo* [Memoirs of the Institute of Oriental Culture] 80 (1980): 86–100.

but now wears bejewelled clothes, which he probably obtained by cheating you." (Itong naparito na kastilang yniong minamahal na taga-Maynila, ay segurong ka-pubrepubrehan doon sa kaniyang bayan ay ang m̃ga dinadamit ay palahiyasan, ay seguro dinaya sa inyo.) The memorandum continues with Octabio's comment on the *vicar forane*'s words: "I have come to realize that the person poor in his own land loses incentive to work and takes advantage of his fellow-poor. And the reason he [that is, the *vicar forane*] said that *mestizos* used to be barred from entering was because they were bright and knowledgeable and difficult to cheat." (Natalastas co ay yari tauo mahirap, sa kaniyang bayan at natatamad magtrabajo, at ang pinagda-dayaan ay tao rin Pubre, at caya aña ypinagbabaval noon[90] na huvag papasoc ang m̃ Mestiso ay yaoi mañga m̃ marurunong,[91] at matatalinong ay di mapagdaraya-dayaan.)

It is not clear from the context who the Spaniard mentioned in this memorandum was. All that can be said is that he happened to be present when Octabio was summoned to the Tayabas church. In any case, it appears that the subject of *mestizos* came up through association with the Spaniard who was there, which suggests that he was a Spanish *mestizo*. It was the *vicar forane*, not Octabio, who explained why the Cofradía did not admit *mestizos*, that is, Spanish *mestizos*. We can infer from the context, however, that Octabio agreed with the reason given. That, to recapitulate, was that Spanish *mestizos* were despicable people who, though they had no real economic power, made a grand show and fooled others with their superficial learning.

A final question is why the "poor people" for whom the Cofradía were organized are almost always referred to by the Spanish word *pobre*. The use of *pobre* in the Poem is unsurprising, since the version we have is a Spanish translation. But Apolinario's letters and Octabio's memorandum were written in Tagalog, yet even there the Spanish *pobre* is used. Why, moreover, did Apolinario and Octabio repeatedly capitalize the word?

Probably the word *pobre* entered everyday speech from the sermons of the Spanish parish priests. They praised poverty in their sermons, "those who are poor," and the term was adopted in the daily language of the common people. Their reaction to the word *pobre* was not simple. Apolinario used the word to assert the value of their existence. When he said that the Cofradía was for poor people, he meant not simply those who were poor in economic terms but those who, though poor in material goods, were rich in spirit and lived righteous lives.

IV. Organization and Leadership

How was this poor people's *cofradía* organized and led? According to the AC Papers, the following titles for members existed: *hermano mayor, hermano menor interior (hermano menor), fundadores, cabecillas,* and *hermanos.* It is clear that Apolinario was the *hermano mayor* and Octabio the *hermano menor interior.* The *fundadores* were the posts obtained by *cabecillas* when they submitted 4 *votos* after recruiting 48 members. The

---

[90]The *vicar forane*'s use of the word *noon* is interesting. The prohibition on membership for *mestizos* is touched on in only three of Apolinario's letters (May 12, May 26, and July 5, 1840). His letter of September 1, 1840 (Appendix II-E-6) already includes the statement "at hangang may napasoc ay tangapin at huvag tatanguihan, tagasaan mang bayan." This suggests that *mestizos* may have been permitted to join the Cofradía after that time, depending on their economic status.

[91]*Mañga m̃ marurunong* is an extremely sarcastic expression. The *vicar forane* may have used it, but it must also express Octabio's own sentiment.

cabecillas were rewarded with that post in recognition of their achievements in expanding membership. In the AC Papers, the *fundadores* and *cabecillas* are listed together, and there is no way to tell who is which. In 1841 there were twenty-three male and sixteen female *cabecillas* or *fundadores*. Since the titles listed above were all Spanish, they may have been titles in general use in *cofradías* at the time.

A close reading of Apolinario's letters, however, reveals that the members of the Cofradía de San José used a different system of titles for their ranks and their relationships among themselves. For instance, Apolinario addressed the members as a whole as "all of you" (*cayong lahat*), "all of them there" (*canilang lahat dian*), or "elders and brothers" (*mañga magulang at capatid*) in his letters. *Magulang* means "parents" or "elders"; *capatid* (*kapatid*) is, literally, "brothers." *Magulang* corresponds to *cabecillas* and *fundadores* in the Spanish list, while *capatid* (*kapatid*) corresponds to *hermanos*.

When Apolinario referred to himself in addressing members, he most often used the term "your father" (*ama ninyo*). He often used "my children" (*m̃ anak ko*) or "those who are taken care of" (*m̃ cuidados*) for the members, in addition to the terms mentioned above. He referred to Octabio as "my right hand man" (*aking camay na canan*), which we can take to mean "alter ego." If we consider Apolinario's mother to be the mother of the Cofradía, as discussed in part one, the hierarchy of titles in Tagalog was as follows:

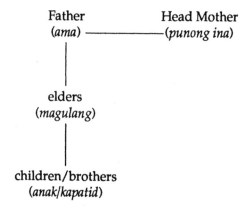

This structure clearly mirrors that of the family in Tagalog society. The diagram clarifies the image the members held of the Cofradía as a whole and their perception of their relationship to other members. To its members, the Cofradía was an extended family. No doubt they believed that as *anak* or *kapatid* they were supposed to follow the teachings of the father and the elders who led the family and to cooperate with one another. The mother of the organization was expected to preserve the tranquillity of the family as a whole and to function as the focus of the children's sense of belonging, just as the ideal mother in a Philippine family would.

The organizing principle of the Cofradía was, then, that of the family. Yet the family formed in this way was not one bound by ties of blood, of course; moreover, it was a family that was required to grow rapidly, day by day. To give this fictive family the spiritual support needed for its development and solidarity, Apolinario emphasized two points: spontaneity and unity. As mentioned in connection with the discussion of efforts to expand the Cofradía, Apolinario urged the *cabecillas* to cooperate actively, united in body and spirit. Such spontaneity was required of everyone who joined the Cofradía: ". . . no one was ever strangled or threatened with dagger;

rather everyone has joined the group voluntarily, and no one was whipped when communicating." (ang sinoman ay hindi natin pinisel sa leeg o tenoonan ñg sondang ñg paq.ᵉq.ᵉsama dito sa caysahan condi pavang bolontad ñg loob at valang dina-an sa palo, ñg paqeq.ᵉpag-osap).[92]

Thus, the members were to follow God's will of their own accord and to make spiritual progress; those who lacked that inner desire would necessarily be left to themselves, loathsome to God as they were, according to Apolinario's way of thinking, ". . . we are only trying to make the blind to see, and when you have become aware, yet do not follow the will of God, you must be loathsome to Him" (cami nagpapamata lamang con sanan sa ysang bulag at saca ñg m̃ mulat cayo ay hindi ypatuloy ang calivanagang banta; ay dapat yatang carumijan ñg Dˢ).[93]

On the subject of unity, Apolinario wrote that "so that we be together and follow each other like one body" (caya ñg tayo ay magcaoompoc ay magsunuran parang isang catau-an). That letter is dated July 5, 1840, when investigation of the Cofradía had just begun. In his letter of January 18, 1841, when oppression had grown much more severe, he counseled: "Therefore all of this that happened to us was brought about by our lack of obedience" (caya na ñga ang lahat ay domating sa atin ay dahilan din lamang sa masasamang pagsusunoran). In these two letters Apolinario demanded that the members act in concert, for this would unify them emotionally, as well. To Apolinario, external actions had to be an unfeigned expression of *loob*, the inner self. The unity of *labas*, the exterior, and *loob* was the core of his teaching. If the Cofradía members acted as one, they would become one in spirit; this was what he meant by unifying the Cofradía. Apolinario also used the phrase "small but radiant glow" (minti bagang diq.ᵗ) in his July 5 letter. This expresses the ideal form of existence for the Cofradía: a state in which its members were welded into a whole, awake to the love of God, and burning with piety. In terms of the members' practice, that state could be described as one of constant prayer. In short, the Cofradía family was to be a group of people awake to God's will and united in prayer.

What manner of man was the head of the Cofradía family? According to the baptismal record in the Lukban church, he was born on July 22, 1815.[94] The membership list of the Cofradía drawn up on January 4, 1841, however, states that he was twenty-eight, and the affidavit written by Spanish officials in early November of the same year gives his age as twenty-seven. Neither agrees with the baptismal record. If we follow the baptismal record, he was seventeen when he founded the Cofradía and nineteen when he set out to undergo religious training in Manila's San Juan de Dios Convent Hospital. His parents were Pablo de la Cruz and Juana Andrea, listed as fifty and forty-five years old, respectively, in the 1841 membership list. Since no honorific title (Don, Doña) precedes either name, apparently they were ordinary peasants, not members of the *principalía*. In his letters Apolinario emphasized that he grew up poor and uneducated: "They should remember that I am a poor man, without any source of wealth, and my relatives grew up in poverty" (ang canilang alalahanin acoy ysang Pobre, na valang pinagcuconan ñg yaman, at laq.ᵉ sa cahirapan ang aquing pulangan).[95] And the Poem states:

---

[92]Letter by Apolinario dated March 15, 1841.

[93]Letter by Apolinario dated February 1, 1841.

[94]Gregorio F. Zaide, *Great Filipinos in History* (Manila: Verde Book Store, 1970), p. 147.

[95]Letter by Apolinario dated September 1, 1840.

If by misfortune, I say, I have been hard up,
I ask your profound understanding that I should be pardoned
since I am ignorant
and a beginner who knows not how to write.

Si por desgracia, digo, he sido escaso
pido a vuestro profundo talento me sea indulgente
supuesto que soy un ignorante
y un principiante que aun escribir no sabe. [474]

Wealthy youths, after completing the first level of schooling in the parish schools or private schools of their *pueblos*, could receive further education in *colegios* in Manila or Naga. Coming from a poor family, Apolinario could not receive that more advanced formal education. Nevertheless, he was well educated by 1839, when the Cofradía began its remarkable growth. We can infer from various parts of the Poem that his parents were deeply religious and were the de facto promoters of the foundation of the Cofradía. As he grew up, probably Apolinario was greatly influenced in his religious life by his parents. He also appears to have been intelligent. When he was nineteen, his parents sent him to the San Juan de Dios Convent Hospital; through the friars he gained deeper religious knowledge and greater cultivation. He made startling progress in his knowledge not only of Catholic doctrine and liturgy but also of society in general. He developed into an authoritative leader, writing letters of instruction and guidance to the Cofradía members about once every six days. Apolinario was also a healer (*esculapío*), with special abilities that were highly respected by the people of his society. Evidence of his healing abilities is provided by a letter from Octabio to Apolinario dated July 29, 1841. Octabio had broken his arm and in the letter asked Apolinario to teach him how to heal it.

Apolinario may have been brought up in a poor family and may have lacked an impressive formal education, but we cannot help noting the ironic ring his words have when he refers to himself as poor and uneducated. For instance, in his letter of January 18, 1841, Apolinario attributed the official persecution of the Cofradía to the members' failure to cooperate. He went on to write, as though criticizing the attitude of Octabio and other members toward him, that "I am of no worth to you and to the brothers, for if I were otherwise, I would have been obeyed even if I am poor, but what can I do since I am merely a child of uneducated farm hands." (acoy valang cabolohan sa yio at sa m͠ga capatid con mayroon sanay di maralita may susondin anong gagaw-in ay anak n͠g hindi nag-aral at tavong taga boquid.)

This passage is filled with indirect self-assertion. With ironic expressions Apolinario pressed for reversal of the worldly values to which Cofradía members still clung, the view that only the lives of wealthy, educated people had meaning. By standing that sense of values on its head, he was able to assert confidently his own function and power as the leader of the Cofradía:

Well although I have the countenance of a beggar,
all of you who are here gathered
are my children, and it is my duty
to lead you through the rough times of this world.

I am your Father and Captain, and yet

in the presence of this multitude I am laid bare,
look and consider, my fellow-members,
this authority which I hold.

Pues aunque yo tengo la representación de un mendigo,
todos los que estáis aquí reunidos
sois mis hijos, y está a mi cargo
el dirigiros por el piélago de este mundo

Yo soy vuestro Padre y Capitán, y sin embargo
en presencia de esta multitud me he descubierto,
mirad y considerad, compañeros todos
este bastón que tengo empuñado [542 43]

What was the basis of Apolinario's authority as the leader of the Cofradía? He was only a *donado* at the San Juan de Dios Convent Hospital, but in his own eyes he had the same qualifications as a full member of the religious order participating in the sacraments. Moreover, he was able to become a friar in this way due to the mysterious grace of the Virgin Mary:

Examine this closely and understand it with your heart,
this is a mystery of the Mother of Jesus
Why have I put on
this black and sad habit?

The scapular is that to which my will has tended
as well as the rosary which my neck has rightfully carried;
on my waist I have girded a belt
which I believe angels have fastened around me.

Reconoced bien esto y penetradlo con vuestro corazón
pues es un misterio de la Madre de Jesús
¿por qué acaso me he vestido yo
este hábito negro y triste?

El escapulario es a lo que mi voluntad se ha inclinado
y justamente el Rosario que traigo el cuello;
a mi cintura me he ceñido una correa
que creo que los ángeles me la han atado. [544–45]

Since Apolinario's inner desire was to become one of the black-robed friars, he tells us, he donned the scapular that symbolized the friars of his own volition. But the girdle that symbolized the friars' vows of chastity, poverty, and obedience was wrapped around his waist not by his own will but by the hands of angels, undoubtedly an act of the Virgin's mysterious grace. His status as a friar, granted by the trancendental Virgin's mysterious grace, was the primary basis of Apolinario's assertion of his authority as head of the Cofradía.

Perceiving himself as thus invested with spiritual authority, he commissioned a portrait of himself and had the Cofradía members venerate it, as if he were a saint.[96] His letters frequently contain the word "directive," *bilin*, which implies coercive force, and at times even used the word "fate," *tadhana*, which can only be issued by an absolute being, by God.[97] His use of such terms must have derived from his sense of absolute authority. He did not hesitate to proclaim that those who opposed his absolute leadership would be punished with flames of wrath:

> If by chance anyone finds himself resentful
> and disappointed by what I said,
> let him rise and approach me
> so that I as superior will give him a suitable punishment.
>
> My brothers, consider this well
> and know that although I am a benign superior,
> I also feel the fire of anger
> when I am annoyed and disobeyed.
>
> *Si acaso hubiere alguno que se encontrase resentido*
> *y disgustado de lo que he dicho,*
> *levántese ya acérquese a mí*
> *que yo como superior le daré el condigno castigo.*
>
> *Hermanos míos, considerad bien esto,*
> *y reparad aunque soy un superior benigno,*
> *también siento el fuego de la cólera*
> *cuando me incomodan y desobedecen.* [608–9]

Apolinario possessed another aspect, however, that contrasted with that of the authoritarian leader. He presented himself as undertaking a life of suffering for the sake of the Cofradía, continuing to struggle despite his exhaustion. The following verses from the Poem present this self-image in Apolinario's own words:

> Which understanding can fathom
> their delight and my weariness?
> Which heart by chance can
> measure heaviness or lightness in our breasts?
>
> Who can give sufficient proof
> that you enjoy and I suffer?
> The trials of the body are permanent
> and perhaps they suffer only that much.
>
> All you hearers, I tell you also
> that I am alone and you are many,

---

[96]Poem, quatrain 546; Letters by Apolinario dated June 1 and July 28, 1840; Father de los Santos's affidavit.

[97]Letter by Apolinario dated July 5, 1840.

I am the father who is laden with fatigue
and it is you children who rest.

¿Qué entendimiento podrá calcular
el gozo de ellos y mis fatigas?
¿Qué corazón por ventura podrá
tantear la pesadez ó alivio de nuestros pechos?

¿Quién podrá dar pruebas suficientes de que
vosotros gozáis y que yo padezco?
los trabajos del cuerpo son permanentes,
y acaso sólo los padecen muchos.

Oyentes todos, os digno también
que yo estoy solo y que ustedes son muchos,
yo soy el padre que estoy lleno de fatigas
y vosotros los hijos que respiráis. [334–36]

Another example is found in the final quatrain:

Enough already, I conclude by exhorting you
to contemplate my works, day and night,
the anxieties suffered on your account,
the hunger and other torments.

Basta ya, y concluyo exhortándoos
a que contempléis mis trabajos día ya noche,
los desvelos que paso por causa de vosotros,
mis hambres ya demás tormentos. [610]

These images combined replicate the image of Jesus Christ presented in the *pasyon*, which was recited during Lent in the Tagalog community. This custom originated in the early eighteenth century. The standard version of the *pasyon* at that time was written by a Tagalog layman, Gaspar Aquino de Belen.[98] Aquino de Belen's *Pasyon* consisted of 196 stanzas, each consisting of five octosyllabic lines, covering the period from the Last Supper to the Resurrection.[99] Since the custom of reciting narrative poetry had been widespread in the Philippines before the Spanish invasion, recitation of the *pasyon* rapidly became an established custom in Tagalog society. Barrion writes that the event in the church calendar celebrated on the grandest scale was

---

[98]Gaspar Aquino de Belen, "Ang Mahal na Passion ni Iesu Christong P. Natin na Tola," in Tomas de Villacastin, *Mang̃a Panalangĩin Pagtatagobilin sa Calolova nang Tavong Naghihin g̃alo,* trans. Gaspar Aquino de Belen, 5th ed. (Manila: Imprenta de la Compañía de Iesus, 1760; orig pub. 1703).

[99]For more on this version of the *pasyon*, see Bienvenido L. Lumbera, "Tradition and Influences in the Development of Tagalog Poetry (1570–1898)" (PhD dissertation, Indiana University, 1967), pp. 98–113; René B. Javellana, SJ, "The Sources of Gaspar Aquino de Belen's Pasyon," *Philippine Studies* 32 (1984): 305–21.

Lent and that the Lenten practice of reciting the *pasyon* was a major religious activity aimed at spreading Christian doctrine and awakening believers' conscience.[100]

Since the *pasyon* was transmitted orally in most cases, it acquired many variations reflecting popular tastes and the reciters' imaginative powers. Naturally enough, people preferred to recite their own versions.[101] That was the context in which a new version of the *pasyon* was published in 1814.[102] The new pasyon is said to have been circulated from *pueblo* to *pueblo* in manuscript form and to have become popular before its publication in 1814. However, even now we do not know who the author was. At present the dominant theory is that the author was an indigenous priest or intellectual conversant with Catholic doctrine and contemporary Church ceremonial. For this reason the new *pasyon* is called either the *Pasyon Pilapil*, after Father Mariano Pilapil, the censor at the time it was published, or the *Pasyon Henesis*, after a major feature of its content. The author's intent appears to have been to revise the *pasyon* to bring its content into line with religious knowledge and practice at the end of the eighteenth century and to restore consistency to its content, which had become variegated because of embellishments added by the common people.

Parts of the *Pasyon Pilapil* are identical to the Aquino de Belen *Pasyon*. Like its predecessor, it was written in stanzas of five octosyllabic lines and made use of the stylistic device of dramatic dialogue. However, the *Pasyon Pilapil* also had some original features. The addition of passages from Genesis and the Apocalypse at the beginning and the end of the *Pasyon* provides a Christian view of the cosmos extending from the beginning to the end of human history. In addition, the details of the narrative have been given a more Philippine cast. Philippine values and sensibilities are seen in the descriptions of the characters and their relationships. The image of the Virgin Mary has also been Philippinized, and the narrative weight given to her has grown conspicuously.[103] Recitation of the *Pasyon Pilapil* was widespread in the Tagalog region in the first half of the nineteenth century,[104] and the custom continues today.

---

[100]Barrion, *Religious Life of the Laity*, pp. 66–67.

[101]Father Joaquin Martinez de Zuniga, who lived in the Philippines from 1796 to 1818, wrote: "Both men and women are much attached to reading verses. They represent them dramatically as they read them and are tireless in this. Every night during Lent passing through the streets one can be sure to hear the *Pasión de Nuestro Señor Jesucristo* recited in verse in many houses. A Franciscan Father, seeing this inclination of theirs, put it in verse for them and had it printed. Though it is well done and, as they themselves admit, the verse lively and well written, they do not wish to read this one but rather other *Pasiones* which they have made themselves, full of fables which they like very much because they emphasize the marvelous, something which they especially enjoy. These fables do not contain anything against religion. Nonetheless many parish priests forbid them to read them, because besides the foolishness which is found in them, the young men and women often make use of the pretext of reading the *Pasión* in order to make love to each other." Schumacher, *Readings in Philippine Church History*, p. 179.

[102]*Casaysayan nang Pasiong Mahal ni Jesucristong Panginoon Natin Sucat Ipag-Alab nang Sino mang Babasa* (Manila: Imprenta y Libreras de J. Martinez, 1935; orig. pub. 1814).

[103]For more on the *Pasyon Pilapil*, see Lumbera, "Tradition and Influences," pp. 156–67; René B. Javellana, SJ, "A Historico-Critical Study of the Tagalog Pasyon of 1814: Casaysayan nang Pasiong Mahal ni Jesuchristong Panginoon Natin Sucat Ipag-alab nang Puso nang Sinomang Babasa" (MA thesis, Ateneo de Manila University, 1983); Javellana, "Pasyon Genealogy and Annotated Bibliography," *Philippine Studies* 31 (1983): 451–67.

[104]Buzeta and Bravo, *Diccionario Geográfico*, vol. 1, p. 157.

The image of Jesus Christ presented in the *Pasyon Pilapil* is, of course, that of the Savior enduring hardship and persecution. At the same time, it is the image of a poor, uneducated man of the lower stratum of society who gathers followers not through wealth or official authority but through the power of his teachings and leads them, through his statements of unconditional truth, to confront the established authorities and powers. In that sense, the image of Jesus Christ in the *Pasyon Pilapil* is that of the ideal leader of the Tagalog people.[105] Apolinario attempted to model himself on the image of Jesus Christ presented in the *Pasyon Pilapil,* an image deeply embedded in the popular mind. His leadership derived from his followers' identification of him with this popular conception of Jesus Christ.[106]

Finally, let us touch briefly on Apolinario's two aides, Octabio and Father Ciriaco de los Santos. Octabio, Apolinario's right-hand man, is identified as an unmarried man of twenty-one in the 1841 membership list. He appears to have been a native of the village of Igang.[107] Igang is now in the *pueblo* of Lukban, but it may then have been part of the Majayjay *pueblo,* for the list says Octabio was from Majayjay. His parents, Don Aniceto Flores San Jorge and Doña Eufemina de la Rosa, belonged to the *principalía* class, as indicated by the honorific titles preceding their names. Both held the rank of *cabecilla* in the Cofradía. His father was responsible for the entire Majayjay district. Octabio was Apolinario's loyal and devoted aide. He enforced Apolinario's many *bilin,* handled members' requests and complaints, and endured investigation and torture by the Spanish officials.[108] Without Octabio, the Cofradía could not have developed as it did.

Father de los Santos was Apolinario's spiritual adviser. According to his affidavit of November 20, 1841, he was supernumerary coadjutor (*coadjutor supernumerario*) of the Santa Cruz church in Manila and private chaplain (*capellán particular*) of Don Domingo Roxas, a Spanish businessman. He stated that he first met Apolinario in January 1840 and joined the Cofradía in September of that year. This agrees with the timing in the Poem, in which he is first mentioned in connection with events early in 1840.[109] It is reasonable to infer that he was involved with the Cofradía when its expansion movement was in full force. His function within the organization is described as *capellán y mayordomo.* That is, he was the chaplain of the Cofradía and was also the organization's treasurer, managing the alms and dues collected. It was he who prepared the *Esclavitud,* the title awarded to members for achievements in the expansion movement.[110] Father de los Santos had another important function, which will be discussed more fully in part six: preparation of the application for official recognition of the Cofradía. Since he had received the formal education of those in

---

[105]The *Pasyon Pilapil* was translated into other Philippine languages beginning in the middle of the nineteenth century and became popular over a wide area. It was translated into Pangasinan in 1855, Bikol in 1867, Pampangan in 1876, Iloko in 1889, and Samareo in 1916. See Javellana, "Pasyon Genealogy," pp. 457–59.

[106]Ileto was the first to argue that Apolinario's image as a leader was linked to that of Jesus in the *Pasyon Pilapil.* See Ileto, *Pasyon and Revolution,* pp. 62–72. The author is indebted to Ileto for this insight.

[107]Poem, quatrain 226.

[108]The letter in Appendix II-F-5 reports on Octabio's final interrogation.

[109]Poem, quatrain 371.

[110]Ibid.

holy orders and was able to converse in Spanish, his presence unquestionably had a great effect on negotiations with the Spanish authorities.

What underlay Father de los Santos's involvement with the Cofradía? The first possibility that comes to mind is friendship with people from his home area. That is probably the most plausible motivation, given the human relationships and patterns of behavior within the Tagalog community at the time, and even today, for that matter. There is, however, no evidence to support this. Setting aside that point, let us consider another factor that was important in the social context of the period: Father de los Santos was supernumerary coadjutor of the Santa Cruz church. In the Philippines at that time, most parish priests were friars. The secular priests who would normally have occupied these positions were excluded, for most friars were Spanish, while most secular priests were indigenous. The result of this ethnic discrimination was that indigenous secular priests spent their entire lives working under Spanish priests as supernumerary coadjutors. Father de los Santos appears to have been one such priest. In the latter half of the 1840s a movement to oppose such discrimination finally began among the members of religious orders, but Father de los Santos' involvement with the Cofradía de San José predated that movement by several years. He probably sympathized with the autonomy, in terms of both structure and doctrine, of this indigenous organization. Cooperation with the Cofradía may have been a way to assuage his frustration over his own position within the Church. In this respect, the Cofradía was an embryonic nationalistic movement arising during a period of social change.

V. A New Way to Heaven

While Cofradía dues imposed a considerable financial burden on ordinary peasants, as discussed in part two, several thousand peasants joined the Cofradía within two years of the commencement of the movement to expand membership. What was their reason for doing so? The answer can be found in the vow and prayer of those joining the Cofradía, entitled "Written testament of servitude to beloved Saint Joseph" (*Sulat na Paquiquialipin sa mahal na Poong San Josef*). At the induction ceremony, one who wished to join the Cofradía incorporated his or her own name at the beginning of the vow and prayer, then chanted it in its entirety. The gist is as follows: "I humbly swear to my father and protector, Saint Joseph, and to the Blessed Virgin Mary. As a sign of my obedience, I will pay my dues and will repeat the *Pater Noster*, the *Ave Maria*, and the *Gloria Patri* seven times a day. I will share the seven sorrows and the seven joys that you [Saint Joseph] experienced when you married the Virgin Mary. Therefore, please accept me as your fortunate servant and direct your merciful gaze upon me. When I encounter suffering and woe, please succor me. Please give me comfort for my soul, a quiet conscience, a happy life, and a fortunate death. Receiving protection from you, my father, and zeal and joy through the grace of Jesus and Mary, may I receive forgiveness of my sins and [finally] see you [the Holy Family] in heaven and stay by your side forever."[111]

People joined the Cofradía seeking happiness in this world and salvation in the next through the help of Saint Joseph. They hoped to be released from physical and spiritual pain (*saquit*) and suffering caused by the lack of materials (*cahirapan*) through the intercession of the Cofradía's patron saint. In the Catholic concept of intercession, the saints intercede with God to grant people's prayers and bestow grace.

---

[111]Appendix II-C.

The Cofradía members usually sought Saint Joseph's intercession through novenas in his name. As we saw in part two, Cofradía members said novenas both in conjunction with events in the liturgical calendar and when they encountered special problems. Though the members hoped for happiness in this world, that is, worldly benefits, through these novenas, their ultimate wish was to receive spiritual tranquillity, not material riches or physical comfort, through the saint's intercession. In their view, happiness in this world was linked to salvation in the next.

In the Poem, Apolinario used the following words to explain the end of an individual's life and the salvation of the soul after death: "The surprise attack on you by death, which God gives to every person, is not that far away."[112] Thus, to be able to receive "eternal joy"[113] after the sudden onslaught of death and for "our souls not to perish," "we must lead model lives" and "always act virtuously."[114] "In this world we must withstand unending physical labor and abandon the joys of this world," for "joys abound in heaven."[115]

Apolinario taught that to enter the Kingdom of Heaven and receive eternal life, one must live a chaste, ideal life on earth. Beyond the limited world of the present is the eternal world of heaven, a world overflowing with joy and happiness in reward for chastity, virtue, and good works in this world. Cofradía members' vivid image of the heaven of supreme bliss is expressed in one of their hymns. Called "Hymn to the Glory in Heaven That Will Be Attained by the Faithful" (*Dalit sa Caluvalhatian sa Lañgit na Cararatnan ñg mga Banal*), the hymn consists of forty-three quatrains.[116] A small notebook made of rough sheets of paper stitched together that is among the AC Papers contains a handwritten copy of this hymn, as well as a copy of another hymn and a list of the names of those who joined the Cofradía from February 1839 onward. The content and the handwriting make it almost certain that this was Octabio's notebook. It is probable that he took this notebook to the meeting on the nineteenth of each month and led the members in singing the two hymns.

"Hymn to the Glory in Heaven That Will Be Attained by the Faithful" begins:

A delightful day
would be made even more joyous
if our source of comfort
could be seen by our eyes.

Even earthly beings
can be loved much
and it is God who mandates
and decides one's fate.

And when the obedient faithful
are brought back to life

---

[112]Poem, quatrain 58.

[113]Ibid., quatrain 180.

[114]Ibid., quatrain 208.

[115]Ibid., quatrain 209.

[116]The complete hymn is recorded in appendix one of Ileto, *Pasyon and Revolution*. However, because of copying errors in quatrains nineteen and twenty, the total number of quatrains is forty-two instead of the actual forty-three.

they will be further blessed
to the measure that we say.

Arao na capitapita
lalong caligaligaya
cun ang macaguiguinhava
matingnan ñg ating mata.

Catao-an lupa mang hamac
mamamahal ding divalas
at ang Dios ang nag-aatas
at nagbibigay ñg Palad.

Saca cun oling buhayin
ang banal na masunorin
lalo ring pagpapalain
sa sucat nating sabihin.

After extolling God's great powers, the hymn continues from the eleventh quatrain onward roughly as follows: "In heaven, all flesh is purified and ennobled, like the body of Christ. There the differences between young and old, male and female, high and low, and rich and poor, as well as sins that are the traces of individual histories and physical imperfections, are wiped out. All people become wholly one. In addition, there are no physical or spiritual troubles, no heat, cold, hunger, thirst, despair, loneliness, fear, jealousy, pride, idleness, or lust. Therefore people become able to love one another wholeheartedly. In heaven, people are replete in body and spirit and can experience all the good and true things impossible to realize on earth; they can gain true riches. People glow brilliantly in heaven with a light that puts the sun and moon to shame. In heaven, the kinship ties of this world disappear and God becomes father and mother and friend to people. Also, in heaven all people are granted the highest knowledge, and all commune with angels, martyrs, and virgins." The heaven depicted in these verses is one in which "all differences of status, age, sex, and property ownership are denied, and there is complete equality, homogeneity, and anonymity"[117]—what Victor Turner calls "communitas."

The hymn containing this image of heaven was written by an Augustinian friar, Father Pedro de Herrera, in the seventeenth century. Since it was an authorized hymn of the Church, the image it presents was by no means exclusive to the Cofradía but was, to varying degrees, shared by all nineteenth-century Philippine Catholics, who were strongly motivated to aspire to heaven. Their orientation to the next world may have been the result of the Spanish authorities' stressing images of heaven to ease the indigenous people's dissatisfaction without making substantial changes. It is also possible to argue that the people themselves, feeling dispossessed socially and economically, sought release, the result being an increased desire to reach heaven. In any case, one of the underlying reasons *cofradías* flourished in the nineteenth century was this popular aspiration to heaven. In that respect the Cofradía de San José was a social phenomenon reflecting its times.

---

[117]Yoshirō Takeuchi, *Bunka no rikai no tame ni: Bunka kigōgaku e no michi* [To understand cultures: Toward a semiotics of culture] (Tokyo: Iwanami Shoten, 1981), p. 301.

What was distinctive about the Cofradía, which was committed to the ultimate goal of salvation in the next world, was the way in which its members sought to achieve eternal life. At the time, the Church encouraged the accumulation of indulgences as the way to salvation. These were usually granted for making donations to a church or religious order or for purchasing the various devotional objects that the churches and religious orders sold (rosaries and scapulars, for instance) rather than for performing pious or charitable acts.[118] Under this system, the wealthy could acquire many indulgences and thus attain salvation, while the poor were excluded from salvation. I quoted Mas y Sans' comment that "Chinese *mestizos* were even more pious and wealthier than the Filipinos [Spaniards born in the Philippines]" in part three. If these words are analyzed in the historical context I have just described, they acquire a bitterly sarcastic note. Did the Church and the Spanish secular authorities regard Chinese *mestizos* as pious believers simply because they were wealthy?

The starting point for the establishment of the Cofradía de San José was the search for a way to eternal life through truly pious acts rather than the power of wealth. There is overwhelming evidence for this view in the way to salvation expressed in the Poem. The exclusion of *mestizos* from the Cofradía and the formation of an organization only for "poor" indigenous people derived from that goal.

Nonetheless, it is true that within the Cofradía indulgences were received in exchange for donations. As we have seen in part two, the membership as a whole received a partial indulgence through the *Misa de Gracia*, which was celebrated on the nineteenth of each month upon making an offering to the church. In addition, the *camisas* that were given to members who had been especially successful in expanding membership were probably purchased from some church and came with indulgences. Nonetheless, these indulgences were, fundamentally, graces granted for members' pious acts, not simply rewards for almsgiving. In addition, the fees for these indulgences were paid out of the dues collected from the membership as a whole and from the alms that members collected during their journeys. The cooperation of all the members helped those who lacked the financial means to acquire the precious indulgences. This cooperative, egalitarian approach is characteristic of the Cofradía.

Thus, the Cofradía de San José turned its back on a world in which money was the road to heaven and fervently sought a way to heaven through pious acts. The Cofradía's attitude toward faith was clearly a call to a different way of life from the life of faith that the Church taught. The parish priest of Lukban, Father Sancho, included among his criticisms of the Cofradía its teachings that "those who joined the *cofradía* were promised indulgences and God's infinite mercy" and that "no one who was not a member of this *cofradía* could enter the Kingdom of Heaven [*reinos de los Cielos*]."[119] Father Sancho's criticisms were well founded. The Cofradía did assert that only its members would receive plenary indulgences and go to heaven. The reason was that the life of faith of the Cofradía was the correct life for those truly awakened to God's love, the only believers whom God would save.

---

[118]José Rizal and Marcelo H. del Pilar, among others, harshly criticized this practice during the Propaganda Movement of the 1880s and 1890s. See, for instance, chapters sixteen, eighteen, and twenty-nine of Rizal's best-known novel, *Noli Me Tangere*, and the chapter on the economic situation in del Pilar's famous work *La Soberana Monacal en Filipinas* (*Monastic Supremacy in the Philippines*).

[119]Sancho, "Relación Espresiva," *La Política* 1, no. 21 (1891): 251.

In his letter of July 5, 1840, Apolinario instructed the members on this point: "Do not think of the past as if you were to go through it again, since I have given you the ability to do things that spark genuine love for Saint Joseph and for Our God the Father, who is one in three persons. It is as if there is a small but radiant glow, and should our children be immediately awakened by our brotherhood and grow up in this way of living, then, even if we were to die, it would be said that we had bequeathed them something. Inquire in your own minds and give an answer about where our deeds take us. I suspect it is for the life of soul and body. I shall now end my admonition to everyone. May God the Father, the Son, and the Holy Spirit save all; may the Virgin Mother and wise Saint Joseph fill us with every blessing here in our sorrowful world and grant us heaven where He reigns without end." (Huvag ang aalaala ay ang nacaraan na para ñg pagdaranan pa yamang cayoi aquing ypinagpapabor ñg cahinusayang gaua na sucat ycapagalab ñg sintang tunay cay S. Josef at sa A. A. D.ˢ na ysa tatlo sa pagcatavo nia, minti bagang diq.ᵗ con ang m̃ batang masusunod sa atin ay agad maguising nitong ating Capisanan at siyang pagcalachang asal; at ano pa tayo ay m̃ matay man ay may masasabing ating pamana sa canila, somogot cayo at tumanong naman sa yniong saliring caysepan na cun ytong ating m̃ gava ay saan cajandaan, sa banta co ay sa cabuhayan ñg caloloa at catau-an Ytahan co na,t aquing pavacasan ytong abang capaaalalahanan sa canilang calahatan, Ang D.ˢ Ama at Anac naman, Espiritu Stong sumacop sa tanan, at ang Ynang Virg.ⁿ maalam Santo S. Josef tayo ay lagacan ñg ganap na bindecion deto sa ating lupang cajapisan at papagcamtin ñg Lañgit na cahari-an Siya navang valan hangan.)[120]

Joining the Cofradía cut one off from one's past corrupt life; it signified entry into a new life, a life that made love of God blaze in one's heart. This new life was embodied in the members' flesh and spirit as they became a single existential entity. Symbolically, the Cofradía, its members living in this world of new meaning, was an incandescent entity awakened to the love of God and burning with prayer in body and soul. That incandescence would over the years be passed from parent to child and from child to grandchild, finally becoming one eternal life. The ultimate purpose of the Cofradía, which Apolinario articulated and each member envisioned, was the building of a heaven on earth linked directly to the Kingdom of Heaven of supreme bliss.

VI. PERSECUTION BY CHURCH AND STATE

In April 1840 the Cofradía de San José made its activities public by petitioning the Lukban parish church to recognize it as a *cofradía* and conduct monthly masses for it. Why did the Cofradía enter into a relationship with the Church and request recognition at that particular time? One major factor was official action. The expansion movement, which had begun in 1839, had enabled the Cofradía to spread to *pueblos* in three provinces in the southern Tagalog region. Church or *pueblo* officials, growing suspicious of the Cofradía, conducted inquiries into Apolinario's activities at the San Juan de Dios Convent Hospital.[121] In his letter of July 5, 1840, Apolinario wrote: "I will probably not be allowed to stay in Manila any longer. I have already been

---

[120] Appendix II-E-4.

[121] In many *pueblos*, several *cofradías* were competing for influence at the time. Thus, it is likely that the entry of a new *cofradía* would make the established ones feel threatened and would stimulate a variety of investigations.

threatened with divestiture of my habit." That day he began preparing an application for recognition of the Cofradía, to be submitted to the Manila archdiocese.[122]

The application, or *precintacion*, was completed in September and submitted to the archdiocese. In the meantime, however, official pressure on the Cofradía had intensified. In mid-July the town mayor (*gobernadorcillo*) of Lukban, Satornino Cristobal, began imposing restrictions on the Cofradía members who went there to attend the monthly meeting.[123] The restrictions appear to have been ordered by the Lukban parish church. In a letter dated July 29, Cristobal wrote Apolinario that if Apolinario would entrust Cristobal's cousin with the monthly mass for the Cofradía, the cousin would act as an intermediary between the church and the Cofradía. It is possible that this cousin was a coadjutor of the Lukban church. Perhaps nothing came of that offer of aid, or perhaps the Cofradía's relationship with the authorities in other *pueblos* had also worsened. Whatever the case, on August 3 Apolinario wrote Octabio ordering him to dispose of all letters and documents dated through 1839, as mentioned in part one. Circumstances had arisen that necessitated concealing past activities carried out without official recognition.

I wish to make it clear that the Lukban church and other Spanish authorities did not begin to be suspicious of the Cofradía *because* it lacked official recognition. Rather, when something about the Cofradía's activities themselves made the authorities suspicious, the fact that it was an unauthorized organization deepened their mistrust. On the Cofradía's part, however, the tightening restrictions on its activities led to a desire to receive recognition from the authorities so that it could continue its activities unhampered.

On September 1, 1840, after nearly two months of work, the application documents were completed and signed by thirty-four members, beginning with Apolinario.[124] The application is discussed in detail in quatrains 566–81 and 595–97 of the Poem. In the application Apolinario requested the archbishop to "protect and pardon [him] and equally protect the many people in the Cofradía."[125] This phrasing suggests that he had already been charged with a crime. Since the archbishop of Manila was away, having set out on the visitation (*la visita*) at the beginning of September, the Cofradía's representative called at the residence of the vicar general in the pueblo of Bulacan in Bulacan Province and handed the application to him. The vicar general responded within the month, stating that in view of the fact that the headquarters of the Cofradía was in Lukban, "abiding by conventional thinking, take [the application] to the archbishop [actually a bishop] in Camarines."[126]

On October 19 the Cofradía was dealt a devastating blow: led by Father Sancho, the authorities made a surprise raid on the Cofradía's monthly meeting. They arrested 243 members and seized the treasury, Apolinario's letters, and his portrait. The raid was not the result of an arbitrary decision by the Lukban parish priest but was based on a warning from the *vicar forane* for Tayabas Province. According to Father Sancho's report, written after this event, around the middle of that year he

---

[122]Preparation of the application to be submitted to the Manila archdiocese is mentioned in Apolinario's letters of July 5, July 6, July 28, and September 1, 1840.

[123]Letter by Apolinario dated 1840. Though this letter bears only the year, its content indicates that it was written in mid-July 1840.

[124]Appendix II-E-6.

[125]Poem, quatrain 567.

[126]Ibid., quatrain 595.

had received the following warning from Father Antonio Manuel, his immediate superior, who was the *vicar forane* for the province and the parish priest of Tayabas *pueblo* (*el Vicario foraneo Cura parroco*): "A large number of men and women claiming the protection of Saint Joseph and calling themselves a *cofradía* gather in Lukban and contribute a set amount for a nonsensical purpose. They are spurred on and led by one Apolinario de la Cruz, former *donado* at San Juan de Dios. This man has already been cast out by the congregation in the capital [*la Congregación de la Capital,* probably a reference to the San Juan de Dios Convent Hospital]. His letters and sermons [*exhortos*] are read with great interest by the participants in the monthly meetings. Afterward, the participants share food and drink in an atmosphere of brotherly love, then adjourn to their various *pueblos*." Father Sancho continued: "Judging from these statements, the high mass I celebrated each month in honor of Saint Joseph on the payment of anonymous persons proceeded from this group. I decided to refuse to celebrate mass for them and take the necessary steps to do away with this scandalous *cofradía*."[127]

Following this, the report contains a lie, introduced by Father Sancho to evade responsibility for having continued for several months to celebrate the monthly mass for the Cofradía despite his superior's warning that it was a suspicious group. In fact, as mentioned above, the Lukban church was already aware of the existence of the Cofradía. While viewing the Cofradía with suspicion and applying various restrictions to it, the church accepted considerable sums in offerings to perform the monthly mass (thirteen to sixteen *pesos* per mass).[128] Father Sancho now began exerting severe pressure on the Cofradía in an attempt to evade responsibility for his church's lack of control over the organization.

On November 17, almost a month after the raid, a man named Lucas de Torres, apparently the *gobernadorcillo* of Tayabas *pueblo*, sent Apolinario the following letter: "We cannot belong to a *cofradía* that has not received permission from the bishop [*Ylustrísimo*]. We have received an order [*Decreto*] from Naga [seat of the Nueva Cáceres diocese] to excommunicate those who have joined this *cofradía*. Corporal punishment in the courtyard of the Tayabas church has been ordered for Cabesang Ysco and his wife [the couple at whose house the monthly Cofradía meeting was held] and for Octabio." The diocese of Nueva Cáceres was already ordering the Cofradía suppressed.

Why did the Church seek to crush the Cofradía? According to Father Sancho's report, the Cofradía was a treasonous organization hiding behind a religious mask. He listed the following reasons:

"[1.] This so-called *cofradía* continued to meet, disregarding an order of excommunication issued by the diocesan of Nueva Caceres and posted in the Lukban, Sariaya, and Tayabas churches.

"[2.] This *cofradía* not only arbitrarily imposed fines on its members but also collected one *real* a month for membership dues. It is quite impossible to understand what the intended use of these dues collected from the five to six hundred members could be.

"[3.] The *cabecillas* were threatened by being told that if they did not strive to expand the membership they would not be able to participate in the great victory.

---

[127]Sancho, "Relación Espresiva," *La Política* 1, no. 21 (1891): 250.

[128]Appendix II-E-2.

They were repeatedly requested to dedicate themselves to the task with the same passionate faith as those who devote themselves to converting the heathen.

"[4.] Those who joined the *cofradía* were promised indulgences and God's infinite mercy.

"[5.] The *cofradía* excluded *mestizos*.

"[6.] Those who attempted to leave the *cofradía* were scorned and severely punished.

"[7.] A particularly important point was that no one who was not a member of this *cofradía* could enter the Kingdom of Heaven [*reinos de los Cielos*].

"[8.] The influence of the former *donado* is growing daily; it may become worship [*un culto*] in future. People's veneration of him already approaches worship. He is already in the position of contradicting the orders of superior civil or ecclesiastical authorities."[129]

The second and fifth reasons appear to have been advanced as evidence that the Cofradía was secretly preparing a rebellion, while the first, third, sixth, and eighth reasons were apparently intended to prove that it was defying the legitimate authority and discipline of the Church. The fourth and seventh reasons seem to have been advanced to show that the Cofradía was spreading teachings opposed to the doctrines of orthodox Catholicism. More of Father Sancho's reasons have to do with religious heresy than with political rebelliousness, an assessment probably based on his understanding of the true nature of the Cofradía. The Cofradía's teachings did indeed contradict the Church's, and to that extent did defy the authority of the Church. Nevertheless, the organization continued, repeatedly and obstinately, to seek recognition from the Church.

Clearly, at this stage the Cofradía harbored no active intent to force a confrontation with the Church. Still less did it aim to undermine Spanish rule through the force of its accumulated economic power, as hinted in the second of Father Sancho's reasons. I believe that the activities of the Cofradía can be regarded as a kind of sectarian movement with respect to the Church. Father Sancho and others perceived it as a group in rebellion against the political status quo because their vision was clouded by an external factor. After the Spanish colonies in Latin America won their independence, Spanish officials in the Philippines felt that their rule there was endangered as well and were inclined to unrealistic fears. There was no basis in fact for their view of the Cofradía as posing a threat of political rebellion.

The 243 Cofradía members arrested in the October 19 raid were confined in the Lukban *pueblo* office. The governor of Tayabas Province, Don Joaquin Ortega, was asked for directions on the disposition of those arrested. He stated that this troublesome matter did not fall under the *gobernadorcillo*'s jurisdiction but was part of the duties of the ecclesiastical judge of the province (*el jusgado eclesiastico de la Provincia*). He refused to become actively involved and had all those arrested released.[130] Ortega remained passive not only in this incident but throughout the suppression of the Cofradía, which led Church authorities to criticize him as a liberal. In the 1840s, the religious orders began rebuilding their strength and their position as the protectors of the Philippine government. At the same time, liberal government officials were being sent from Spain to staff the government offices. Thus a confrontation between the religious orders and the liberals was developing within the ruling class.

---

[129]See note 119. The bracketed numbers have been added to clarify Father Sancho's reasons.

[130]Sancho, "Relación Espresiva," *La Política* 2, no. 31 (1892): 100.

In December 1840 the Cofradía sent a document appealing the injustice of the October raid to the Seor Fiscal in the Audiencia,[131] but the authorities took no action. In Lukban, surveillance and restriction of the Cofradía became so strict that the organization found it impossible to continue its activities there. At the beginning of 1841 the monthly meeting was moved to Majayjay *pueblo*. In February representatives of the Cofradía, led by Father de los Santos, went to Naga to submit to the Nueva Caceres diocesan authorities the application for recognition that had been rejected by the vicar general of the Manila archdiocese in September 1840.[132] The reply was finally delivered to Octabio in late May by a messenger who had been sent to Naga.[133] Recognition was not granted. In his letter of May 24, 1841, Apolinario directed Octabio to prepare for another trip to Naga; this time, he wrote in desperation, he wished to deliver the application in person. Pressure to disband the Cofradía was gaining strength daily, and Apolinario and the other leaders believed that receiving official recognition was the only way to salvage the organization.

In March 1841 Apolinario had been dismissed by the San Juan de Dios Convent Hospital and had gone to live in Father de los Santos's house (which may have been the parish rectory). In June he submitted the application for the fourth time, this time to the Audiencia.[134] Official recognition had become a matter of life or death to the Cofradía. The Superior Gobierno (office of the governor general), which had received the application for recognition through the Audiencia, decided to refuse it and ordered a series of measures to crush the Cofradía.[135]

On July 8 the Superior Gobierno issued an order for Apolinario's arrest.[136] In mid-July orders proscribing the Cofradía de San José were issued in the three *pueblos* of Lukban, Tayabas, and Majayjay.[137] In addition, the parish church in each of these *pueblos* established a Cofradía ni San Francisco Xavier to undercut the Cofradía de San José.[138] With the highest secular authority moving to suppress it, persecution of the Cofradía was growing in both quantity and quality. Its very survival was now in jeopardy.

Though persecution worsened daily, Apolinario clung to hope, writing on July 22, "I still can say nothing about our application, which is before the Audiencia." This tells us that the Superior Gobierno was imposing measures to suppress the Cofradía before refusing the application. How should we interpret Apolinario's continuing to pin such hope, even then, on the decision of the Spanish authorities? As will be discussed in part seven, he was evidently sustained by his strong faith, his conviction that right was on his side and that God would not abandon him.

In September the Superior Gobierno ordered the governors of the provinces concerned to raid the Cofradía's monthly meeting in Majayjay on the nineteenth.[139] That

---

[131]De los Santos affidavit. The *Audiencia* was the tribunal which performed the triple function of hearing important cases, advising the governor general, and sometimes initiating legislation. The *Fiscal* was a state attorney.

[132]Cruz, "Declaración," *La Política* 2, no. 32 (1892): 114.

[133]Letter by Octabio dated May 20, 1841.

[134]De los Santos affidavit.

[135]Cruz, "Declaración," La Política 2, no. 33 (1892): 130.

[136]De los Santos affidavit.

[137]Letter by Octabio dated July 14, 1841.

[138]Letters by Octabio dated July 14, July 21, and July 22, 1841.

[139]Sancho, "Relación Espresiva," *La Política* 1, no. 23 (1891): 289.

information reached the Cofradía in advance, and most of the members avoided arrest. Octabio's house was searched, however, and he was arrested and tortured in the *pueblo* office. Octabio's father and a few other members were interrogated in the same way.[140] Thus the Cofradía approached its final crisis.

VII. AN APOCALYPTIC UPRISING

After the raid on October 19, 1840, several of Apolinario's letters discussed how Cofradía members should perceive the crisis threatening the organization. The following three passages from letters reveal Apolinario's interpretation of the persecution being inflicted on the Cofradía.

"This letter has no other purpose, my brothers, but to encourage you to be steadfast in these times. Whoever falters, I might disown. This seems just like a spectacle that shields the sun's rays. Through God's mercy, soon light shall be upon us. Whatever misfortune befalls us, let us bear it, for it is destined. God disposes and he himself will change things for us."

"Valang dahilan ytong aquing sulat m̃ capatid condi ona ang canilang loob ay hovag ioorong sa m̃ panahong yto at ang tomalicod ay di co na yata aari-ing casama yto ay para lamang ysang pañganoring tomaquip sa cicat ñg arao ano pa at sa ava ñg D.ˢ ay maglilivanag din tayo at ang anomang carovaguinan ay tiisen at nasa panahon, sapagcat Dios ang may bigai at cia rin naman ang bibihis sa atin. . . ."[141]

"The sufferings we now endure will end up in glory. Those who waver in being a member of our group must consider whether perhaps their minds are darkened. Those who forget this moment must worry about where it leads when our destined day for glory comes, which will be granted to everyone. . . ."

"At ang m̃ga hapis na ating dinadala ñgayon ay luvalhati naman ang casasapitan, at ang m̃ga loob na nag oorong sulung ñg paq.ᵉq.ᵉsama sa ating caysahan ay dapat mag isip at baca nadidiliman lamang macalilimot sa panahong yto ay mag alaala at ang casasapitan ay baca con domating ang arao na tadhana sa ating calovalhatiang dapat ypagvagui ñg sino pa man. . . ."[142]

"Consider the best that you can do at the present moment, since everything that has transpired is of divine will. All the trials you have endured are not punishment. They are a great grace toward the enlightenment of this confraternity. You have seen a glimmer of the five joyous mysteries as well as the sorrowful. Needless to say, the glorious mysteries will prevail forever."

"Pacaysipin mo ang lalong magaling na gauin sa panahong yto at ang anomang nasapit at nagda-an ay calooban ñg Langit; ang m̃ parusang binata mo yaon naman ay hindi parusa condi tulong malaquing gracia na ycalilivanag nitong Cof.a yayamang napag aninao mu na ang limang Mistiriong tuva, hapis naman ay gayon din, sa bagay ay luvalhati naman ang yiral na valañg hangan. . . ."[143]

Apolinario explained the Cofradía's situation in terms of the orthodox Catholic interpretation of history and salvation. He regarded the persecution by the Superior Gobierno and the Church as the will of God. God had sent the members this ordeal to teach them the way to eternal glory, that is, to instruct them in the mysteries of the rosary. To share in the glory of heaven, one must first know the joy of the Gospel and

---

[140]Appendix II-F-5.

[141]Appendix II-E-8.

[142]Appendix II-E-9.

[143]Appendix II-E-12.

must be able to withstand ordeals. The members must prevail by understanding their present suffering, not allowing their hearts to waver. If they can do this, they will be able to share in the final triumphal glory.

This explanation had the same persuasive force upon the members as Apolinario's other teachings. His interpretation of reality was not likely to spark resistance to official persecution, for he taught that the members' proper path was to have firm faith and endure.

As persecution intensified, however, some members were unable to endure and either left the Cofradía or broke its rules. Apolinario's letters of 1841 often mentioned punishments for those who had violated the rules or failed to perform their duties. The following letter was discussed in part four. I quote from it again here because punishments within the Cofradía are mentioned before and after the passage quoted earlier:

"I ordered that you should be responsible to them. Why then did you not do what was necessary and inflict on them the rightful punishment? Because this is what I say: No one was ever strangled or threatened with a dagger; rather everyone has joined the group voluntarily, and no one was whipped when communicating. Thus I have no other instructions for you except that with regard to our followers those who refuse to obey and share in our suffering at this moment should be given the proper punishment."

"Acoy nag-orden na ycau ay binibigyan co ñg cuedado sa canila, baguin at di mo gauen ang m̃ catampatan, at bagay sa canilang casalanan, sapag at ganito ang sasabihin co, ang sinoman ay hindi natin pinisel sa leeg o tenoonan ñg sondang ñg paq.ᵉq.ᵉsama dito sa caysahan, condi pavang bolontad ñg loob at valang dina-an sa palo, ñg paqeq.epag-osap. Caya aco ay valang bilin sa yio, na con tongcol sa tavo na m̃ga basalial natin, condi ang aayau somonod at domamay sa hirap sa panahong yto ay gau-in ang carampatan, at ocol sa ganganoong casalanan."[144]

In another letter Apolinario instructed Octabio on how to punish traitors:

". . . whoever errs, you should whip. Whoever needs censure, you should reprimand . . . and if you defer a response to the betrayal of members and not mete out justice, you will be answerable to me (for males, it must not exceed seven whips of the *suflina* and for females five *palamita*), whether dealing with small or great offenses, it will be more difficult if recriminations take place in the afterlife; when one becomes a follower, it is better for the head to mete out just punishment."

"Ang magcasala sa yio at dapat mong abriguahin ang carampatang paluin ay paluin at ang dapat pañgaralan ay pañgaralan, . . . at palalamiguin mo pa ang m̃ pagtatraydor ñg A. m̃ casama, hindi gauen ang pagcajosticia, ay magbabayad ca sa aquin (con lalaq.e huvag lumalu sa pitong lantac ñg suflina, at sa babayi ay limang palamita, munti at malaquing casalanan lalong mahirap cun doon pa tayo magtototulacan sa huling buhay con napasasacup ang ysang basalios ay carampatang gauin ñg ysan puno ay jostipica at dapat sa casalanan."[145]

Several other letters contain such statements as "You make the decision and give Mr. and Mrs. Cabesang Franco the appropriate punishment. You are the judge in my

[144]See note 92.

[145]Letter by Apolinario dated June 8, 1841. *Suflina* and *palamita* appear to be types of whips, though I have not yet been able to ascertain precisely what they are. Please note that the original text lacks a closing parenthesis.

absence."[146] The frequency of such comments suggests that agitation and disaffection were spreading. To make matters worse, external pressure grew much harsher in July 1841, when the Superior Gobierno, which had the support of the army, ordered Apolinario's arrest and the proscription of the Cofradía. At that point the Cofradía leaders' perception of the situation began gradually to change. Once the Superior Gobierno added its force to the persecution, further passive endurance would endanger the Cofradía's very existence. If the Cofradía were dissolved, all would be lost: the ties between the members, their reason for living, and, ultimately, their way to the Kingdom of Heaven. Thus the Cofradía was forced into a new stance: armed resistance.

In his letter of August 13, 1841, Octabio reported to Apolinario that he had visited the village of Isabang (*nayon ñg Ysabang*).[147] The letter does not mention the reason for his journey. Since we know that two months later, on October 21, the Cofradía members gathered in this village to start their uprising, it appears that preparations for the uprising began around the time of Octabio's visit.

When considering the uprising, we should remember that within the Cofradía the movement to resist persecution with force was still explained in terms of a Catholic belief structure. The cruel persecution by the authorities, which the Cofradía had never anticipated, made the members think that the Apocalypse was at hand and that the Antichrist, the embodiment of evil, was rampant. The time of the Last Judgment had arrived, they were told. God's faithful would have to rise, fight the traitors, and witness to their faith. This kind of call to arms explained the crisis facing the Cofradía in terms extraordinarily persuasive to its members, familiar as they were with the apocalyptic world of the *Pasyon Pilapil*.

In its September 1841 order to crush the Cofradía, the Superior Gobierno commanded the Tayabas provincial governor, Ortega, to arrest all the Cofradía leaders. Ortega put off carrying out the order, however, then left for Manila on September 28, leaving the *gobernadorcillo* of Tayabas *pueblo* to handle the matter. Since his wife was herself a member of the Cofradía, he too was less than active in pursuing the arrest of its leaders. The leaders, who escaped thanks to this chain of events, gathered in late October in the *pueblo* of Bay on the southern shore of Laguna de Bay. There they met Apolinario, who had fled from Manila.[148] The group made its way through San Pablo, Tiaon, and Sariaya to Isabang. Judging from Father Sancho's report, the journey was made on October 21. As noted in part three, the news that Apolinario had arrived in Isabang "was transmitted with unbelievable speed. Numbers of young and old, male and female, people of every position in society, drawn by the prestige of the founder [of the Cofradía], transformed that isolated village into a lively, if crude, camp in a matter of hours."[149]

The people swelling the camp included some twenty-five hundred armed men as well as Aetas, aboriginal tribespeople who supported the Cofradía and were armed

---

[146]Letter by Apolinario dated February 23, 1841.

[147]Isabang was a settlement within the *pueblo* of Tayabas. Since Octabio called it *nayon ñg Ysabang*, while Father Sancho described it as *sitio de Isabang*, Isabang may not have been a *barrio* yet.

[148]Sancho, "Relación Espresiva," *La Política* 1, no. 23 (1891): 289–90; José Montero y Vidal, *Historia General de Filipinas desde el Descubrimiento de Dichas Islas hasta Nuestro Días* (Madrid: Tello, 1895), vol. 3, pp. 39–40.

[149]Sancho, "Relación Espresiva," *La Política* 1, no. 23 (1891): 290.

with bows and arrows. Counting the Aetas and the Cofradía women and children, the force numbered several thousand.[150] After Apolinario's arrival in Isabang the wife of the Tayabas *gobernadorcillo* conveyed his wish to say a novena in the Tayabas church and negotiated with the *pueblo* officials concerning this request. One can readily imagine that in this crisis Apolinario would wish to pray for the grace of God through the intercession of Saint Joseph, the Cofradía's patron saint. While the Tayabas *principalía*, thrown into a panic by the situation, were hesitating over their decision, Governor Ortega returned from Manila on October 22, and the negotiations ended in failure.[151]

Immediately upon returning to the *pueblo* of Tayabas, where the provincial office was located, Ortega issued a special amnesty to the members of the Cofradía on condition that the organization disband immediately. That was out of the question for the Cofradía. The following day, October 23, Ortega assembled a force of about three hundred men, consisting of hastily called out municipal policemen (*cuadrilleros*), several village heads who happened to be at the *pueblo* office with men they had brought for corvée labor (*polo*),[152] those laborers, and the Franciscan parish priests from Lukban and Tayabas. Ortega led this punitive force in an attack on the Cofradía members crowded into Isabang. Upon arriving at the battlefield, however, some of his force deserted, while others defected to the Cofradía. To make matters worse, the Aetas rained arrows upon the governor's force. The Aetas probably harbored long-standing resentment against the Spanish authorities, while Ortega's force included Cofradía sympathizers. Abandoned by his subordinates and left alone on the field of battle, the governor was slaughtered by Cofradía members.[153]

The day after winning this first battle with the authorities, the Cofradía moved its camp to Alitao (or Ypilang, as Apolinario called it in his affidavit), a more advantageous location militarily. Alitao, situated about seven kilometers north of Isabang as the crow flies, was nestled in a narrow plateau on Mount Banahaw. The plateau was bounded to the north and south by the Iyam and Ypilam rivers, originating on the mountain, and to the east by forest. The Cofradía prepared for battle by raising a double palisade along a line connecting the two rivers and digging crisscrossing emergency water channels behind this fortification. In the center of the camp they built a makeshift church of bamboo and palm fronds and decorated its interior with colorful hangings and religious pictures. In the week before the authorities attacked, Apolinario commenced a novena and conducted other rites there. Quarters for Apolinario were built beside the church. There he spent his days in prayer and meditation, isolated from the ordinary Cofradía members.[154]

The Spanish colonial government was shocked by the news of Ortega's murder. Aware of the seriousness of the affair, the government sent an army to Tayabas, via both land and sea, to attack the Cofradía. The governor of Laguna Province had already sent several dozen soldiers to the *pueblo*. On October 30 the punitive force, commanded by Teniente Colonel Joaquin Huet, assembled in Tayabas. The force in-

---

[150]Cruz, "Declaración," *La Política* 2, no. 33 (1892): 131.

[151]Montero y Vidal, *Historia General*, vol. 3, p. 41.

[152]According to Montero y Vidal, they were *individuos de resguardos*. Montero y Vidal, *Historia General*, vol. 3, p. 41.

[153]Ibid.; David Sweet, "A Proto-Political Peasant Movement in the Spanish Philippines: The Cofradia de San Jose and the Tayabas Rebellion of 1841," *Asian Studies* 8 (1970): 108.

[154]Sancho, "Relación Espresiva," *La Política* 2, no. 26 (1892): 30–31.

cluded four hundred regular soldiers (of whom sixty were cavalry), a total of four hundred *cuadrilleros* and *resguardos* (guards), and thirty artillerymen. That day Huet issued a special amnesty for the members of the Cofradía in the name of the governor general and appealed to them to surrender. The offer was bluntly rejected,[155] for the Cofradía members were certain of victory.

A description of the Cofradía stronghold of Alitao is included in the affidavit of an eyewitness, Gregorio Miguel de Jesus, a forty-one-year-old native of Isabang. He stated that Alitao was defended by approximately three thousand people, armed with pistols, guns (*fusiles*), catapults (*trabucos*), firelocks (*escopetas*), three cannons, and a great variety of other weapons. "They knew nothing of what was about to happen there. But since they were assured of victory and believed their cause [*su causa*] was just, they were determined to do everything necessary for their defense." In fact, the commanding officer of the Alitao force, Purgatorio,[156] loudly assured the people assembled that all of them would be able to escape the government forces' attack.[157] Apolinario also promised his followers that they would prevail, prophesying miracles: "As soon as the opposing forces appear, the earth will crack open, and those who dare to attack the Cofradía will be swallowed up."[158] And "during the battle two voices would emanate from Tayabas and be answered by two rumbles from Mount Amolog. The mountain would open and the *Yglesia* (lit., 'Church') would appear, uniting all the brethren. Manila would be inundated; the waters from the sea would drown all who were not cofrades, the latter being aided by a great armada."[159] Since the members believed this battle to be the battle of Armageddon, they had absolute faith in these prophecies and promises of victory.

A vivid description of this apocalyptic battle is found in the final chapter of the *Pasyon Pilapil*, "Ang Paghuhukom ng Ating Panginoong Hesukristo sa Sanglibutang Tao" (The Judgement of Our Lord Jesus Christ on All Mankind). Following is a summary of that chapter:

The Gospel According to Saint Matthew states that Jesus will definitely return to this world and judge the entire human race. But even those of deep faith do not know when this will be. As that day approaches, however, fearsome signs will appear in the heavens and on earth, in the winds and on the seas, and the universe will be thrown into confusion. The most fearsome of these signs will be the advent of the Antichrist, the worst traitor. He will lead those of little faith and rule the world for three years. Then the prophets Elijah and Enoch will appear to save all people from becoming faithless traitors. The two prophets will be killed by the Antichrist, but will be resurrected after four days. When the three years are over the angel of Christ, Michael, will come to earth and destroy the traitors and their king, the Antichrist. God will then give humanity forty days for repentance. When the final day arrives, thunder will roar, the earth will tremble, and fire will fall upon the world and destroy it. All people and all things will be rent asunder, burned up, and destroyed. Finally, at the sound of the trumpets (*pacacac*) that the angels blow, the dead will rise in the Valley of Josaphat. The resurrected people are all thirty-three years old. They are divided into the faithful and the traitors. The flesh of the traitors gives off a

---

[155]Montero y Vidal, *Historia General*, vol. 3, pp. 44–45.

[156]This was the nickname of Apolonio Juan de la Cruz, a man from the *pueblo* of Tayabas.

[157]Cruz, "Declaración," *La Política* 2, no. 35 (1892): 155.

[158]Montero y Vidal, *Historia General*, vol. 3, p. 45.

[159]Ileto, *Pasyon and Revolution*, p. 75.

stench that reaches the highest heaven, but the flesh of the faithful emits a sweet perfume, and their faces are wreathed in a glow brighter even than the sun's flames. Jesus Christ descends to earth with a band of angels and judges all the people. When he has finished the Last Judgment, he calls to the faithful: "Come, my intimate friends, / whom God the King, my Father, / has truly blessed, / now receive / the joy of paradise."[160] Then, burning with wrath, Jesus shouts at the traitors: "Go now and receive / fire in the hellish kingdom / that has been prepared / for you and all the demons / for all eternity."[161] The earth suddenly splits open where they stand and swallows up all the evil people and demons and those with ferocious hearts.

Apolinario's prophecies were based on this apocalyptic vision, deeply embedded in his followers' minds. They burned with the conviction that they upheld the true teachings of Jesus Christ and that they alone would triumph and be saved.

The government army launched its attack on the Alitao camp late on the night of October 31. As the battle was about to begin Apolinario drew his sword, said to have been taken from Ortega at the battle of Isabang, and blessed his followers one by one "in the name of the Father, and of the Son, and of the Holy Spirit," whereupon they became extremely excited, believing that this blessing made them invincible.[162] They bravely charged the government force with their handmade bows and arrows, axes, and rifles, and one by one joined the heap of dead and wounded. Appalled by the carnage, the *cabecillas* marched into Apolinario's quarters to threaten him with death if he did not immediately produce the miracles and rescue he had prophesied. They were too late. The punitive force had already reached Apolinario's quarters and he had escaped, crawling through a predawn cloudburst into the forest behind the camp.[163]

In four hours of fierce fighting the battle, begun in the middle of the night in bad weather, ended in a bitter defeat for the Cofradía: three hundred to five hundred members were killed, and about five hundred, including three hundred women, were taken prisoner. The remainder of those who had attempted to hold the camp slipped off in the driving rain into Mount Banahaw's forests. Apolinario was captured on November 2 and was executed by firing squad on November 4. Approximately two hundred other prisoners were also executed that day.[164] A great tragedy in the history of the Tagalog people had come to a close.

CONCLUSION: FEATURES UNIQUE TO THE COFRADÍA DE SAN JOSÉ AND THOSE SHARED WITH OTHER COFRADÍAS

In 1870, a generation after the Cofradía de San José tragedy, the activities of a subversive *cofradía* were discovered in the same area of Tayabas Province. This *cofradía*, calling itself the Cofradía de San José, San Apolinario y San Apolonio, held regular meet-

---

[160] *Pasyon Pilapil*, stanza 2,638. This English translation is drawn from René B. Javellana, SJ, *Casaysayan nang Pasiong Mahal ni Jesucristong Panginoon Natin na Sucat Ipag-alab nang Puso nang Sinomang Babasa, With an Introduction, Annotations, and Translation of the 1882 Edition* (Quezon City: Ateneo de Manila University Press, 1988), p. 233. This work was consulted only at the time the English version of this paper was being prepared.

[161] *Pasyon Pilapil*, stanza 2,644. See Javellana, *Casaysayan nan Pasiong*, p. 233.

[162] Cruz, "Declaración," *La Política* 2, no. 33 (1892): 131. This is an illustration of the characteristic Philippine belief in invincibility and invulnerability, an interesting point but one beyond the purview of this paper.

[163] Sancho, "Relación Espresiva," *La Política* 2, no. 29 (1892): 74.

[164] Ileto, *Pasyon and Revolution*, p. 79.

ings at the house of the widow of Apolonio Juan de la Cruz (Purgatorio), the commander of the Cofradía forces at Alitao.[165] The new group had added Apolinario and Apolonio to the ranks of the saints. The Cofradía de San José had been reborn and was developing anew. The leader of the new organization, Januario Labios, claimed to be able to communicate directly with Apolinario, Apolonio, and the Virgin Mary. He also asserted that they had given him instructions on how to rebuild the Cofradía and systematize its religious practices.

The new *cofradía* claimed that if its members resolutely followed its teachings they would enjoy eternal bliss after death and would be absolved from the tribute (*tributo*) and granted independence (*independencia*) in this life. It is not clear what this *cofradía* meant by *independencia*. Since its rise coincided with the period in which Manila was enthusiastic about the liberal policies of Governor General Carlos María de la Torre (served 1869–1871), it is possible that this word reached the group via Manila. Thorough government investigation, however, revealed no connection between the new *cofradía* and the liberal movement in Manila. Thus, it is likely that these peasants understood *independencia* to mean freedom from the *tributo* and the *polo*. In any case, the new group made salvation in the next world and happiness in this one its goals, and the religious practices incumbent upon its members were intended to serve these ends. The first duty of members was daily prayer. When the Spanish authorities attacked the group, which had secluded itself on Mount Banahaw, in 1870, they seized several notebooks containing the life of Jesus Christ written in Tagalog, a number of documents recording prescriptions for medicines, and the texts of prayers. The new *cofradía* also recited the *pasyon* and other prayers—probably the rosary, the *Pater Noster*, the *Ave Maria*, and the *Gloria Patri*—with some prayers to be said every day and others on occasions specified by the *cofradía*.

Second, the new group required members to make a pilgrimage to Mount Banahaw as a penance (*penitencia*). This act of penance eternally separated the members from the past, impure world and ushered them into a new world of faith. That new world of faith was supposed to herald the human relationships that would be realized in the heavenly kingdom to come. The new *cofradía* not only rejected the *polo* and payment of the *tributo*, the central institutions of colonial exploitation, but also lacked all respect for parish priests, asserting that their own church was on the mountain. Since this *cofradía* was so plainly rebellious toward the colonial authorities, in 1870 the Spanish officials embarked on a policy of suppression, searching out the members on Mount Banahaw and arresting many.

Pilgrimages to Mount Banahaw and the neighboring peak, San Cristobal, remain popular in Lent today, and Ileto appears to regard their origins as lying in this new *cofradía*.[166] As mentioned in part one, however, the Cofradía de San José had also conducted pilgrimages to Mount Banahaw. The Cofradía de San José and today's pilgrimages to Mount Banahaw are linked by the passionate faith of the Tagalog people.

This brief overview of the major features of the reborn Cofradía should help clarify the characteristics of the Cofradía de San José. The aim of this paper is to present as clear a picture as possible of popular Catholicism in the Philippines in the nineteenth century through a detailed discussion of one manifestation, the Cofradía de San José. More narrowly, its goal is to elucidate the *cofradía* movement in Tagalog society in the nineteenth century. In conclusion, then, I will attempt to distinguish be-

---

[165]The information on this new *cofradía* is from Ileto, *Pasyon and Revolution*, pp. 80–91.

[166]Ibid., pp. 86–91.

tween characteristics peculiar to the Cofradía de San José and the those common to all *cofradías*.

The first distinctive feature of the Cofradía was its leadership. Usually the parish church played the central role in organizing *cofradías*, and the *principalía* class of the *pueblo* dominated the group's leadership. The Cofradía de San José, however, rejected church leadership; peasants organized it on their own. The nature of its leadership is closely related to the following three features. The second distinctive feature of the Cofradía is that it made its first priority the salvation of Tagalog peasants, who were experiencing increasing relative deprivation in the face of the economic advances made by Chinese *mestizos*. Third, the Cofradía sought to win salvation in the afterworld not through indulgences, as the Church taught, but through prayer. The life of prayer that the members of the Cofradía pursued meant living in a world of new meaning divorced from the defiled world of the past. Therefore individuals had to participate in the Cofradía of their own free will. Fourth, Cofradía members sought their own sense of religious sufficiency though religious practices, such as the pilgrimage to Mount Banahaw, which were not approved by the Church, and through their meetings (at a member's house, not a church, and including a communal meal that had great significance for the members). Finally, their leader, Apolinario, claimed transcendental authority received through the mysterious grace of the Virgin Mary and attempted to personify the image of Jesus Christ depicted in the *Pasyon Pilapil*.

At the same time, the Cofradía de San José shared many of the characteristics and religious practices of other *cofradías*. First, the goal of the Cofradía de San José, like that of other *cofradías*, was salvation, a matter of the greatest concern to the Tagalog people of the time. Second, it shared with other *cofradías* a dual structure, with a formal and an actual set of titles and relationships. While the Cofradía had a formal hierarchy using titles borrowed from Spanish religious orders (*hermano mayor, hermano menor interior, fundadores, cabecillas, hermanos*), its actual relationships were modeled on family relationships in Tagalog society (*ama, magulang, anak*). Third, the activities of the Cofradía de San José were similar to those of other *cofradías*. These included the duties of members (daily prayers, high dues, a monthly *Misa de Gracia* on a day associated with the group's patron saint, attendance at regular meetings, a devotion to Mary outstripping faith in the patron saint, a related deep devotion to the rosary, prayer for worldly benefits through novenas, the custom of reciting the *Pasyon Pilapil* during Lent) and titles and ranks based on piety. Finally, recitation of the *Pasyon Pilapil* was common to other *cofradías* and was widespread among the Tagalog people in general. Through this their sacred book they shared the Catholic view of salvation and eschatology, which formed their basic worldview. Both the shared and the unique characteristics of the Cofradía de San José indicate the Catholic belief and practice prevalent among the Tagalog people in the nineteenth century.

A Note on Orthography

The Tagalog orthography in the AC Papers differs from the orthography of present-day Pilipino. When quoting sources or using terms that occur in these sources, I have followed the spelling found in the sources. Otherwise I have used modern Pilipino orthography.

ACKNOWLEDGMENTS

I am indebted to many people for assistance with this paper. Lilia F. Antonio, Assistant Professor at the University of the Philippines, patiently helped me decipher difficult spellings and meanings in the AC Papers. Vicente Marasigan, SJ, and Rene B. Javellana, SJ, of Ateneo de Manila University gave me valuable instruction in Catholic doctrine, organizations of believers, and Church history. Bartholomew Lahiff, SJ, of the Department of History and Political Science of Ateneo de Manila University repeatedly urged me to complete the paper as quickly as possible. During my fieldwork in Lukban, Armando Racelis, the mayor of Lukban, and Angelo Q. Peña, the president of Southern Luzon Polytechnic College, gave me warm support. My research in the Philippines was supported by the Japan Foundation Scholars Abroad Program. During this period (March 1982 through April 1983), I had the use of research facilities as a visiting fellow at the Institute of Philippine Culture, Ateneo de Manila University. I am deeply grateful to these individuals and institutions for their assistance. In addition, I received the assistance of two friends, Viveca V. Hernández and Michiko Yamagishi, in editing and proofreading the Japanese manuscript.

AFTERWORD

After completing this paper, I conducted historico-anthropological research on Philippine folk Catholicism on the island of Luzon for a fifty-day period beginning in late March 1985. I spent about ten days studying the papers in the Philippine National Archives, at which time I discovered a valuable document concerning the Cofradía de San José. This document, found in a bundle of papers catalogued under "Cofradía," is the Cofradía de San José's account book. Several pages are missing from the beginning and the end of the document, so that the title and the total number of pages are unknown. The surviving document totals 447 pages recording income and disbursements from December 1832 to July 1841, together with notes (*notas*).

The discovery of this voluminous document has provided a clearer picture of the Cofradía's activities. The *notas* record many fascinating details not found in the AC Papers. At this point I do not judge that radical revision of the present paper is necessary, but I hope to write a supplementary paper soon. The newly discovered document should make it possible to define more precisely the significance of the Cofradía de San José in the context of social unrest in Tagalog society in general at the time. In addition, it provides a rich source of data on the early history of the Cofradía.

The Cofradía, founded on December 12, 1832, began its expansion movement in May 1839. The most valuable aspect of the newly discovered document is its detailed record of the way this movement developed. It also provides evidence dramatically reinforcing the interpretation of the exclusion of *mestizos* offered in the present paper.

In my next paper, I plan to consider in particular Apolinario's leadership. The newly discovered document describes in detail two portraits of Apolinario produced by the Cofradía, thus making it clear for the first time that not one but two portraits of Apolinario were painted. My analysis in the present paper, naturally, has focused on only one of those portraits, that is, on only one aspect of Apolinario. Since the image of Apolinario is the prototype of the "Philippine Christ," I intend to discuss both portraits in my next paper.

This paper was originally published under the title "19 seiki Firipin no minshū katorishizumu: Sei Yosefu Kyōdaikai no katsudō o chūshin ni shite" [Popular Catholicism in the nineteenth-century Philippines: Focus on the Cofradía de San José Movement] in *Ajia, Afurika gengo bunka kenkyū* [Journal of Asian and African Studies] 30 (1985): 1–77.

REFERENCES

MANUSCRIPT MATERIALS

Apolinario de la Cruz Papers. Philippine National Archives, Manila.

Galán, Fray Bartolomé. "Informe sobre la Provincia de Tayabas." MS dated April 8, 1823. Ayer Collection Box 1350, Newberry Library, Chicago.

Matta, Juan Manuel de la. "Apolinario de la Cruz: Relación en que se Da Cuenta de Haber Estallado la Conspiración en Tayabas." MS dated November 16, 1841. Ayer Collection, Newberry Library, Chicago.

PUBLISHED MATERIALS, THESES, AND DISSERTATIONS

Agoncillo, Teodoro A., and Milagros Guerrero. *History of the Filipino People*. Quezon City: R. P. Garcia Publishing Co., 1970.

Anderson, Gerald H., ed. *Studies in Philippine Church History*. Ithaca: Cornell University Press, 1968.

Aquino de Belen, Gaspar. "Ang Mahal na Pasion ni Iesu Christong P. Natin na Tola." In Tomas de Villacastin, *Manga Panalanin Pagtatagobilin sa Calolova nang Tavong Naghihin galo*. Translated by Gaspar Aquino de Belen. 5th ed. Manila: Imprenta de la Compañía de Iesus, 1760 (orig. pub. 1703).

Barrion, M. Caridad, OSB. *Religious Life of the Laity in Eighteenth Century Philippines: As Reflected in the Decrees of the Council of Manila of 1774 and the Synod of Calasiao of 1773*. Manila: University of Santo Tomas Press, 1961.

Blair, Emma Helen, and James Alexander Robertson, eds. *The Philippine Islands, 1493–1898*. 55 vols. Cleveland: Arthur H. Clark, 1909.

Buzeta, Manuel, and Felipe Bravo. *Diccionario Geográfico, Estadístico, Histórico de las Islas Filipinas*. 2 vols. Madrid: Imprenta de D. José C. de la Peña, 1850.

Casaysayan nang Pasiong Mahal ni Jesucristong Panginoon Natin Sucat Ipag-Alab nang Puso nang Sino Mang Babasa. Manila: Imprenta y Librerías de J. Martinez, 1935 (orig. pub. 1814).

Constantino, Renato. *The Philippines: A Past Revisited*. Quezon City: Tala Publishing Services, 1975.

Costa, Horacio de la, SJ, and John N. Schumacher, SJ. *The Filipino Clergy: Historical Studies and Future Perspectives*. Loyola Papers 12. Quezon City: Loyola School of Theology, Ateneo de Manila University, 1979.

Cruz, Apolinario de la. "Declaración de Apolinario de la Cruz." *La Política de España en Filipinas* 2 (1892): 113–14 (no. 32), 130–31 (no. 33), 155 (no. 35).

Delaney, John J. *Dictionary of Saints*. Garden City, NY: Doubleday, 1980.

Dolendo, Teodorico T. "Los Sucesos del Mag-Puli." *Renacimiento Filipino*, August 21, 1911, pp. 220–23; September 21, 1911, pp. 367–69.

Ebisawa, Arimichi. "Kirishitan no konfuraria (kyōdaikai)" [Christian cofradías]. *Ajia bunka kenkyū* [Asian cultural studies] 11 (1975): 31–48.

Estatuos de la Pía-Unión de S. Antonio de Padua y Rezo para Todos los Martes. Manila: Tipo-Lit. de Chofré y Comp.ª, 1895.

Fernando, Pablo, OP. *History of the Church in the Philippines (1521–1898)*. Manila: National Book Store, 1979.

Francisco, Gabriel B. *Kasaysayan ni Apolinario de la Cruz na May Pamagat na Hermano Puli*. Np, 1915.

Guía de Forastero en las Islas Filipinas, para el Año de 1842. Manila: Imprenta de D. Miguel Sanchez, nd.

Hardoman, John A., SJ, ed. *Gendai katorikku jiten* [Modern Catholic dictionary]. Translated by Kangorō Hama. Tokyo: Enderle Shoten, 1982.

Ikehata, Setsuho. "Firipin kakumei no rīdāshippu ni kansuru kenkyū (1896 nen 8 gatsu–1898 nen 4 gatsu)" [A study of leadership in the Philippine Revolution, August 1896–April 1898]. *Tōyō bunka kenkyūjo kiyō* [Memoirs of the Institute of Oriental Culture] 80 (1980): 41–194.

———. "San-Hose shintodan no hanran: 19 seiki Firipin ni okeru komunitasu undō" [The uprising of the Cofradía de San José: A communitas movement in the nineteenth-century Philippines]. In *Sennen ōkoku teki minshū undō no kenkyū: Chūgoku, Tōnan Ajia ni okeru* [Studies of popular millennial movements in China and Southeast Asia], ed. Chūsei Suzuki, pp. 441–90. Tokyo: Tokyo Daigaku Shuppankai, 1982.

Ileto, Reynaldo Clemeña. *Pasyon and Revolution: Popular Movements in the Philippines*. Quezon City: Ateneo de Manila University Press, 1979.

Javellana, Rene B., SJ. "A Historico-Critical Study of the Tagalog Pasyon of 1814: Casaysayan nang Pasiong Mahal ni Jesuchristong Panginoon Natin Sucat Ipag alab nang Puso nang Sinomang Bahasa." MA thesis, Ateneo de Manila University, 1983.

———. *Casaysayan nang Pasiong Mahal ni Jesucristong Panginoon Natin na Sucat Ipag-alab nang Puso nang Sinomang Babasa, With an Introduction, Annotations, and Translation of the 1882 Edition*. Quezon City: Ateneo de Manila University Press, 1988.

———. "Pasyon Genealogy and Annotated Bibliography." *Philippine Studies* 31 (1983): 451–67.

———. "The Sources of Gaspar Aquino de Belen's Pasyon." *Philippine Studies* 32 (1984): 305–21.

Kobayashi, Yoshio, ed. *Kirisutokyō hyakkajiten* [Christian encyclopedia]. Tokyo: Enderle Shoten, 1960.

Lumbera, Bienvenido L. "Tradition and Influences in the Development of Tagalog Poetry (1570–1898)." PhD dissertation, Indiana University, 1967.

Manuel, E. Arsenio. *Dictionary of Philippine Biography*. Vol. 2. Quezon City: Filipiniana Publications, 1970.

———. *A Lexicographic Study of Tayabas Tagalog of Quezon Province*. Quezon City: University of the Philippines, 1971.

Mas y Sans, Sinibaldo de. *Informe sobre el Estado de las Islas Filipinas en 1842*. 2 vols. Madrid: np, 1843.

Molina, Carmen. "Cases of Idolatrous Practices in the Tagalog Region During the XVII Century." Paper presented at the ninth conference of the International Association of Historians of Asia, November 1983, Manila.

Montero y Vidal, José. *Historia General de Filipinas desde el Descubrimiento de Dichas Islas hasta Nuestro Días*. Vol. 3. Madrid: Tello, 1895.

Nantes, Pantaleon. *Kasaysayan at Talâ ng Bayan ng Lukban, Quezon*. Manila: Benipayo Press, 1952.

Pastrana, Apolinar, OFM. "The Franciscans and the Evangelization of the Philippines (1578–1900)." *Boletín Eclesiástico de Filipinas* 39, no. 435 (1965): 80–115.

Phelan, John Leddy. *The Hispanization of the Philippines: Spanish Aims and Filipino Responses, 1565–1700*. Madison: University of Wisconsin Press, 1959.

Pilar, Marcelo H. del. *Monastic Supremacy in the Philippines*. Quezon City: Philippine Historical Association, 1958.

Rivera, Elena Zarco. "Christ in the Tagalog Pasyon." MA thesis, College of Arts and Sciences, University of the Philippines System, 1976.

Rizal, Jose. *Nori me tanhere* [Noli me tangere]. Translated by Gen Iwasaki. Tokyo: Imura Bunka Jigyōsha, 1976.

Sancho, Manuel. "Relación Espresiva de los Principales Acontecimientos de la Titulada Cofradía del Señor San José: Formada por el M. R. P. Fr. Manuel Sancho, Cura del Pueblo de Lucban." *La Política de España en Filipinas* 1 (1891): 250–51 (no. 21), 289–91 (no. 23); 2 (1892): 30–32 (no. 26), 74–75 (no. 29), 99–101 (no. 31).

Schumacher, John N., SJ. *Readings in Philippine Church History*. Quezon City: Ateneo de Manila University Press, 1979.

———. "Syncretism in Philippine Catholicism: Its Historical Causes." *Philippine Studies* 32 (1984): 251–72.

Sturtevant, David R. *Popular Uprisings in the Philippines, 1840–1940*. Ithaca: Cornell University Press, 1976.

Sweet, David. "A Proto-Political Peasant Movement in the Spanish Philippines: The Cofradía de San José and the Tayabas Rebellion of 1841." *Asian Studies* 8 (1970), no. 1: 94–119.

Takeuchi, Yoshirō. *Bunka no rikai no tame ni: Bunka kigōgaku e no michi* [To understand cultures: Toward a semiotics of culture]. Tokyo: Iwanami Shoten, 1981.

Tormo Sanz, Leandro. *Lucban (A Town the Franciscans Built)*. Translated by Antonio Serrano. Manila: Garcia Publishing Co., 1971.

Turner, Victor W. *The Ritual Process: Structure and Anti-Structure*. Chicago: Aldine, 1969.

———. *Dramas, Fields, and Metaphors: Symbolic Action in Human Society*. Ithaca: Cornell University Press, 1974.

Wickberg, Edgar. *The Chinese in Philippine Life, 1850–1898*. New Haven: Yale University Press, 1965.

Woods, Robert G. "The Strange Story of the Colorum Sect." *Asia* 32 (1932): 450–54, 459–60.

Zaide, Gregorio F. *Great Filipinos in History*. Manila: Verde Book Store, 1970.

APPENDIX I

The List of the Letters Written by the Members of the Cofradía de San José

(A)   From Apolinario de la Cruz to Octabio Ygnacio S. Jorge
      Before the year of 1840:
      6/29/1837
      11/9/1838
      In the year of 1840:
      5/12, 5/18, 5/26, 6/1, 7/5, 7/6, (*), 7/28, 8/3**, 9/1, 11/16, 11/18***, 12/8,
      12/22
      In the year of 1841:
      1/4, 1/12, 1/18, 1/24, 2/1, 2/16, 2/23, 3/2, 3/9, 3/15, 3/29, 4/1, 4/26, 5/1,
      5/18, 5/24, 6/1, 6/8, 6/22, (****), 6/29, (*****)
      * This letter indicates only the year, but we can judge from the content that this
      was written in the middle of July, 1840.
      ** Sender of this letter is Ciriaco de los Santos, but calligraphy is Apolinario de
      la Cruz's.
      *** This letter was addressed to Octabio Ygnacio S. Jorge's parents.
      **** This letter does not have date and name of sender, but we can judge from
      the content that this was written by Apolinario de la Cruz between June 22 to
      June 29, 1840.
      ***** This letter was written in Antipolo being addressed to Octabio Ygnacio S.
      Jorge but without date and name of sender. Judging from the content, sender is
      certainly Apolinario de la Cruz.
(B)   From Padre Ciriaco de los Santos to Octabio Ygnacio S. Jorge
      In the year of 1841:
      7/5*, 7/12*, 7/20*, 7/27, 8/10, 8/16, 8/24, 9/14
      * The calligraphy of these letters are Apolinario de la Cruz's.
(C)   From Octabio Ygnacio S. Jorge to Apolinario de la Cruz
      In the year of 1841:
      5/20*, 6/23*, 7/14(a)*, 7/14(b)*, 7/21*, 7/22, 7/29, 8/13, 8/19. 9/15**, 9/21**
      * This letter has no name of sender, but judging from the content, sender is cer-
      tainly Octabio Ygnacio S. Jorge.
      ** This letter is addressed to Padre Ciriaco de los Santos.
(D)   From other members to Apolinario de la Cruz
      7/29/1840   (From Satornino Cristobal)
      11/17/1840   (From Lucas de Torres)
      2/24/1841   (From ? probably to Apolinario de la Cruz)
      9/8/1841   (From Sta. Maria and others)
      9/15/1841   (From Gregorio Miguel de Jesus)
      10/23/1841   (From Doroteo Cayetano)
(E)   From other members to Octabio Yygnacio S. Jorge
      6/30/1840   (From Gregorio Miguel de Jesus)
      8/11/1841   (do.   )
      8/18/1841   (From Pafosto de S. Juan)
      9/15/1841   (From Gregorio Miguel de Jesus)
(F)   Others
      10/25/1841   (From Catalina de Sn. José to Gregorio Miguel de Jesus)
      10/25/1841   (From Catalina de Sn. José to Padre d. Estevan de Sn. Miguel)

APPENDIX II

Selected Documents of the Cofradía de San José

Contents:

A. Letter to confirm that Octabio Ygnacio S. Jorge has assumed the control of the Cofradía Apolinario de la Cruz gave up, with the date of Feb. 6, 1837
B. Cofradía's petition presented to the church of Lukban on April 1, 1840
C. Prayer recited by the neophyte when he enters the Cofradía
D. Paper to certify that Fahosta Maria has received Ang Votong Esclavitud, attached to the letter of Apolinario de la Cruz dated July 28, 1840
E. Letters of Apolinario de la Cruz

    1. November 9, 1838
    2. May 12, 1840
    3. May 18, 1840
    4. July 5, 1840
    5. August 3, 1840
    6. September 1, 1840
    7. November 16, 1840
    8. November, 1840
    9. February 1, 1841
    10. February 16, 1841
    11. June 22, 1841
    12. Written in Antipolo without date

F. Letters of Octabio Ygnacio S. Jorge

    1. July 14, 1841(a)
    2. July 14, 1841(b)
    3. July 21, 1841
    4. July 22, 1841
    5. September 21, 1841

SOME NOTES ON TRANSCRIBING THE MANUSCRIPTS

I employed the following rules in transcribing the original manuscripts:

1) All the spellings, with the exceptions stated below, are spelled in accordance with the original.

2) When inconsistency was found among the spellings and stylistics even in a single paper, or in a single letter, I followed the originals as they were, without trying to standardize them.

3) The indecipherable spellings are shown in parentheses.

4) In the following five cases, I made some changes to the original.

<1> When two parts of a word are spelled separately, I put these together as a single word. However, words such as *mag acala, or mag oonion*, are spelled as in the original, because it becomes more difficult to grasp their meanings if spelled *magacala,* or *magoonion.*

<2> When two words are spelled as a single word, I put them down separately.

<3> When words other than proper nouns were capitalized, and there was no reason for them to be capitalized, I put them in lower case. On the other hand, when proper nouns were found without capitalization, I capitalized them.

<4> When two commas were attached beneath a *t*, with the exception of abbreviated forms, I have omitted them. For example, *mahigpit̗* or *pagpapasalamat̗* have been spelled *mahigpit* and *pagpapasalamat* with the „ omitted. In case of *lat̗,* which is the abbreviated form of *lahat,* this has been spelled *la,t* as have all the other abbreviated forms.

<5> Abbreviations such as *Sm̃a* and *St̃o* have been standardized as *Sma.,* and *Sto.* However, in the case of *St̃ong. Quarisma,* I have followed the original. When in the manuscripts, the abbreviated forms are employed without a period to indicate they are abbreviated, such as *Yllostmo* (abbreviated from *Yllustrisimo*) or *fha* (*fecha*), I have also followed the original without adding a period.

[II—A]

Sa mahal na ñgalan nang Sma. Trinidad, Dios Ama Dios Anac Dios Espiritu Santo tatlo sa pagcapersona ysang Dios na totoo. Amen.

Acoy se Octabio Ygnacio de S.ⁿ Jorxe, tauong tunay sa bayan nang Majayjay, baguntauo, edad de 18 a.ˢ anac sa tunay na matrimunio ne Aneceto Flores de S.ⁿ Jorxe, at ne Eufimiana dela Rosa, sacop nang Cavezera ng Pagsanjan, nang taong 1837 binigyan nang catibayan at monting capangyarihan nang caniang pañgaseuaan, ang aquing yniuang Cofradia, nang Smo. Rosario na huag bagang magulo ang mañga pagsimana, at mañga iba pang obligacion, nang ysang Religiong Cofradia, caya pong aquing mañga magugulang ay nang mayroong pinauang ponong dapat pagtanganan, nang anomang bagay na caotosan domarating dito sa ating Carohan, caya po ysinalin co mona sa cania, ytong aquing alagang Cofradia, ni S.ⁿ Fran Ama natin, at ang esclavitud nang m.ˡ na Virgen at sampon nang Santo S. Josef, at aquin po namang binigyang catibayan toloy caming nafirmahan sa tapat nang aming mañga pañgalan na fha 6 de Febrero de 1837, caya po ynoolit co rin sa inyong aquing mañga magugulang na huag po ninyo calilimotan, ang ona nating pagsasamahan, na para rin po nang acoy dirian, ang pagsonod ninyo sa aquing pinagcatiualaan, alang alang po sa mñga pañgalan nang caniang hinahauacan toloy po nating gagaoin ang Santa Novena nang N. S. del Rosario, siam na hapon, ating pagdadasalanan at sa cataposan nang ycasiam na arao nang nasabing novena, at saca ysosonod pa ang cay S.ⁿ Josef, na pitong ligaya, at pitong hapes niya, saca cong matapos cayoi mayroon limosang justong ganang ysang Misa para sa mañga caloloua sa Porgatorio, siya nauang ualang hangan magparating man saan, Cahimanauari po ay tayoi bigyan pa nang mahabang buhay at lacas nang cataoan ang Stong Bindicion po ninyo ang siya ang ynaantayan sa tuing horas dini sa aquing pagcalagay sa Convento de N. P. S.ⁿ Juan de Dios de Manila. Toloy pong mapagsirvehan co ang Abitong Bindicion ng nasabing M.ˡ na Santo.

Ypinagtatagobilin co sa inyong lahat sa tuing ycaualong arao ng Oct.ᵉ ay inyong gagaoin ang Santa Novena, nang nasabing N. S. del Rosario fha 6 de Febrero de 1837 a.ˢ

Ermano Apolinario de la Cruz
Octabio Ygn.º S. Jorge

[II—B]

Aquing sinalin ang ynihaying present.^{on} sa cay Pry Manuel Sancho sa Locban na siyang lug.^r Padre curra. =

Exmo Yllmo Señor

Apolinario de la Cruz natural del pueblo de Locban prov. de Tayabas, donado del Convento de S. Rapael y Hospital de N. P. S. Juan de Dios, en union a mis compublanos a bajo fermantes postrados a las benignas plantas de V. E. Y. y con el mas profundo redemiento y sumision nos presentamos y desimos=

Que por nuestras intenciones y devocion y en bien de la humanidad de nuestro pueblo deseamos establecer en Nuestra Cofradia, una regla fexa para q en cada dies y nueve, del mes estubiese patente el Divinisimo en nuestra Yglecia, que a fesar de nuestras pubresas ofresemos pagar los derechos parroquiales que se nos exegen, y como esta gracia o concision correspunde a las atribusiones de N. Caseres, y como por la gran destancia que medio aquello Diosesi, no lo executamos sino que se nos ha perecido conveniente ocurrir a las altas pacultades de V. E. Y. a fin de que se sirva concedernos lesencia para el fin que tenemos indecado en casaso que no podemos conseguer se serva V.E.Y. por vos rasgo de aquedad, coadyubarnos para aquel Diosesano, reconmendando al mismo tiempo se nos a consediese la gracia que aspiramos. Y para conseguierla a V.E.Y. rendidante pedimos y suplicamos a si serva decretar que es gracia y mersid que imploramos.

—Pablo de la Cruz   —Octabio Ygn.^o S. Jorge
—Aniceto Flores de Jorge   —Bened.^{to} de los Stos.
Nang 1° Mierc^s nagsifer^a ytong apat catauo na nasabi sa ytaas,
    sa 1840=b. Abril

[II—C]

SULAT, NA PAQUIQUIALIPIN
Sa Mahal Na Poong San Josef.

O Casantosantosang Josef, Ama at Pañginoon co: Acong si *Eufeminiana dela Rosa* ay nagpapatirapâ sa iyong mañga paá, alipin ni Jesus Sacramentado, at nang Casantosantosang Virgen Maria, na ypinaglihing di pinanictan nang casalanang Original, mulâ na ñg caniyang pagcatauo, homahain aco at napaáalipin sa iyo, at nang caiyo na bagang tatlong mañga Pañginoon cong si Jesus,

Maria, y Josef, ay sumaaquing pusô ; at ang tandâ nitong caalipnan ay bubuisan quita, at pagdarasalan arao arao, catamistamisan cong Ama at Pañginoon, ñg pitong Ama namin, Aba Guinoong Maria, at Gloria Patri, pacundañgan sa iyong pitong saquit, at ligaya na quinamtan mo, noong casama mo, ang iyong yniybig na Esposa. Yniaámô co, mahabaguing Ama, na silayan mo aco ñg mañga mata ñg iyong auâ, at tangapin mo aco, at ypaquibilang sa iyong mañga mapapalad na alipin, at alang-alang sa iyong mañga capaitpaitang hirap, ay ipag adya mo aco sa mañga saquit, at cahirapan na macararating at mangyayari sa aquin ; at alang-alang sa iyong capayacpayacang ligaya ay magauad sa aquing Caloloua ang aliú, at catahimican ñg isang mabuting Conciencia, buhay na maganda, at mapalad na camatayan ; na doon baga,i camtan co alang alang sa tolong mo, mahal na Ama, ang yñong mañga pagcacalingâ nina Jesus, ni Maria ; at nang cun aco,i sumigla at maaliú na, at mangyari cong camtan ang capatauaran ñg aquing mañga sala, ay maquita co cayo,t paquisamahan, at purihin sa Lañgit magparating man saan. Siya nauâ.

[II—D]

Acoy si Fahosta Maria Soltera Anac sa tunay na matrimonio ni Temotheo Gma. de Leon y de Franca Geroni.[a] tavong namamayan sa mismong Cavezera ng Tayabas, tinanggap co ang Buto Esclavitud ñg dia 27 ñg Julio ñgayong taong lumalacad, sa ml. na comb.[to] nang Sto. Hospital ñg Nra. P.[e] S. Juan de Dios sa Maynila sa di lanting buto at capilla ng Nra. Señora del Carmin yguinavad ñg Camay ñg Ating Hermano Mayor nitong Sta. Cofra, at di man carampatan sa m̃ narinito boong calahatan aquing binigyang Caruga na magpatingdig nang caniyang tavo ytong se Pahosta Maria, casama ñg m̃ cabicelahis ñg Ating Cofradia, at ytong aquing binigyang Caruga ay casama ñg mga cavicellahis, sa huli ñg Padron nitong Cabilogan Carohan ng Amang Sto. San Josef yari ng fha. ng nasabi sa ytaas ñgaong taong de 1840 a.[s]

S. Juan De Dios de Manila

Lenagyang fe. nitong Hermano Mayor ng Ateng Cof.[a] na si
Apolinario de la Cruz

[II—E—1]

Malaqueng toua co,t pasasalamat ang onay sa A. P. Dios de man po aco dapat cayo nava po ay sapiteng malovalhate nitong aquing madlang comosta at madlang pavilin na cayo pong lahat dean m̃ magogolang at capated at con aco naman ay seyang madaraang ipagtatanong ay malacas ang catao-an na para nang dateng acoy manggaleng dean at gayon din se Catalina at se Lociano ava ñg ateng P. D.

Valang ybang dahilan ytong aqueng solat conde ytong na bibilin sa ybaba nitong regla manayiñga cayo at enyong dengen at talastacen ninyo ang mañga cadahelanan ñg caotosang nanggaleng sa ating ponong Yna ay ganito caya dapat sondin nateng lahat at seyang naguing cahatolan at bigay niayan sa sa ateng Cofradia dahilan sa ateng m̃ga cacolangang pagsonod ñg otos.

Ang caonaonahang bilin co ay magmola ñgayon ay ang pag ordinanza ay vala nang sosolong at hinde na naman macapagpipisan na para nang date, at maghihivahivalay na tayo ay anong gagao-en acoy ang naghalamang de maca-pagdelig sa enyo, ay mañga magogolang co,t capated hinde co sa pagpapabaya sa nasa aqueng pohonan con baga sa pohonan, ay anong gagaoen naten, ay quenapos ñg capalaran at magbabaet cayo m̃ga capated houag den cayong macalilimot ñg mañga pagtavag sa Dios bagaman tayo ay nagcajivahivalay at ang ycalava ay hovag cayong magpipisanpisan, at vala nang pahintolot at saca aco naman ay vala nang capanyarihan na para nang date Cayo ren ang may cagagavan, caya tayo nagcaganito, ay m̃ valang pag isesep at alaala, sa gaga-linggaling ay nagpacasera cayo sa mañga pagsonod ñg m̃ga caotosan sa aten. Aba senong enyong tatavagueng Pañgenoon ngayon, seno ang tatacbohan ngayon ninyo, sa aquen ay vala nang maidadaeng sa aquen ñgayon Aco ay valañg calacasan na parañg date at ang ycatlo ay ytong se Catalina ay enyong conin deni at hinde co na maaalagag At ñg cayo naman ay hovag napapagod ñg mañga paglovas deni sa aquen, at con aco na lamang ay vala mang parini ay acoy hindi naghihintay. Caya con anong veca niñio sa tanong cong yto sa iniong lahat dean sa ay con anong padecer ninio cay Catalina, aco man yatay magdamet nang malibag ay anong masaquet sa enyo rean, at ang isa ay ang vica ñg Caca ay cayo rao ay taga bayang hinde dapat maquepagbate, sa amin at cayo rao ay ay sacop nang bandong aayao gomalapong Caya cayo ay ipinoera sa amin, at saca ytong bilin niya, cayo ay mañgagsonorang magaling na para ñg date pero hovag maglalapet at hovag dao namang magogonanap ang m̃ onang pagsasama, at m̃ga pañgaral sa enyo at vala reng halaga pala sa enyo, Caya ñga,t nagcacanito ay m̃ heja co cayo ang may sala at cayoi ang may otang nagseserbe ay hinde tapat na gava ang enyong pagsonod sa aquen, at pagtalima, Caya valang ibang may sala conde cayo Ito na lamang at valang

ybang bilin ang loha co at habag sa enyo ay seyang tomotolo at tayo ay nagcaganito loha co ang paligoen.

H.º Apolinario dela Cruz

Guenava co at (　　　　) sa enyong lahat at ñg maalaman ang casaisayan
ñg a 13 nang Noveemb.ᵉ ñg taong 1837 anos pa yto ñgyare ay ñgaon lamang
nalabas ñg 9 de Nov.ᵉ ñg de 1838 anos ang caotosang yto ay seyang dapat
sonden naten at cayo ay m̃g magtanda ñg m̃ga panononod, sa lahat ñg bilin
sa m̃ga sa ytaas at ybaba ñg Regla D. g. m.ˢ s.ˢ

Lecha at decta ñg Caca ñg 11 de Dez.ᵉ sa ateng lahat ay ang hirap co ay
con natatanto yata ñg senoman sa enyo ay banta co ay ang lohay mananabog
hangan ñg aco ay bauian nang titulo at sampon ni Apolinario ay cami ay ñg
gogolanet caya ang inaantay ren namin ang mataemtim sa enyong loob na pag-
sisice at cami ay ñg macacavas sa pagsisiseng hirap m̃ anac co ang hirap namin
ay hirap caniyio sa banta co ay hinde caya yto na lam̃g at ñg aco ay hovag
lalong (　　　　　　　　　) ang m̃ pangan̄garal sa yio ay naon con
ngâon cayo ay ngavacavac at cami nativalag sa laot ñg dagat.

[II—E—2]

S. Juan de Dios de Manila dia 12 de Mayo de 1840 años

Domateng din navang maluvalhati sa yiong harapan ang aquing ylang catagang
bilin sa m̃ cautosan ñg A. Cof.ᵃ at langcap naman ang aquing madlang comosta
sa canilang la,t dian at lubos na pagpapasalamat con cami naman ang canilang
ytatanong ay valang sacunang anoman ava ñg A. P. D. at ñg m.¹ na Virg.ⁿ

Pues ang ona cong bilin na mahigpit sa canila ay pagcatanto baga ñg m̃
nalalaman sa sulat ay manyari lamang canilang maatindi at ñg con ypagcaloob
ñg D.ˢ marating na ang laong m̃ binabanta nitong ating Cof.ᵃ

At ganito ang canilang gav-in sa yca y 16 o 17 ñg buang lumalacad ay
canilang pag osisain na na mangyaring matanto nila ang cahalagahan ñg derichos
ñg misang ating pagbabayaran, ganito ang pagtaratu, sa misang ating Emporta,
con ang misa cantada aninio ay may repeque na ysang pasada ang alas 12 at
alas 2, ay lumismo, at ang Avi Maria at sa omagang bagong magmisa bilang
ay apat na pasada ang repiq.ᵉ at misa ñg ysang padre lamang, ay con magcaano
ang gastos ñg ganoong claci, o con mababayaran ñg 13, o catorce, o 15. o 16.
pesos ay caya cayo na ang bahalang tomarato atomavad ng cahalagahang nasabi
sa ytaas.

At con maricebe na ang salapi, at magcasondo na cayo ñg trato, ay hilin̄gin nilang aquing pinagcativalaan na magperma sa ating Quaderno ang cindico at padreng ñg misa ñg ating Entencion.

At ang ypagpapahayag mo naman sa lahat na m̃ capatid natin sa naturang Cof.ᵃ ay con sinong may calogalan, ay manyari baga na sumimba, at ñg canilang maq.ᵗᵃ ang pinagcacapatirang cabuhay.ⁿ ñg calolova at ang hindi man macasimba na may capansanan ay caramay rin ng paq.ᵉnabang, at ang gagav-in naman con matapos ang misa, ay magpipisan ang calahatan, sa ladong cabaac ñg simbahan, canan man, o caliva, ay mangyayari, caya albirtohan mo ang m̃ cavi.ˡˡᵃ na con matapos ang misa ay con saan ang talaga na pagcacapisanan ay cinyalan at pagcaraca ay gamiting ang Sto Rosario, ysa lamang parte alinsonod sa arao conpormi ang ating dating guinagavang rosario, sa m̃ capisanan, datapuva ay con matapos ang tatlong abapuó, at porijet ybantog ay casunod nam.ⁿ ang pitong A. Maguinoong M.ᵃ at Gloria Patre, bati sa m̃ Stos na Capayapaang Esclavitud at ypamono ang Esclavitud ñg madalang para sumagot ang lahat at ang natitira na candila cay San Josef ay hovag ypapapatay hangan di matapos ang masabing rosario at yordin mo nam.ⁿ sa m̃ capatid na ang m̃ pagpipisan o pagq.ᵉq.ᵉta ay ang maghahanapan pa ñg alac at ybang bagay ang lahat ñg iyan ay baval, tarcuval con p.ᵃ ñg m̃ magagandang pagq.ᵉq.ᵉta. Caya sa cataposan Octabio ay icau na ang bahala con yinyong yhatid ang pelac, ay dalahin ang Precintacion, at baca sacaling ytanong ng cura ang bagay dahilan ay ang papel ang yabot at con hindi mang umosisa (ay) sabihin nilang yto po ang aming ypinaghain ñg papel sa yio, Caya po sa tuving 12 ay aming babayaran na mola ñgayong arao na yto, at ang yba nam.ⁿ ay sa bait na nila para rin at hahabang lobha, sampon sa m̃ alvirtincia at pag ootos sa tavo, at vala naman na casiquip.ⁿ at valang pilitan ng paq.ᵉq.ᵉcapatid, at sampon ñg m̃ pagtangap. hangang may napasoc ay bucas ang pinto hovag lamang ang m̃ tauong mistisa sapagca at ytoy sa Dogu ñg Pobre, at sa nasabing salapi sa ytaas ay pate na ang cantores ay casama na roon, at con sacalit magcucolang ñg salape ang Cof.ᵃ ay si Cabisang M.ᵃ at si Cavisang Binidicto, ang Pensador, at yaon nam.ⁿ ay sa sa salapi rin ng calahatan ang ybabayad, at maalaman co namang madali ang naguing halaga at m̃ hechora, at ang demanda, ay ang lalacad ay ang dalava na talaga sanang sa buan ñg Abril, ang ang dalavang sa Mayo ay Junio, At ang ama naman, at Josta Fernandes, ay sa buvan ng Junio ay rebajahin mo ang calahati ñg disenuebe, bilang ay ang dalava ay naman ycavalo na ñg holog sa calahatan, D. ang lumagac sa yio at tomolong sampon ñg m.ˡ na Virg.ⁿ at poong S. Josef na ating Pintacasi.

[II—E—3]

Acoy magpapasalamat ang onay sa A. P. D. at sa m.ˡ na Virg.ⁿ sa yio at

sa canilang lahat na m̃ capatid at magulang con datnin bagang matahimic n̄g
aquing madlang sulat langcap ang comosta naming lahat at tayo naman ay n̄g
valang caramdaman at con cami ang canilang maytatanong ay ava n̄g D. ay
malalacas na para n̄g dati.

Ang bagay dahilan n̄g aquing sulat ay nang matanto mo ang m̃ pagcapa-
daraan n̄g lavindalavang Esclavitud nang m.[l] na Virg.[n] na canilang dala=Ang
dapat mong gavin ay pagsabihan mo ang may m̃ roon, n̄g nasabing Esclavitud
na silang m̃ga susuotan baga ay bago mo suotan ay papan̄gompisalin mo at
panayum ona n̄g Endul.[a] plenaria, puera lamang ang dalavang Mig.[la] Pasq.[la]
at Franca. Serafena, at yaon ay nacatupad na rini, sa Maynila, datapovat ang
m̃ yba ay lalong mabuti ang magconfezar at magcumolgar, at bagu naman
suotan ay tatlong Pte. ng Ros.[o] ang ypatapos sa canila, at saca basahiñ mo at
sumagut ang magsusuot pero pataas ang mocha sa tabla para n̄g m̃ naona na
na aquing ypinagbigay cargo sa iyo.=Caya ang dalavang nasabi sa ytaas ay
suotan mo na lamang at sabihin mo ang canilang arao at ang caotosan nam.[n]
at ybig co naman na maalaman, con anong m̃ arao n̄g magsitangap. at ang
lahat namang tantos n̄g tavo n̄g Cof.[a] at nanyari sa ateng misa na ypinagma-
malasaquit sa Amang Sto San Josef at sampon n̄g naguing casagutan n̄g Cura
at ng Zendico, at con siya pomirma at ang Padreng nagmisa cantada at cong
nagcautang o hindi ang Cof.[a] ay maalaman co bagang maaga at n̄g maypalagay
co ang lalong cabagayan n̄g A m̃g pagsusonoran, =at pagluvas n̄g Ynang Enta
ay ang Quaderng n̄g pamisa ay ypadala mo rini at pafepermahin co si P.[e]
Cereaco, gayon din naman ang m̃ga calacaran n̄g m̃ tavo ay maalaman co,
Yto na lamang Dgue m.[s] a.[s] SSS.

Yto naman ang dapat mong procurahing ypagpajayag sa m̃ga Cavicellajes
n̄g Pondador nitong ateng Cof.[a] ypag utos sa canicanilang tavo na ang nacaba-
basa n̄g sulat ay magmimoria n̄g Stong Esclavitud ni S. Josef, at m̃ Misterio n̄g
Sto Rosario at ang hindi maalam ay paturo n̄g Esclavitud at Rosario, at con sila
namay mayroong m̃ casama sa bahay na ybig pomasoc, bucas animo at valang Zuna
huvag lam.[g] ang naturang Mistisa, datapuvat tagalog ay ricibido, at yto namang
may m̃ saq.[t] sa panahong pagliligpitan n̄g Diesynube, ay despensado at gayon din
ang nasa malaq.[g] capansanan, at sa m̃ pagsimba sa arao na misa Diej.[a] ay valang
sapilitan, at saan m.[n] naruroon ay cagamay n̄g capaq.[e]nabangan sempre tavo n̄g
Cof.[a] at maalaman co rin nam.[n] con ang m̃ baguhan ay napagsabihan moñg
lahat n̄g m̃ yhahanda p.[a] sa catubosan n̄g canilang caluluva, at ang lahat na
m cavicella ay hovag papapagtahanin n̄g pagqta. ng tavo, para na animo silang
nagcocombrete n̄g m̃ Ereges, at doon sa lan̄git tatamohin ang ava ni S. Josef
at n̄g m.[l] na Virg.[n] at camtan naman nilang lahat na sang Cof.[a] ytong masusunod.= (Sa n̄galang n̄g A. A. Estu. Sto.) sa lahat n̄g horas at gayon din
ang madlang Endolg.[e] n̄g Aq[g]. Sto. Abitu n̄g laravan n̄g Sto. San Juan de D.[s]

Manila 18 de Mayo 1840 a.[s]

H[o] Apolinario dela Cruz

[II—E—4]

Alas honorifecas manos y Ermanos, Ermanas
    Manila y Hospital de Nro. P. S. Juan de Dios dia 5 de Julio de 1840 años

Malaquing tuva co at pagpapasalamat ang onay sa A. A. D.[s] at sa Ynang m.[l] na Virg.[n] gayon din cay S. Josef na Ateng m.[l] na pentacase ñg boong Cof.[a] ñg Smo. Rosario, na cayong lahat ay datnan ñg aming madlang comosta, na valang sacunang anom.[n] ang canilang m̃ catau-an at calolova, At con cami naman ang canilang maytatanong ay bagong nagsipanggaling sa saq.[t] na talaga ñg A. P. D. at nagtatagal sa cahirapan sa yiong ang cadahilanan, ñg m̃ pagcacalinga sa arao at gab-y at lahat nang oras.

    Poes m̃. magugulang co,t capatid, ang onaona cong bilin sa buong nalolooban ñg aquing maraletang Cof.[a] ay tayong lahat ay hovag macalilimot ñg pagtavag sa D.[s] at sa m.[l] na Virg.[n], gayon din sa m.[l] nating Ama, na marating din nateng matahimic ang ang m̃ cabanta-an ñg ateng loob. doon sa m.[l] na By.[n] na calovalhati-an, at ang ycalava cong catanoñgan ay con totoong m̃ boto ñg loob ñg boong Comon, ang pañgañgatau-an sa Cof.[a], ay canilang onavain ang sa ganan aq.[g] padecer, ñgaón, yayamang nasapit na at naratin ang m.[l] na pinto ng A. Diesynuebe, ay mag acala na naman tayo na tomoloy sa dacong loob. Caya yto ang ating gagauin, mintras acoy naririni pa sa Comb.[to] ñg m.[l] na Sto. ay maglacad tayo ñg ysang Presintacion sa Yllostmo, at aber con maconsegui na magcaruon ñg Smo. Sacramento sa Altra ytong maghapong arao na atin guinagavang feista at ypagcapama naten sa D.[s] at sa A. Calolova, aco ang yayari ñg nasabing Precintacion, dini at ang mabotohan co ay piferma sa Escreto, =Ang ycatlo cong bilin ay hovag na oling mariñgig ñg aquing tay-ñga na ang pomapasoc sa Cof.[a] ay tatangguihan, at magbabayad sa áquin t̃a m̃ cavicella hovag lamang (Dogong Mistesa,) hangang mayroon ay conin, hovag ang cajostohan lamang sa caniyang Nomero, Datapuva ay ñgayon ay bocod bocod na ang tatlong bay.[n] samacatuvid ay di na para ñg ona na macajejeram ñg tavo sa ybang bayan ñgayon ay sarilenan sapagcat seyang dapat m̃ capatid ang ganoong Pondaceon Ytitic sa alaala ang aquing m̃ sinabi at ypinagpahayag m̃ guilio na capatid.   Huvag ang aalaala ay ang nacaraan na para ñg pagdaranan pa yamang cayoi aquing ypinagpapabor ng cahinusayang gaua na sucat ycapagalab ñg sintang tunay cay S. Josef at sa A. A. D.[s] na ysa tatlo sa pagcatavo nia, minti bagang diq.ᵗ con ang m̃ batang masusunod sa atin ay agad maguising nitong ating Capisanan at siyang pagcalachang asal; at ano pa tayo ay m̃ matay man ay may masasabing ating pamana sa canila, somogot cayo at tumanong naman sa yinong saliring caysepan na cun ytong ating m̃ gava ay saan cajandaan, sa banta co ay sa cabuhayan ñg caloloa at catau-an Ytahan co na,t aquing pavacasan ytong abang capaaalalahanan sa canilang calahatan, Ang D.ˢ Ama at Anac naman, Esptu Stong sumacop sa tanan, at ang Ynang Virg.ⁿ maalam Santo S. Josef tayo ay lagacan ñg ganap na bindecion deto sa ating lupang cajapisan at papagcamtin ñg Lañgit na cahari-an Siya navang valan hangan.

Acoy si Octabio Ygnacio San Jorge anac na tunay sa matremonio ni Aniceto Flores S. Jorge at ni Eufemeana dela Rosa natural sa Pueb.º ng Mahayhay Prov.ª ñg Lalaguna, Acoy binigyan ñg camay pajentolot ñg ating Amang pono nitong Cof.ª na mag otos sa m̃. casunoran at pagpapalagay baga ñg Capisanan, caya aquing binasa at ypinatalastas ang ating m̃. dapat comflehang pagsunod. at ang magbigay casuayan at gauin co ang parang camay nia ang nagparusa, Manila 5 de Jolio de 1840 a.ˢ

H.º Apolinario dela Cruz

Lesta cong guinavang panibago na hinguil sa m̃ paghanap nang cani caniyang tavo para maaun din na mabuti ang ateng Cof.ª ñg Smo. Rosario, at nang huvag namang nag aalañgan ang loob nang ysa,t ysa ñg pagtangap ñg magsisipasoc at maq.ᵉq.ᵉcapatid sa cay Sto S. Jose, Atila mandin cayo ay sumosonod. lamang ay m̃ vala sa loob. con cayo sana ay ibig sumonod. ay pagcaramayan ñg calolova,t catau-an hovag ang paembabau lamang at yian ay hivag ypaghalong biro lamang at sucat acalaen naman ñg m̃ cabicelea na yto ay paq.ᵉq.ᵉnabangan natin at mamanahin ñg m̃ eredero natin, caya ang cani caniyang Nomiro ay magcalaman puera sa naq.ᵉta na ay ytong bagong hahanapin ay ciya namang sundin m̃ capated. aco na ang humahalic sa canilang m̃. m.¹ na yapac at ylalim nang capangyarihan, at aquing ytinatavag sa m.¹ na patron ng A. Cof.ª na magcabohos ang m̃ loob ñg tavo, con baga sa cajoy o sang halaman ay mamolaclac ng sagana at toloy magbunga nang madlang caalivan,

Lesta ñg m̃ cabicella na maghahanap ñg tavo sa cani-caniyang Nomiro ay na ytong masusunod. Yari nang dia 5. de Julio de 1840 anos.

			Nomiro ñg cani caniyang y-palalagay na tavo
Pmte.	Pablo dela Cruz	N.	12.
	...Yseduro de S. Juan	N.	12.
	...Aniceto Flores S. Jorge	N.	24.
	...Sant.° dela Cruz	N.	12.
	...Domingo Necolas Sant.°	N.	12.
	...Dionices Medina	N.	12.
	...Benedectu de los Stos.	N.	24.
	...Franco de los Stos.	N.	12.

Viodos y Solteros

...Leoncio de S. Juse	N.	12.
...Luis dela Cruz	s.N.	12.
...Mariano de S. Jose	s.N.	12.
...Serapin de S. Jose	B.N.	12.
...Juana Andrea	N.	6.
...Paula Alfonza	N.	6.
...Eufeminiana dela Rosa	N.	36.
...Petrona Greg.ª	N.	6.
...Thomacina de los Stos.	N.	12.
...Paula de los Stos.	N.	12.
...Prefecta dela Consep.ᵒⁿ	N.	36.
...Maria Veola	N.	24.
...Greg.ª de S. Jose	N.	12.
...Franca de S. Jose	N.	36.
...Baldo de S. Buenabintura	N.	12.
...Greg.° Mig.¹ de Jesus	N.	48.
...Fahusta Fernandes	N.	12.
...Seperiana Magdalina	N.	12.
...Becintina Franca	N.	12.
...Rafaela dela Rosa	N.	12.
...Celveria dela Cruz	N.	12.
...Semplecia de S. Jose	N.	24.

498

...Jacinta Pasquala	N.	6.
...Francisca Serafina	N.	12.
...Micaela Grig.ª	N.	12.
...Cecella Grig.ª	N.	12.
...Arsena de S. Jose	N.	12.

...Andrea de S. Jose ....N. ....12.
...Abarista de S. Jose...........................N. ....12.
...Miguila Pasq.la ....N. ....24.

♯ 680 ♯

Ang aquing tadhana sa m̃ capated ay ganito: ang aayau homanap nang tavo ay huvag nang omasa ñg aquing Vectoria na yoovi rean, at marahil ay acoy dini na malagac sa lupang Maynila con aco ay ñgayong nagbabanta nang maghobad nang Sto Abito, ay doon cayo maraming m̃ casuayan ay maalaman co lamang at ñg cayo ay napapabayaan co na na mag ysa rean, Caya ñg tayo ay magcaoompoc ay magsunuran parang yisang catau-an, m̃ cabecellahis cayo ang maglalagay ñg cajostohan sa Nomero sa tapat nang pañgalan na natutoca sa ysa,t ysa, lumabis ay huvag magculang sa m̃ Nomero, at ang pahintolot lamang ñg nagtanggap ñg maq.eq.ecapated ay sa sampo nang buan, at mahirap na ang m̃ pagpasoc, caya animo ay mintas maaga ay palista at cong macaraan ang termino ay may yba nang Regla na susundin ang pagpasoc sa paq.eq.ecapated cay S. Jose.=Ang aquing bigay na camortajan, at parosa sa bavat ysa catavo ay condi macapaglagay sa caniyang lugar, sa buang aquing termino ay ang apat catavo ay magbabayad ñg ysang diesynuebe para ñg pagbabayad ñg Comonidad, at ang magmamaniho naman nito ay se Octabio Ygnacio S. Jorge na aquing parang catauang seyang susundin ñg m̃ casama, Lagacan tayo nang m.l na bendecion ñg tatlong D.s at ñg Ynang maavain sa tavong domadalañgin, gayon din naman ang A. Sto. S. Josef na patron ñg Cof.a

De mano y forma del Sto hospital de S. Juan de Dios de Manila
Dia 5 de Jolio de 1840 anos

Hermano Apolinario dela Cruz

[II—E—5]

Al Sr D. Octabio Ygnacio S. Jorge Hermano Mayr Ynt.no de la Sta Cofradia del Sant.mo Rosario y Voto del Sr. S. Jose.

Ang cadahilanang nitong aming maralitang sulat ava ñg ating P. D. ay domating dining malualhati ang sulat na galing diyan at natanto nam.n m̃ga malalaman sa yong sulat.

Puez ang bilin co naman at hinihingi sa yio ay ang Quadernong limpio at mahosay ñg m̃ga nagastos mula ñg pumisan ang 19, at lumabas ang Misa de Gracia sa Bayan ñg Lucban at saca ang m̃ga sulat mong nañgaririyan at yni-yngatan na may mañga fecha ñg tauong 1832 años hangan 1839 a.ˢ ay iiong pag aalisin na sa casama ñg ating m̃ga papeles, at ava ñg ating P. D., at ñg Ýng. Virgen, ay linisin mo ang apunte at mahusay hangan sa buan ñg Julio nang tauong 1840 a.ˢ Caya co ypinagbilin na pagsirain mo na ang mañga naapunte sa natalikdang taon.   Para huvag ñg may macapagtitinging sinosinu huvag lamang ang magmula sa buvang sinabi ng tauong 40.   At ang yio namang yguinagajac na cacatolongin co ay hovag mo na mona monang paparinihin, totoo nga, at malaqui ang trabajo ay yisang Libro itong guinagaua paanong macapagda-dalaan ñg pagsulat.   Caya (   ) mo sa yba nang arao tumalaga at aquing ypagbibilin, At ang sinabi co naman sa ysang sulat namin caylan ca may calugalang, at maluag na macahingi ca ñg Lucm.ᵃ sa yiong Maes( ). at yba pa Datapuvat huvag mong masabi na aco ang quiquitain mo ani hindi ang Among.   At ang sinabi mo na hindi pa nacapagsoot ng Esclavitud ay huvag mo nang paluvasin dini, at ang gaoin mo namang diyan sa canilang tatlo ay pasimbahin ñg arao ñg Lunes o Jueves o Sabado. Caya naman at pagcatapus na macasimba ay suotan mo na riyan sa iniong bahay datapvat pabilhin mo ñg titingisan candilang sa sa ycaualohin at sindihan mo sa laravan bago gaoin ang catampatang ogali pʳᵃ ñg naonang m̃ga sinuotan mo at cun matapos ay iyong papagdasalin (   ) sa Herm.ᵗᵃ ñg Nra. Sra. de la Porteria ñg tatlong parte ñg Smo. Rosario J. H. L. Et.ᵃ Canilang ypatongcol ang naonang parte sa m̃ga tauong nasa casalanang mortal, at ang ycalauang parte ay sa m̃ga naghihingalo at manganganac, at nasa biglang camatayan ng oras na yaon, at ang ycatlong parte ay ypatongcol naman sa Buhay at Patay, na naguing casama sa gaganitong Cofrad.ᵃ at saca ysonod ang oraciong (na O Virg M.ᵃ Amparao de pecadores) saca mo yseñal ang m̃ga pagtupad na caotosan para ñg nasa sa Esclavitud.   At ang ytinatanong mo nam.ⁿ cagamitan sa yiong camay ay dian mo maquiquita sa ysang sulat, at cami namay uala pang masabi sa ating pleto sapagcat hindi pa nagcacasamasama ang naonang presentacion, at ang aming holing bilin sa yio at sa boong cumunidad ay ang pagpapacatibay ñg loob at pananalig sa ating P. D.ˢ at sa Ynang m.ˡ na Virg.ⁿ gayion din naman sa ating mahal na Patron, at pintacasing Sr. S. Jose, at huvag magpapacaraig sa m̃ga balita, at tocso ñg capuva rin tavo at tayo namang lahat, ay yngatan ñg ating P. D. at ñg m.ˡ na Virgen, at pacabuhayan mahabang taon, at arao, at huvag mong calimotan naman na hindi ipadala ang apunte ñg m̃ga nagastos sa paririning dezpacho at aming nesesita at cun caylan ca naman may lugar na macaparini, at tomatalaga naman sa canilang lahat sa iyan na pag otosan ytong Saserdote si P. Ciriaco de los Santos.

Sta Cruz de Manila a 3 de Ag.ᵗᵒ de 1840 a.ˢ

[II—E—6]

S. Juan de Dios de Manila y 1º de Septeembre de 1840 a.ˢ

Maluvalhati cang datnan ñg aquing madlang comosta sa iyo at boong Capisanan, at con aco naman ang canilang madaraang ytatanong ay malacas ang catau-an na para ñg dati.

Ang bagay dahilan ay ito ang precintacion natin ay naya,t yari na, ycau ang aquing ynaasahang camay na mag aabiyad na yiay madespasu at ynaantay co sa ysang Viernis, ang precintacion at valo catavo, na ating salitaan na, at yaong Quaderno ay aquing guinava at ñg hovag magulo, ang magcacasunod ay cia mo ring susondin sa Cellado, at hovag magcacabagobago ang hanay, at ang ysang valang tavo ay talaga co cay Ambrocio, at ycau na ang bahala, ang seradura ay narian ang dalavang Zeradura, ang padala mo ay nagsubra ñg saicapa,t tatatlong bahagui bilang yiang dalava ay ay aquing ybilini na ñg candila, at ang ycalava ay sa darating na dicenuebe ay huvag mo nang cunin ang salapi sa Tayabas, ytanda mo na lamang at yñgatan na mona ni Greg.º at ñg huvag yscandalusa, sa tavo at nacapagbibigay ñg masamang onion, caya ang tantos na lamang ay siya mong ytanda, at con loobin ñg A. P. D. at domating ang banta ay saca cunin, gayon din ang diyan sa inyo ay hovag na monang yahon ang salapi at tavo na lamang ang bilañgin, at tantos na na bagang malaquing ligalig, at paghingi co ay saca pagpisanpisanin, at ang sulat ay hovag mong pamalayan sa marami, na para cay Domingo Niculas Sant.º ay ibigay mo ñg lihim at pañgosapan mo na siyay hovag nang ooli oling sumilip ñg nasabing pondo, at con mariñgig co pa oli ay sa obispo co sia ypaparte, at ang bilin cong mahigpit ay sa bawat pipirma ay sabihin mo na hovag moñg ybabantog sa calahatan, at antain mo ñg manaog ang provedincia, lalo sa m̃ ponong bayan at con nanyari na ay saca ypagpapahayag sa lahat at antay co naman totoo sa ysang Viern.ˢ ang tavo at papel, at ang hinihiñge mong m̃ papeles ay antay ca mona, at tutoong labis sa camay co ang trabajo co, at saca panahong ñgayon na tayo ay magbobloñga na yata con ava ñg D.ˢ at ang lagay ñg Pegura ay ipasalin mo sa papel na para matapos co na ang ating veda, ang luhod at patindig ay maq.ᵉ-ta co lamang at mapalagyang signipica Caya con may lugar ay macasama na sana ñg Precintacion, compormi ang lagay ñg narian at hichora sa cuvarteta lamang papel Caya sa lahat cong bilin ay icau na ang bahala at ang tanong mo naman na cong matatanggap ang bata, con qᵉnacargo ñg magulang ay oo, at manyayari sa bata ang sa sa ycavalo, at hangang may napasoc ay tangapin at huvag tatanguihan, tagasaan mang bayan at nagcacasampu o siyam sa ysang bayan ay tanggapin, at ñg tayo,i domami.

Yñgatan ca ng A. P. D.ˢ at ng m.ˡ na Virg.ⁿ at pintacasi nating S. Josef at camtan mo naman ang m.[1] cong bindicion sa oras oras.

Apolinario dela Cruz

Acoy ang enyong Ermano Mayor ay nagbibigay ñg madla,t maraming comosta sa canilang lahat na aquing boong capatid sa Cofradia cahimannavari pa,i cayong lahat ay sumacativasay ang ona at mabuting pagsasamahan, at valang cagulohan, at sacunang ano pa man, at con ang mayor po nam.[n] ang ipagtatanong ay ava ñg A. P. D.[s] ay malacas at valang caramdaman; =At ang bagay dahilan ñg buong capahayagan co, sa calahatan caliva co,t canan, m̃ maguinoo at dili, ay ganito, hovag na namaq.[e]pagsama sa Cof.[a] diang maralita na para nito, cong ang dahilan din lamang ay mag oosisa ñg pondong salapi, tutuong sa tulong at ava nang ating P. D.[s] at ñg m.[1] na Virg.[n] sampon ni S. Josef ay cahit acoy bata ay mayroon din namang ycapagpaparusa at lalo ang Elleo'tricimo na may capanyarihan sa buong Maynila, na omaacu dinitu, sa aquing ypinagmanejo sa bayan yto, at m̃ ynacala, at ang ycalava ay ang canilang alalahanin acoy ysang Pobre, na valang pinagcuconan ñg yaman, at laq.[e] sa cahirapan ang aquing pulangan, ay sapagca,t ava yata ñg A.P.D.[s] ay itong Cof.[a] ay bago natayo ay pinagcagugulan co, ñg pagod at puyat arao gaby, at ang mga quita sa limang libong piso na napuhonan co ay di co masabi con saan co q.[e]nuha magmula ñg taong 1832 na yto bagay aquing pondarin at sa balang arao ay maq.[e]q.[e]ta rin nila rito sa ateng calalagyan, na para na ñga baga ñgayon na mayroon nang nag aacalang magbigay exemploñg masama sa m̃ pagsasamahan natin, caya capatid cong lahat con hindi ninyo pajalagahan ang ysang nagpagod ay cayo na po ang magmaniho, at di na aco pariri-an, sa ating Capisanan, at saca mamaya,i con canilang maq.[e]ta na ang calivanagan ay vala condi sa paghañga, at magbibigay pa na cunvari, (ay) siya ang pondadores con mamahayag sa yba, ay di macatupad ñg caysahan, at ang saycapat ay natatamad pa Yto na po lamang aquing Capisanang capatid ang aquing pahayag sa Lucban, at cabisirang Tayabas, gayon din sa Mahayhay at yba pang taga Saryaya, at sa lahat ng pueblo na naq.[e]q.[e]pagdalita rito, sa aquing Cof.[a] at saca yñgatan tayong lahat ñg A. P. D. ñg m.[1] na Virg.[n] at patrong San Josef sa tuvituvina ay aboloyan ñg gracia, at ytangol sa m̃ tocso ñg Dimonio, y

S. S. S. Q. S.[o] Manos Besus y plantas
de los Ermanos y Ermanas el pobre el
Apolinario dela Cruz

S. Juan de Dios de Manila a 1[o] de Septeem.[e] de 1840

Con domating at sumapit ang arao ñg 19 nitong Septeemb.ᵉ ay itong sulat ay basajen sa boong comonidad, ñg matanto ñg lahat ay pagcariñgig ñg yba ay ang nasa lupa ay oling basahan mo at ytoy capaalalahanan sa marami at ycalilivanag natin at ang Quaderno nang Pamisa ay ybalic mo oli, at sa arao ñg Jueb.ˢ ay bago mo patloguin dian ang lalacad ay pasimbahin mo mona at magbigay ca toloy ñg ysang p.ª sa Nra. Sra. de la Posteria, at ñg tayo ay tuloñgan, sa salapiñg cumonidad, at saca ang apat na candila na bilin co cay Ynang Ynta mo ytanong at bayàran mo sa salaping pondo; at ang m̃ peperma naman ay pagsabihan mo na hovag pamalayan sa di m̃ permantes, at si Ambrocio ay magperma sa lugar na ysang butas, n.ˢ D. gue m.ˢ a.ˢ S. S. S.

Aponte ñg tavong peperma na sa Precintacion ay na ytong masusunod sampon ñg nacaperma na ay naririto, at ñg juvag macagulogulo ay ñg ytong masusunod at hovag magcabagobago ang talodtod,

Hº Apolinario dela Cruz

+ Octabio Ygnacio S. Jorge	— D.ⁿ Gabriel de los Stos.
+ Serapio de S. Jose	+ D.ⁿ Pedro de S. Antonio
— Pablo dela Cruz	+ Atanacio de S. Franco
— Santº de la Cruz	+
+ Greg.º Mig.ˡ de Jesus	+ Lurinso Trinidad
+ Julian Greg.º Banaag	+ Luciano de S. B.ª V.ª
— D. Bernandino de S. Juan	+ Juan Abila Sta. Getrodˢ
+ D.ⁿ Leoneco de los Stos.	+ D.ⁿ Franco de los Stos.
— Jose Baupta. Renoso	+ Agapito de la Cruz
— D.ⁿ Juan Enx.º de Leon	+ Mauricio Barme
+ Felipe Gmo. de la Cruz	+ Arcadio Santº
+ D.ⁿ Cereaco de los Stos.	— D.ⁿ Pedro de S. Juan
+ D.ⁿ Venedicto de los Stos.	+ Pausto de S. Juan
+ D.ⁿ Aniceto Flor.ˢ S. Horge	— Rafael de los Stos
+ Vecinte Abila de los Stos.	+ Feleciano S. Horge
— Mariano de S. Josef	+ Mariano Bartolome
+ D.ⁿ Jose Ram.ˢ de S. Juan	

[II—E—7]

Malaqui ang tuva at pagpapasalamat naming lahat na m̃ga Pondadores nang A. maralitang Cof.ª at maties din natin ang m̃ caruvaguinang lahat dito sa ybabao ñg lupa at ang ycalavay maraming comosta sa boong Cof.ª at con cami naman ang madaraang ytatanong ay magaling ava ñg A. P. D. at nang m.¹ na Virg.ⁿ

Ang cadahilanan ñg aming sulat ñg Pari, bucod sa comosta sa canilang lahat di-an ay ganito sa boong capatid ay aming ypinahahayag na cahimannavari ay ang boong comon ay hovag macalilimot sa A. P. D. at sa m.¹ na Virg.ⁿ at ytong m.¹ na Patron ñg ateng Cof.ª ay lalong pacatitibain nila ang boong loob, at ang silay siyang malaqui sa lahat caming m̃ Pondadores dini ay di tumatalivacas sa canilang lahat at sinoman ang tatanoñgin ñg m̃. nayinguit sa pondo ñg salapi nitong ating capisanan ay nasa cay Padre Ceriaco de los Santos sa Bayan ñg Santa Cruz, at siya ang nacaaalam. at ang m̃ yba pa ay di cu natoran, at silay precinteng lahat onay sa P. D. at sa mag oosisa, at ang Padron naman at yba pang aponte ay antay namin dini sa Maynila at ytalaga ang loob ng tutoong comiquilala sa pagsasamahan at ang hindi nam.ⁿ ay cami di macapilit lalo,t ang aacalain ay na ay nasa caligaligan yto na lamang toloñgan ñg A. P. D. ytong Cof.ª at ang salaping m̃ natitipon ay antay sa oras oras ñg A. Padre celador y capillan, at ang anomang Novedad ay maalaman naming mañga rini at hovag ang nacalalamig na D. gue m.ˢ a.ˢ S. S. S. de todos los Pondadores y los dimas.

Ycao ñg aming pinagtitivalaan ang bahalang omatindi sa ating m̃ capatid at magulang Yari ñg a 16. de Nov.ᵉ sa Combto ñg S. Juan de Dios de Manila de 1840.

H.º Apolinario dela Cruz

[II—E—8]

Alas manos de D.ⁿ Aniceto D.ª Eufeminiana y D gue. m.ˢ S. S. S.

Malaquing tuva co at pasasalamat ang ona ay sa A. P. D. at sa m.¹ na Virg.ⁿ con datnan cayong tivasay nitong aquing maralitang sulat langcap ang maraming comosta sa canilang lahat dian at con cami naman ay canilang itatanong ay malacas sa ava ñg A. P. D.

Valang dahilan ytong aquing sulat m̃ capatid condi ona ang canilang loob. ay hovag ioorong sa m̃ panahong yto at ang tomalicod ay di co na yata aari-ing casama yto ay para lamang ysang pañganoring tomaquip sa cicat ñg arao ano pa at sa ava ñg D.ˢ ay maglilivanag din tayo at ang anomang carovaguinan ay tiisen at nasa panahon, sapagcat Dios ang may bigai at cia rin naman ang bibihis sa atin aco naman ay di nagbibiling hovag dadalavin ci Octabio sa Tayabas, sapagcat atin laman ay dapat aboloyan at ñg hovag masira ang caniang

loob. at ang m̃ tavo naman ating m̃ capatid ay pagsabihan nila na con
(   ) ñg Disenuebe ay hovag macalilimot ñg pagsimba bagamat tayo ay
nasa ligalig at macababavi rin tayo sa cahapisan, at con magagava nila ang
cobransa rian sa Mahayhay ay cobrahan ang macabibigay ay ycao Cancito ang
bahalang mag aparte rean, at ang cabicilla naman sa Lucban na may m̃ poso
ay mañgobra at ycao ang mag apunte rian at solong naman ang loob nila at
ang Pilac na marerecoje ay dalahin rini at yiñgatan ñg Pari vala na acong
ibang bilin condi yto lamang at ang bilin sa Ynang Ynta ñg caysan catauan ay
bavat magaling ay ciang gauin y D gue. m.ˢ a.ˢ S. S. S. L. S. B.

H.º Apolinario dela Cruz

Manila—Nuviembre año de 1840

[II—E—9]

Alas manos Senor D.ⁿ Octabio Ygnacio S. Jorge mi cuedado de la Sta Cof.ᵃ

Malaquing tuva co at pasasalamat onay sa A. P. D. at sa m.¹ na Ynang Virg.ⁿ
gayon din sa ating m.¹ na Patron ñg Santa Cof.ᵃ con datnin cang tivasay at
valang damdam ang catauan langcap ang aming madlang comosta ñg Pari sa
iyo at sa buong caysajan ñg ating (   ) at con cami naman ang canilang
ypagtatanong ay ava ñg A. P. D. ay vala caming damdam na para ñg dati.
Ang malaquing dajelan ñg aming sulat na m̃ga Fondadores nitong ating maralitang Cof.ᵃ ay pacatanto-in mo at con matanto mo ay tambing mong ipagpa-
jayag sa lahat nang capatid na ang aming cautosan ñg Pari ay ganito ; ang sino
senoman ay nacatatanto na ñgayon ay panahong darating ang S̄tong Quarisma
ay ang catampatan sa para nating m̃ de Cof.ᵃ ay hovag paaabot nang Domingo
de Lazaro, at hindi dapat sa m̃ga para nating nag oonion ñg isang calivanagan,
ytong bagay na yto ay ipablica mo sa apat na Bayang ating m̃ casamahan, at
con abotin ñg Lingo de Lazaro ay ang carampatan sa lalaqui ay lumimos ñg
isang misa at con babayi ay isang Sta. Bula de la Cruzada, at apat na candila ng
dia medio m.¹ na perdon, bago mañgompesal, caya mintʋas maaga ay aming
pajayag na sa buong comunidad at nang huvag namang gagahojal ang ysa,t
ysa o mamañgamañga con datnan ñg Parusa, at ang icalava namang ipinatatanto
namin sa lahat na m̃ga casamahan natin, ay pacatitibayin ang loob ñg pagtavag
sa A.P.D. at ang ycalavay sa m.¹ na Virg.ⁿ ycatlo ay sa Ama nating cay Sto
S. Josef. at ang m̃ga hapis na ating dinadala ñgayon ay luvalhati naman ang
casasapitan, at ang m̃ga loob na nag oorong sulung ñg paq.ᵉq.ᵉsama sa ating
caysahan ay dapat mag isip at baca nadidiliman lamang macalilimot sa panahong
yto ay mag alaala at ang casasapitan ay baca con domating ang arao na tadhana

sa ating calovalhatiang dapat ypagvagui ñg sino pa man, Caya ang sa ganang aming paalaala sa ysang natalivacay ay ganito ytong gauang ito ay hindi sa puersa nagda-an sa sinomang ynaq.[t] dito sa bagay na yto, datapovay ang hampas ñg A. m.[1] na Patron ay huvag caming daramay na mñga Fondadores at cami nagpapamata lamang con sanan sa ysang bulag at saca ñg m̃ mulat cayo ay hindi ypatuloy ang calivanagang banta ; ay dapat yatang carumijan ñg D.[s] ang isang ganganoon at vica ñg mñga campon ñg D.[s] ay dapat yhalembava ang ganoon sa babuy na pono ñg domi, na bavat tavong macaqq.[ta] ay nadirimarim, caya dapat mag isip sa panahong yto cayong m̃ capatid ñg aming poso at quinacaliñga sa arao at gab-y ñg m̃ maralitang omaquit nitong cabuhayan ; yto na lamang ang nilayin ñg sino seno man, con dinaratnan ñg m̃ masamang gunamgunam, at con ava ni S. Josef ay ipaquiquilala sa nadidilimang sinabi na, ang isang mabuting palaguiing isip. capara ñg sinasabi at hinihiñgi ñg ating loob na ypagcaloob ang capaytan bagu ang ligayay paratiñgin sa homihiñging camocha na mña natin, ay abañg ybigay ang saq.[t] at carujaguinan ay pagaasava-an ñg nagnanasa at homi-hiñgi ñg ysang cabuhay, ay sa banta coy di masapit ang caligayajang antay, nang isang omaantay=at sigurong vala naman sa bacuran ñg isang nagbacod bagamat nasasaloob. con ganoon nagpaquiquisama sa mabuting caysahan ay valang cabulohan, capara nang humacic ay masama ang binji damo ang cumental na napayndalong hayop ang lumamon, ay talagang sa tavo yto caya itinanim ñg isang nagbuquid ay ang acalay mag ani, ay tavong m̃ may isip at potencia ay alinman caya ang capara dito sa mundu con tayo ay domolog at omorong sa ysang caguinhavahan ñg calolova Yto na lamang ang pajayag co Octabio sa yio at dapat mong ipaaninau sa canilang lahat ang aming monting paalaala ng magulang sa canilang lahat na nalolooban ñg ating Cof.[a] at ang vica naman at pahayag ñg D.[s] Ama sa Anac nia, ang sumayio ay iyo at ang hindi namay labas sa cuenta mo caya cayo namay ditong lahat sumagut at mag isip sa pahayag ñg D.[s] Ama sa Anac nia nang manalañgin sa halamanan at pavisan ñg dugu ; Caming m̃ nagpundar nitong caysahan ay malaq.[e] ang pasasalamat con matutuhan nilang pagcuruin ang ilang comostang talinhagang at capatid y Dgue m.[s] a.[s] de mi cuedado y de las interiores de la Sta. Cof.[a] que se alla de los lugaris cada uno y S. S. S. B. L. y P. de todos ellos. Hermanos y Ermanas de la Sta. Cof.[a] del Señor S. Jose Pundadores de un P. Clerigu y.

H.[o] Apolinario dela Cruz

Manila y S. Juan di Dios, dia 1.[o] de Febriro de 1841

(Postscript of this letter is ommitted.)

[II—E—10]

Alas manos D.ⁿ Octabio Ygnacio S. Jorge

Ang tuva cuy malaqui at pasasalamat ang onay sa P. D. at sa m.¹ na Virg.ⁿ gayon din naman sa 'A. m.¹ na Patron nang boong Cof.ᵃ at cong tivasay ñg aming madlang comosta sa canilang lahat dian na (   ) capated at magulang at con cami naman ang madaraang ytatanong ay ava ñg A. P. D. ay malacas ang catau-ang capara ñg dating tayo ay magquiquita.

Ang cadajelanan ñg aming sulat ay ganito ona ang casagutan sa m̃ga bilin mo at ycalava ay ang sulat nang Cavezang Escu ay natanto naman namin ang calooban nilang ñg mag asava pabayaan mo sila at. ang Dios ang nacaaalam sa canilang ganganoong caysipan, at ang ycalava naman ay sa dalava cong casama ring sumapit di-an ay anoman ang isirang pori sa aquin at sa canilang aquing m̃ga anac, ay salamat at panahon pang silay may bibig na yquinapangongosap sa ating munacala, at ang ycatlo ay con masusunod mo ay sa a 25. nitong buwan ay paparinihin mo ytong m̃ga masusunod at patutuloñgin co sa trabajo ng Fiesta ni S. Ju.ⁿ Dios=Pausto de S. Ju.ⁿ Tay.ˢ Lorenzo Trinidad id. Mariano dela Cruz id. yto ay hostohin mong apat at ynaantay co sa nasabing fecha sa yta-as at con may m̃ carualan ang sinabi co ay nasa iyo ang cayari-an at despuner hovag lamang ang valang domatin at inaasajan cong patutuloñgin sa trabajo rini, at si Matandang Fleciano naman ay nari-an at nagbalic ay icau na ang bajala sa matanda, at mangyaring macabalic na maaga rini at siyang antay ñg Audincia ang caniyang quinucoja sa bicario at cura sa Lucban at cami naman ay valang biling naman sa m̃ capatid ang dating ogaling onion ay paratihin at siya ring caoovi-an Caya ang m̃ tavo ay antay co at yparijan mo naman ang pataTayabas, at saca yaong si Juan na naguing casamang pumaruon sa Camarines ay catampatan mong pañgosapan at aralan ñg m guinavang pirojecio sa cay Matandang Ciano at ñg ycapagcasundo nating lahat at tuloy namang sabijen mo sa cania na siay may paring dapat omacay sa cania ay con ano ang loob nila sa panajong yto ay matanto co, at con sumagut ñg masamang sabi ay sabihin mong tumolong pa cia sa Vicario, at yba pang contrario ñg sila ay macavicturia, yto na lamang Octabio huvag mong malimotan ang m̃ bilin co, sa yio at maalaman co sa ycalavang despacho ang m̃ padecir ng isa,t ysa. Caya ycau na ang bahalang mag atindi sa mga sinabi sa pono,t dolo nang aquing bilin sa sulat at ycau naman ay sumama sa Tayabas datapovat huvag cang haharap sa Vicario at ang yba namang m̃ lalaq.ᵉ ay sucat omaboloy sa pagharap doon sa pagcuha nang testemonio at huvag patigil tiguilin at ñg tayo ay magcacalotas na nang mañga hapisan at ang yba cu pang bilin ay sa despacho mo na ysangguni y D.ˢ gue m.ˢ a.ˢ S. S. S.

H.º Apolinario dela Cruz

S. Juan de Dios de Manila a 16 de Febriro de 1841

At tayo naman ay bago na naman ang General dito sa Felipinas nahalinhan na si D. Luis Lardizabal.

[II—E—11]

Alas manos D.ⁿ Octabio Ygn.º S. Jorge y Dgue en q.ᵉ se allan en el Pueb.º de Majayhay

Ang cadajelanan ñg aming sulat sa yio, una ang huvag cang magpapacatacut o matataranta sa pag atindi mo sa A. m̃. peligricis, at saca ang m nanyari at guinava sa A. m̃. casama duon sa Tayabas, anomat ano mang nanyari, ay maalaman naming maaga, at cu sacali, sila ay tinampalasan, u sinamsam ang m̃ padron o pafeles, ay humiñgi cayo ñg testemoñio, at ypalacad na madali at aming matanto cun paano ang dapat gau-in, at ycau ay alesto (sana) sa m̃ Nobedad diang anoman, at ang ytinatanong cu sa yio na m̃ afunte ay ybilin mo sa sulat at ñg maalaman cu cun ano, at huvag cun cami rini ay humiñgi ñg tubig ay apoi ang ypadadala mo, at mahirap sa A. m̃ pagsasamahan ang ganuon, at cun sa A. pletu ay hindi cu pa maalaman cun magbabalic pa uli sa Naga caya ganitu ang bilin cu, maghahanda cami ñg tavo at alas oras, ay anuman ang maguing cautosan, ay ñg natatalaga na at huvag ang cun casangcapan na ay saca pa magagayac, at cun may ava ang A. P. D.ˢ at ang m.¹ na Virg.ⁿ sampon naman ñg daquela nating patron, sa ycalavang despacho ay saca mu matantu, cararagdagan mo ang paghiñgi ñg tulong sa Amang D.ˢ at huvag cang mababacla sa anomang sigva at panahon ñgayong tayoi nasa tribonada, at sa pag alagad sa tavo ay ang aming bilin ay anoman ang canilang gauin sa A. m̃ cahapisan, ay huvag manimden cundi manggaling sa amin dini ang anomang orden sa A. lahat na casama, at caylan pa tavo aabuloy sa m.¹ na Sto. ñg hirap at dalita at caming nañgaririni ay canilang tutuloñgang manalañgin arao gab-y sa A. Amang Dios. Cahimannavari ang m̃ga ninanasa ñg boo nating loob. ay may Victoriang maluvalhati at magdamdam na ñg munting alibio ang calolovang nagcacasaq.ᵗ sa Porg.º na umaantay ñg A. m̃ nasa ñg buong loob. at cun nacasiñgil sa Tayabas ñg cubranza ay ipadala rini, at nagcacautang na acu sa may salapi, bucod sa nacayañg cung tulong, at cumosta sa m. A. Yna, at sa boong Cumonidad caming m̃ fundadores na naririni at tumatalagang nagderipender sa canilang lahat, at sila na muna animo ang bahalang humanap

ñg Remedio, sa nagbilin ñg gamot sa aquin malaquing tutoo ang cagulohan cu
sa ysa nang despacho, saca mo na maalaman at sa Arzobispo naroroun pa ang
A Pletu hindi pa nanasuc sa Audencia ysusi ycau ang bahala, ñg pag alagad
sa canila, Dgue. m.ˢ a.ˢ S. S. S.ᵒʳ de tudos hermanos y hermanas de la Sta Cof.ᵃ

Apolinario dela Cruz

At ang padrong dala ni Paustu ay ycau na ang bahalang tumiñgin at pacub-
ranzahan mo at vala na acu na ybinilin pa, sinabi cu na cay Paustu at ytanong
mo sa cania at sa caramihan ñg atindi cu ay hindi cu na naylagay sa sulat.

22 de Jonio año de 1841

[II—E—12]

Al Señor D. Octabio Ygnacio S. Jorge en que mi coedado de la Sta
Cofradia del Señor S. Jose: y Abitacion de Nra Señora del Smo Rosario y
Numeracion del Objeto de gran comonidades: a sus flagas:
Lavegan ca navari ñg mahal na gracia at Santong Vendicion ñg caliñga
co at avang laganap sa aquing catitibong pag ybig sa buong Comonidad at
yñgatan cang mahabang panahon nang pintacaseng Sto S. Jose: at ang ycalavay
ang ganap mong pagtiñgin sa madlang caliñga ñg piligricis at tunay na pagcumber-
ting loob na cila bagay huvag mong bigyang postura sa m̃ga pagcaaburidiong
valang casasapitan at lobos na ycapupuot ñg Dios sa ysang tumalicud ñgayon sa
panahong yto; at lubos ang pagcici con magcalutas at maquita ang calivanagan,
caya ang tapat ding pag amo sa canila ang catampatang pagpapaalaala sa m̃
balinong loob. na napadadala lamang sa tucsung siñgau ñg lupa, at ycau namang
aming camay sa canilang boong cadajunan; ay huvag matatacot sa capuva tavo;
ysusi con ang ysang Dios! yntanat sucat catacotan at anoman ang sacuna ñg
loob ay dapat ytavag sa Cania at sa Ynang maavaing may caliñga sa lahat na
sa sangmuduo hovag (sana) ang nahihilem cang palaguing parang vala sa loob
ang anomang guinagava paanong di ca. gagalitan ñg manong mo at mag yinit
sa yio.   Ay pacaysipin mo ang lalong magaling na gauin sa panahong yto at
ang anomang nasapit at nagda-an ay calooban ñg Langit; ang m̃ parusang binata
mo yaon naman ay hindi parusa condi tulong malaquing gracia na ycalilivanag
nitong Cof.ᵃ yayamang napag aninao mu na ang limang Mistiriong tuva, hapis
naman ay gayon din, sa bagay ay luvalhati naman ang yiral na valañg hangan,
ano pa at ano pang cabobolagbagan mo lahat ay natataling hilo sa caybigan
ñg q.ᵉnahihivatigang canlong ñg nanalilum, sa cabulosang silong na nanalogtug

sa Yna mong puno ñg guinubcob at (   )
parusang hinapujap sa nagcalubitbit na nativajelatig. yto lamang ang bilin co
at aral sa mapinong diquit mo at loob na pinipintoho mo sa arao at gab-y
at magtiistiis ca mona at hindi na malalavon at haharapin ca na; cayo ñg
ama ninong nalulugami maralita may sasangguniying salamin cayong m̃
yniybig; di man dapat ay sumondo ñg sunod sa calivanagang loob, magtanong
ang namamañginoon sa nagbibigai hatul, ang hinahatulan namang comohang
hatul, hosticiang napaourali sa valang halagang ogali; maguinoong nagdadalidali,
hinarang ni Cabisang Tinio, at si Aniceto namay tumatacbo quinalavit ni
Octabio, tumatacbo naman ang Cabesang Mario, at si Pajosto ay navala na,
bagu si Ca Cinta ay balo, at si Bulas ay sira ang juicio, binoboncog ni Gudio,
mañgisda at estucador na ci Cumicinadong pagsinipon nang nagcasusupong
ang mag Amang Pañginoon yto naman ang lasapin mo haligapgap cang totoo
ñg pagsundo sa gostong otos ñg puno mo, si Balas ay higalitin mo, sa pagvika
ni Balong Fodio, at ang asavay colonggomo, ytinatanong naman ñg Pañginoon
mo sa matinong napauo sa ysa sira ang olo.

Siya na,t baca di mo na maubos acala-in ang aquing cutyang pabilin at ito
ay salicsiquin mo hangang pono at dolo naririan ang m̃ gagau-in mong dapat
sa nasasacop mong Mestirio hovag ang hahañgal hañgal ca; at cuedadu ca capag
ang m̃ tavo hindi mo mapiguil ang lalacbai ay ang vica ñg iyong yna, nasa
yio na ang dulo.

Dgue. m.ˢ a.ˢ una salve y ......para la madre Protectura de la Sta Cof.ª

La dectamen del Pueb.º de Antipolo

[II—F—1]

Al Sor D.ⁿ Apolinario dela Cruz—H.º May.ʳ de la Sta. Cofradia y boto del
Señor S. Jose=

Ang cadahilanan po nitong aquing maralitang sulat vna, ay ava nang at.
Pañginoong Dios ay sumapit dining maluualhati ang ynio pong sulat, at ang
ycalauay, ang nanggaling diyan matandang babayi sa natalicdang biyahi, ay
pagdating dini sa Pandac ay nagcataong nagbibisita anual ay nang siyai
pomaroon sa bahay nang Matanda sa Nayon ay siyai pinaglilisan, doon na con
saan aña naroroon ang H.º at hindi mo casamang sumoba ay ang sagut naman
nang Matandang Andrea, ay caya ñga aña aco naquisidiyahan doon ay aquing
hinahanap at ang balitay sa Camarenes, ay ang vica ng ysat ysa, ay ypinahanap
doon ay hindi rin maquita, at ang ycatlo naman, ay ˉuala namang Novidad
dini, at sa Locban, ay nagbasa na naman ñg bando, at dini sa Mahayhay ay

nang arao na Domingo, ay malaquing ypinipilit sa santong sermon, ay ang Cofradiang sinasabi na tigagalauang quar.[a] tuving Lingo at ang vicay yari lamang aming bayan ang di napapasoc, at ang vicay vala na aniyang lalalo dito sa Cofradiang ytinatayo=at sa Tayabas naman, ay ang orden ñg Govern.[or] ay capag nahuli ay saSan Antoniohin at ypaloluvas diyan, at sila naman ay valang capisanan, ang ypinahayag nang cavicilla ay ang pagnonovena, at nag-pamisa sila ñg ysa doon, na may recivo, at ang bilin mo po ay aquing sosondin, Ynom.[s]

Mahayjay 14 y Julio, Mierc[s] año de 1841

At caya co po sinolatan ang Pari ay sa caniya co ysinolit ang ybang pafelis, at ang cartilla ñg m̃ demanderes, at ang afunti nang m̃ namatay, ay naroon din at casapin ang casompong mañga fha nang buvan, hindi nga lamang naca-cavit sa fozas.

[II—F—2]

Alas manos D[n] Apolinario dela Cruz=H[o] Maor. de la Sta Cofradia, y boto del Señor Sn Jose=

Ang cadahilan po nitong aquing maralitang sulat vna ay aua nang a. t. Pañginoong Dios ay natanto cu po ang eniong mahal na sulat=Ang ycalavay ang aming novidad, ay uala namang nanyayari, condi ang sa Locban, ay nang arao na Domingo ay sinasaoli ang bando, at sa bayan nang Tayabas; ay ang Orn. ñg Gov.[or] ay capag nahuli, ay saS.[n] Antoniohin, at ang nanyari dini sa Mahayjay ay uala acong masabi condi ang sermon nang arao na Domingo 11 nitong bu.[n] ay ang Mahal na Pañgaral sa Propita, ay yari rao amin lamang bayan ang hindi pa na napapasoc at hindi pa natatalastas Datapuva aña at hangan Manila ay ytoy tanyag na, at ang vicay vala na aniyang lalalo dito sa Cofradiang yto na ytinatayo na tigagalauang quarta Lingo lingo, = At nang domating naman ang Matandang Andrea ay nagcataong paroon sa bahay ang Matanda sa Nay.[n] ay napagpara nang ytinanong sa caniya ang H.[o] Ang sag.[t] niyai caya nga ana aco nagquincidia ay aquing hinahanap doon, ay ang pag-cabalita ay nasa Camar.[s], ay ang vica naman ang nahanap aña sa Manila nang ycalauang biyahi sana lipasan ñg dalaunag Comisionador at ysang aroliante, ay hindi nacuha gayon din sa Camarin.[s]
At sila sa Tayabas ay valang capisanan at ang ypinahayag nang cavic.[lla] ay opan magcahayoran ang magcapatid ang magsipagnovena a tayoi maglilimosan, siya ñga nilang naysipan at nagpamissa nang ysa na may recivo=Nariyan ang

curra sa Locban, at nagtagobilin sa conven.^{to} na siyai pagagamot at malaq ang saquit niya Yno. m.ˢ y D.ˢ gue m.ˢ a.ˢ

Mahayjay 14 de Julio Mierc^s ano de 1841

Octabio Ygnacio S.ⁿ Jorge

At caya co po sinolatan ang among ay sa caniya co po ysinolit ang ybang pafelis at ang cartillang afunti nang m̄ demandero, at ng ysinosulit co sa conv.^{to} ay ang vica mo poy dalhin co na doon, At ang afunti nang m̄ ṅamatay na capated, ay naroon din at casapin ang casompong na manga fha nang buuan hindi nga lamang nacacavit sa foxas, at yba namang toloy.

[II—F—3]

Al Sor D.ⁿ Apolinario dela Cruz Hº May.ʳ de Cofradia del Santesimo Rosar.º y boto del Senor S. Jose =

Ang dahilan po nitong sulat vna ay domating na po ang mañga nangaling diyan, at aming natalastas ang mañga ypinag ootos na madirigir
Ang bocod po ditoy ang aquing ysinolit sa pari ay cong napabigay na po caya sa yio, toloy aquin pong ypinagbebigay alam ang mañga naguing novidad namin dini na sa aquing bahay ay may dalauang lalaqui na nanonibago, at nagmasid ytoy taga Locban = At ang ang bilin mo po cay testigong Esteban ay mabuti at acoy senolatan ng caniyang asaua, ñgayon na con may pag-totolong nang mañga gagauin ay di seya rao pong salam.ᵗ, at hindi naman siya ynaantay doon toloy nangcomosta sa caniya at ang caniyang bianan ay ñg dia 18. de Jolio at ang aming novidad dini ay totoong mahigpit ang m̄. otos at pagbabantay sa Tayabas, at ang pari ay nagala sa m̄ tendajan at nahiñgi ñg limos, at con macacuja ytinatanda ang pañgalan at sa Locban naman ay ang bando ay ang pinapasoc nang limosan sa m̄ tauo, at dini sa Mahayjay ay ypinahahayag sa paopito ang otos ñg P.ᵉ Cura, gomagala rin naman ang aming pari nang pagpapasoc sa sinasabing Cofradia ni S.ⁿ Fran.ᶜᵒ Xavier, at may bagong otos ñgayon dini ang Gov.ⁿᵒ sa amin, na ang lauac ñg mañga Nay.ⁿ at ang layo sa bayan ay sinosucat nang mañga jueses at ang bilin mo po naman may maquiquita na (   ) na ma(   ) ang ferma, ay mayroon datapuvat may mañga estado. Ynom.ˢ

Mahayjay 21 de Jolio año de 1841

[II—F—4]

Al Sor. D.ⁿ Apolinario dela Cruz q. Dios gue. m.ˢ a.ˢ
Hermano Mayor de la Sta Cofradia, y boto del Sor S Jose =

Ang bagay po at dahilan nitong sulat vna ay domating na ang mañga nangaling diyan, at aming natalastas ang mañga otos at dirijir.

   Ang bocod po ditoy ang afunti na nasasa pari ay con napasolit na caya sa yio, toloy co pong ypinagbibigay alam, ang aming naguin novidad dini na mayroon nang naquiquiramdam dini sa bahay dalauang lalaquing taga Locb.ⁿ Ang asaua ni D.ⁿ Estevan, ay aco poy sinolatan, na siyai nagpacomosta at con macacatolong ay siya rao pong salamat hindi naman ynaantay, toloy ypinagpte. sa aquin niya na ang caniyang bianan ay binauian na ñg D.ˢ nang buh.ʸ at nang dia 18 de Jolio, = At bilin mo po ay na con may magmabuting forma dini, ay mayroon di namang nacao°tay datapuvat may mañga estado=Nobidad namin dini ay totoong mahigpit, mañga otos lalo sa Tayabas, ay ang pari doon ay nagala sa mañga tendajan, at nahingi nang limos, at con macacuja ay ytinatanda ang pañgalan, at sa Locban, ay may bando, sa pinofundar na Cofradia nila na mayroon ang nagsisipagmanejo at dini sa Mahayjay ay gayon ding nagala ang quajotor at nagpapasoc sa sinasabing Cofradia na may pintacasing S.ⁿ Fran.ᶜᵒ Havier=At ypinahahayag din naman sa propito,=At may bagong otos na dini sa aming bay.ⁿ ang govierno na ang m̃. nay.ⁿ ay ang lauac at layo sa bayan ay sinosucat nang mañga Jueses. Yn.ˢ q D.ˢ gue m.ˢ a.ˢ

Mahayjay 22, de Jolio año de 1841

Octabio Ygnacio S Jorge

Comosta cay Canɟ Eulogio at nabayaran na ang caniyang nag.ⁿ cuvinta sa Tayabas, nitong Cavˡˡᵃ

[II—F—5]

Al P.ᵉ Capp.ᵃⁿ D.ⁿ Ciriaco delos Stos

   Ang bagay po at dahilan nitong aquing sulat una ay maraming comosta at aua ñg at. P. D.ˢ at nang ating mahal na patron ay malacas na para ñg dati.

   At ang bucod po ditoy ang aming nobidad dini sa Majayjay nang acoy naririni sa bahay co na ualang yba namang nadalao na capated na may yba sa

aming magcacasamajan, = Ay nang arao na Domingo dia 19, y Sipt.ᵉ ay ang oras
ay alas unce sa gaby, ay siya co nang quinaguisnan sa aming bahay ang aming
P.ᵉ Cura, Tiy Ant.ᵉ Ruman, at ang maguinoong Capit.ⁿ at ang Escriv.ᵗᵉ Ofeciales,
Comf.ᵃ Comicionad.ˢ at ang ytinatanong sa aquin ñg cura ay sa naroon ang
tauong capat.ᵈ sa Cof.ᵃ = Ay ang sag.ᵗ co po ay para ñg sinabi sa ytaas, saan
ca aña naghahatid nang pamissa, ang sagᵗ co po ay hindi aco nacacapaghatid
at ualang yhahatid, ay saan aña naroon ang salaping fundo ang sagᵗ co po ay
ay uala rin ay saan aña ysunosulit ang salapi nang H.º ang sagut co po ay sa
yio nacasulit (   ) pa ang ybat yba ay sa ybang arao na at hindi
na muna macacasangcapan, Anoy acoy tinauag at tiningnan ang aquing bolsa
at saca naroon aña ang Yntero Yngm ang llave nang mañga caban ang sag.ᵗ
co po ay ualang susi ang aming caban ay ang laman ay nang mahanap nila
na ualang macuja silang pafil at pilac. ay ang ynosisa naman nila ay ang lajat
na tacbà sampon m̃ sampalan sa paloc co, at nang hinihiñgi ang llavi ñg cajon
sa aquin, na ytong cajong yto ang quinalalagyan nang aquing Quad.º at isang
clace ñg mañga cav.ˡˡᵃ, sampon ñg sampon ñg padalahan tuving biyaji hañgan
pagcacagolo sa Locban, = sa tanong saq.ⁿ ay ang sagut co ay di co po mayybig.ʸ
ang llavi ona nay siyang pagyabat ñg baston sa aquin toloy acoy sinampal sa
mocha, ay yion pala aña ang quinasisidlan ñg mañga tesoro saca nagbubulaan
sa aquin nang macuha nang lajat ay acoy tinauag at cami yomaon na, at ang
P. Cura ay domaan na sa comv.ᵗᵒ at dala ang pafelis at acu namay ypinagsama
sa triv.ˡ at ynilagay aco sa calaboso ysinoot ang aquing ysang paa sa pañgao at
nang quinabucasan oras alas 2, acoy ypinahango oli at tinauag aco oli sa conv.ᵗᵒ
casama ang Capit.ⁿ at pinagbasa nila ang sulat at nang acoy hajampasin ay acoy
nahiñgi ng testim.º ay cami naghabolan ñg paorung aco at acoy sinisicaran at
sinasampal at pagcaracay acoy ypinahampas at pagcalantac ñg pito ay ypinatajan
at ang ytinatanong sa aquin ay sa naroon ang herm.º ang sagᵗ co ay auan
pò man ay sila ay nagauà ñg sumaria at ypinadala sa Alcalde, at ypinahatid
aco oli sa dati cong lagay ang ama namay ypinacaon at ysinilid pati si na para
rin ñg lagay co nacabucod hindi cami macapag osap at ang vica ng capitan ay
ypalolosong cami sa cavisera, Pagsanjan Yno.ˢ

Majayjay 21 de Sept.ᵉ año de 1841
            Hº Yº Octabio Ygnº de S.ⁿ Jorge